HOLY SPIRIT OF GOD

HERBERT LOCKYER

ABINGDON PRESS
NASHVILLE

THE HOLY SPIRIT OF GOD

A Festival Book

Foreword copyright © 1981 by Herbert Lockyer

All rights reserved

Festival edition published by Abingdon Press, October 1983

ISBN 0-687-17323-X

(Previously published by Thomas Nelson Publishers
under ISBN 0-8407-5234-2)

Unless otherwise noted, all Scripture quotations are from the King
James Version of the Bible.

Scripture quotations marked ASV are from the American Standard
Edition of the Revised Bible, copyright © 1901 by Thomas Nelson
& Sons.

Scripture quotations marked NKJB-NT are from The New King
James Bible-New Testament. Copyright © 1979, Thomas Nelson,
Inc., Publishers.

PRINTED IN THE UNITED STATES OF AMERICA

2215395

Contents

Foreword

Over thirty years ago the renowned Union Gospel Press of Cleveland, Ohio, kindly published this study of mine, which has been out of print for several years, under the title *The Breath of God*. An opportunity arose to revise and amend the book for publication under its new title, *The Holy Spirit of God;* sincere gratitude is expressed for permission to release and reprint the same.

In his introduction to Abraham Kuyper's monumental work on *The Holy Spirit*, Professor B. B. Warfield remarked, "The Holy Spirit—a theme higher than which none can occupy the attention of the Christian. . . . Only a spiritually-minded church provides the soil in which a literature of the Spirit can grow."

Within the last half-century or so, such literature has become most extensive, so that one is embarrassed by riches when a study of the far-reaching ramifications of the Spirit's ministry is undertaken. It is superfluous for me to add that I am deeply indebted to scores of writers on this theme. The volume before you constitutes a personal endeavor to express in simple terms for believers the manifold activities of God the Holy Spirit, the Author and Lord of all life.

November 1980   Herbert Lockyer

CHAPTER ONE

Approaching the Theme

Religious teachers and writers are impressed by the fact that Christians everywhere desire a more comprehensive knowledge of the person and work of the Holy Spirit. It may be that a sense of need and insufficiency cause many to inquire. They want to understand how the Spirit's fullness can be received and retained.

In many cases, misconceptions concerning the Spirit and ignorance of His work are responsible for weakness and ineffectiveness in Christian life and labor. If only the Spirit could come into His own, lives would be rich in fruitfulness and fragrant with the perfume of Christ. By realizing all that the third person of the Trinity has for us, facts of promise could become factors of power.

Approaching the theme before us, sublime and sacred as it is, we have to confess that no saint can explain fully to himself or to others the gracious operations of the Spirit. Personally, we can experience His power and witness His work in and through other lives, but our reach exceeds our grasp. Thus, any exposition of the personality and work of the Spirit is more or less imperfect because of our inability to describe our experiences correctly.

All of us are able to know with absolute certainty the facts of His indwelling presence, life-giving energy, and sanctifying power, even though our opinions as to the origin and theory of the Spirit's presence within the soul may differ.

We enter upon these evangelical studies of the Spirit with the confession that the doctrine is, in many respects, mysterious. Because of our finite understanding we may have a true

11

but incomplete grasp of it. It is a revealed fact of Holy Scripture, and as such is to be received and believed. The truth of the Spirit transcends, but does not contradict reason. The Father, the Son, and the Holy Spirit are one and only one God. Each has some characteristics which the other has not. Neither is God without the others, and each with the others is God. The Father says "I," the Spirit says "I." The Father loves the Son; the Son honors the Father; the Spirit testifies of the Son.

The Need of Study

Students of church history have pointed out that the twin truths of the Holy Spirit and of our Lord's return were lost to the church for a long period. Although recognized, declared, and surely believed by the apostles and early fathers, they were lost to vision during the Dark Ages when the church was almost entirely Romish.

The Spirit's manifold operations allied with the "blessed hope" now hold a prominent place in the theology of evangelical believers, thanks to the efforts of spiritually-minded teachers throughout the last 150 years.

And, it will be observed, these twin truths rise or fall together. If we deny the one, we discard the other. In his monumental volume on *Christian Doctrine,* Dale remarks, "There are some who have not discovered that as the coming of Christ was a new and wonderful thing in the history of our race, the coming of the Holy Spirit was also a new and wonderful thing in the history of our race, and that His coming has made an infinite difference in the life of man."

It is imperative to grasp the truth of the Spirit.

Because it is a neglected truth

Although we have more volumes than ever before expounding the graces and gifts of the Spirit, I fear that such enlightenment is sadly neglected by the vast majority of Christians. A recital of the Creed there may be—"I believe in the Holy Ghost"—but where He is unknown, or where the essentials of our faith are tampered with, His presence cannot be realized.

Professor Erdman, in his inspiring book *The Holy Spirit and Christian Experience,* wrote,

> The Spirit cannot be where Christ is denied as redeemer, life and Lord of all. Christ is "the Truth" and the Spirit is "the Spirit of Truth"; all is personal, not abstract, ideal, and the sum and substance of material wherewith the Spirit works in Christ. . . . In brief, the Spirit must be silent altogether in pulpits and churches where a different "gospel which is not another" gospel is preached, and where unrebuked and unchecked . . . prevail, although in a form of godliness, "the lust of the flesh, and the lust of the eyes, and the pride of life" and the things which are "not of the Father, but . . . of the world"; things which are not of the new nature and spirit in which the Holy Spirit dwells and through which alone He can work and testify. . . . We should be warned by the history of the apostolic churches, once so full of the Spirit, but which perished from their places long ago. The same denial of Christ, the same worldliness is our danger today. All that can help us is the presence of the Spirit of Christ, and He will not work save with the Truth of Christ; and He only must dwell in the Temple of God, which temple we are.

Bearing in mind that he is named some ninety-three times in the New Testament, we realize His conspicuous place in this age of grace, which is the dispensation of "the ministration of the Spirit" (2 Cor. 3:8). It is spiritually disastrous to neglect what the Bible reveals of His activities. Preeminence is given to "Church Work," "Social Work," "Mission Work," but the apostles knew only one kind of work, namely the Spirit's work. This is why the Acts is saturated with His presence and presidency, and should be renamed "the Acts of the Holy Spirit through the Apostles."

Of William Arthur's fiery message, "Tongues of Fire," issued in 1856, Campbell Morgan remarked, "It was a book before its time, yet men read it—our fathers tell us—on their knees." Here is a sentence or two from this spiritual classic: "In this age of faith in the natural, and disinclination to the supernatural, we want especially to meet the credo—'I believe in the Holy Ghost.'" May the Spirit enable us to challenge the spirit of the age thus! God forbid that we should live and serve as the Ephesians who had acted ignorantly of the Spirit, and who when brought face to face with His claims, declared that the had "not so much as heard whether there be any Holy Ghost (Acts 19:2).

Because it is a misunderstood truth

Are we not safe in affirming that no other aspect of biblical truth is so misunderstood as that of the ministry of the Spirit? Endless confusion reigns—confusion resulting in heartache and spiritual disaster—because of this lack of understanding.

No one can amass printed material on the Spirit without encountering conflicting theories. And what bitterness is sometimes expressed by one section of believers who cannot endorse the opinion strenuously held by another group! As the late Campbell Morgan so forcefully expressed it, "The greatest peril which threatens the truth of the Spirit's personal ministry today, arises from the advocacy of the truth by those who are not careful to discover there have been launched a number of wholly unauthorized systems, which have brought bondage where the Spirit would have brought liberty."

One aspect of misunderstanding is referred to by Dale, who speaks of those "who are still sitting in the upper chamber, waiting, praying, longing for the coming of the Spirit, not knowing that the Spirit came almost nineteen hundred years ago with a mighty rushing wind and tongue of fire; that He has never left the church; that there is therefore no reason for Him to come again. He is here, for according to the words of Christ, the Spirit having come abides with us forever."

Satan has two methods of procedure in dealing with truth. First, he seeks to hide the vision. When that is no longer possible, when any truth with its inherent brilliance and beauty drives away the mists, then Satan's method is that of patronage and falsification. He endeavors to take it out of its true proportion and turn it into deadly error.

Because it is a perverted truth

This aspect arises out of the one just considered, for misunderstanding and perversion are inseparably allied.

For example, in his concern lest the converts in Corinth should be lured away from "the simplicity that is in Christ," Paul indicates for them three characteristic marks of false teaching: another Jesus, another Spirit, and another gospel (2 Cor. 11:4). It may be profitable to examine this trinity of perversion or compendium of error.

Another Jesus

It was clearly evident to Paul and the Corinthian believers that the Jesus of the false teachers of Galatia and of Corinth was not the Jesus they knew—not the Savior of a lost world the apostle so vigorously preached. And the Jesus of present-day modernism, beautiful and holy though He may be, is still only the peasant of Galilee, not the Christ of God invested with all the prerogatives of deity. The Jesus of modern, cultured thought is not the Jesus of the Gospels and the Epistles; not the Jesus we believe Him to be, who died, rose again, and ascended into heaven, there to intercede for us until He appears in great glory for His redeemed ones.

Another gospel

This different gospel was not the one the Corinthians had received from Paul, namely the gospel of pardon through faith working by love. The perverted gospel he refers to was one based on the old Pharisaic lines of works, ritual, and ceremony.

The old-fashioned gospel of the grace of God is not fashionable in some quarters today. The gospel of redeeming blood, of salvation by faith is treated as worn-out theology. Advancing knowledge has brought us a gospel of ethics, a social gospel, and salvation by works. But as Paul warns us, "If any man preach any other gospel unto you than that ye have received, let him be accursed" (Gal. 1:9).

THE HOLY SPIRIT OF GOD

Another Spirit

From Ellicott's most illuminating *Commentary* on the Scriptures we have this interpretation: "The words, 'another Spirit,' point to a counterfeit inspiration, perhaps like that of those who had interrupted the praises of the church with the startling cry, 'Anathema to Jesus!' . . . Such as these were the 'false prophets' of 2 Peter 2:1; 1 John 4:3; simulating the phenomena of inspiration, perhaps thought of by the apostles as really acting under the inspiration of an evil spirit."

Liberalism in our age has produced "another Spirit," one who has no gracious personality, no deity, but whose works are simply emanations. To quote the findings of the modernistic school of thought, "what the New Testament denotes by 'Holy Spirit' is the divine dynamic energy, pregnant with all the potencies of 'spiritual' or supernatural life, which passed, as in the nervous system of a human organism from head to body, animating and controlling all the members and constituting the whole mystic or spiritual messianic organism, humanity indwelt by God." All of which verbosity is a polite way of bowing out the august person of the Spirit from the biblical revelation of His real substance and service.

A cry for "another Spirit" of a more diabolical sort, however, fills the air. One sure mark of our Lord's speedy return is a greater manifestation of "seducing spirits" (1 Tim. 4:1). And the Spirit Himself expressly warns us against counterfeits of His person and work.

The spirit at the back of spiritualism and all spiritist forces is not the Holy Spirit we love and revere. It is "another spirit," the evil spirit who is the satanic antagonist of the Good Spirit.

What we need, therefore, is a closer study of the Spirit of grace as He is revealed in Scripture. Nothing can rescue the God-dishonoring factions laboring under the cloak of Christianity from deeper apostasy apart from a repentant return to the Holy Spirit Himself. Once He assumes lordship, a true antidote is found for all perversion, apostasy, and spiritual barrenness.

Because it is a Scriptural truth

A. J. Gordon, who has given us one of the most wonderful books ever written on the Spirit's ministry, implied that there is no need to prove His person and prerogatives when they are so clearly taught by Christ in John 14–16. "The discussion," he says, "of the personality of the Holy Spirit is so unnatural in the light of Christ's last discourse that we studiously avoid it." But while such a position is tenable from the standpoint of orthodox believers, we are exhorted to "prove all things." For this reason we set ourselves to the task of outlining what the Bible teaches concerning the reality and resources of the Spirit.

Some belittle the importance of the study before us through a misconception of what our Lord said of the Spirit in John 16:13: ". . . he shall not speak of Himself. . . ." Such a description is taken to imply self-effacement. If in all humanity the Spirit never speaks of Himself, then why should we say much about Him? This, of course, is a misinterpretation of the phrase, as the next qualifying statement proves: ". . . whatsoever he shall hear, that shall he speak. . . ." A comparison of one or two translations will help to clarify the matter.

The American Standard Version has it: "He shall not speak from himself." Weymouth expresses it, "He will not speak as Himself originating what He says, but all that He hears He will speak." Moffat translates the phrase, "He will not speak of His own accord." All of which implies that the Spirit does not act or speak on His own authority or initiative. He does not originate the truth He utters. Receiving it from God, He communicates it to others.

Our Lord's declaration of the Spirit's subordination is in contrast to the attitude of human teachers, as He indicates in a previous chapter: "He that speaketh of himself [that is, acting on his own authority] seeketh his own glory . . ." (John 7:18). Heaven-sent teachers do not speak on their own authority. "I have given unto them the words which thou gavest me . . ." (17:8).

THE HOLY SPIRIT OF GOD

Believing, as we do, that the Bible was inspired by the Holy Spirit, it is not surprising to find His own visible marks across its sacred pages from Genesis 1:1 to Revelation 22:17.

Because it is a practical truth

Conduct is regulated by creed. It is necessary, therefore, to clearly and fully grasp the truth of the Spirit in order that His purposes and character may be revealed in and through our lives. It is not enough to formulate theories about His manifestation. All we discover must have a practical effect upon our lives.

It is true that what we most constantly think about exercises a transforming power over life. A miser unconsciously shows his greed and fascination of gold. The ambitious, unscrupulous man cannot hide the cunning schemes he devises. Pleasure seekers cannot cover up the lustfulness of their mind. "As he thinketh in his heart, so is he . . ." (Prov. 23:7).

Our aim should be to know the truth, the whole truth, and nothing but the truth of the Spirit in such a way as to produce a life of richer devotion and holiness. The Word must become flesh and go out and dwell among men. That such a theme is intensely and immensely practical is emphasized by A. T. Pierson's heart-searching words:

If the Spirit dwells in the body of Christ, and is left free to work His own will, He will quicken the whole body. Members will have a new care one for another, suffering and rejoicing together. There will be a holy jealousy for the welfare and happiness of all who belong to the mystical body, and an earnest and loving co-operation in all holy work. All schism, whether manifest in inward estrangement or in outward separation becomes impossible so far as the Spirit of truth indwells; and all apathy and inactivity in the face of a dying world will give way to sympathetic activity when and so far as the Spirit of life thrills the body; even as all ignorance of God and superstitious worship of forms flee like owls of the night when the spirit of God shines in His divine splendor. In a word, all needs of the church are met so surely and speedily as the Holy Ghost, who still abides in the church as God's only earthly temple, resumes by the consent and co-operation of disciples, His normal control, actively guiding into all truth and duty.

Behind all negligence, perversion, and rejection of the Spirit's operations is the hidden hand of Satan. He fully realizes how detrimental to his satanic plans is a perfect understanding of the work of the Holy Spirit and an entire submission to His way.

The Spirit of Study

No matter what realm of investigation may open to one, the manner in which it is approached largely determines the measure of success in the pursuit of required knowledge. The scientist with his problems; the naturalist and his studies; the scholar with his quest for knowledge, all alike realize that the frame of mind with which they face their tasks prepares them in a very definite way for the discoveries. How then, should we study one of the holiest of themes?

Devotionally

Has not our Lord a somewhat daring word about casting pearls before swine, and giving that which is holy unto the dogs (see Matt. 7:6)? Clearly, one application of such a drastic declaration is that the Holy Spirit will not unveil His magnificence and power unless we seek to maintain a right heart attitude in such a meditation as this. As we read the pages of this book, we must constantly pray that an ever-growing knowledge may be ours and that immediate and implicit obedience to light received will be given. If such a study does not lead to fuller submission to the will of God, to a complete consecration, to a deeper passion for souls, then our goal will not be reached. Light apart from obedience is apt to become darkness, and how great is this darkness!

Dependently

There is no reason to linger here. It is taken for granted that we realize our need of a prayerful, absolute reliance upon the Lord for guidance and tutoring. May we be saved from studying the truth of the Spirit without the direct aid of the Spirit of Truth Himself!

Paul exhorts us to remember that spiritual truths are not discoverable by human wisdom, but are revealed and taught by the Spirit (1 Cor. 2:9–16). What is hid from the wise, who are proud of their wisdom, is revealed unto babes; as R. A. Torrey used to say, "the baby method is the best one for discovering truth."

Doctrinally

As we come to analyze the various aspects of the Spirit's work, we must be prepared to lay aside our preconceived notions or theories. Our judgment must not be confused. We must be ready and willing to think God's thoughts of the Spirit after Him.

The Berean method of searching the Scriptures daily to see whether " [these] things were so" (Acts 17:11) is one to copy as we grapple with any doctrine. And one result occurring from a prayerful, patient, and systematic approach to any phase of scriptural truth is that it becomes a settled conviction. Further, when confronted by the theories, opinions, and speculations of men we instantly receive or reject them, by the law and testimony embedded within our own mind.

CHAPTER TWO

The Personality of the Spirit

Endeavoring to know the Spirit, even as He is known, we must seek after a right adjustment to this Holy One Himself. A spiritual understanding is dependent upon instant and unfailing surrender to truth revealed.

Of course, the Scriptures do not stop to prove the Spirit's reality, but plainly state the fact. Yet some are guilty, either from ignorance or thoughtlessness, of applying neuter pronouns to Him. Others speak of him simply as an influence or an emanation. Both of these are errors so unscriptural and paralyzing to the most pungent exhortations based on the believer's new life in Christ, that I deem it necessary to correct them.

He is an essential part of a divine revelation.

Seeing that the Bible is divinely inspired, the Holy Spirit as its author has had a great deal to say about Himself. Everywhere His prerogatives are before us. And from what He has revealed of Himself, the Spirit means us to understand His part in the divine economy.

He is the direct agent between heaven and earth in this gospel age.

To the Spirit has been committed the sacred task of applying redemption to believing sinners and of making believers holy. He it is who convicts of sin, regenerates, sanctifies, teaches, guides, and inspires us. We are totally dependent upon Him for all that concerns our life in Christ.

He is the administrator of the church's affairs.

This aspect of the Spirit's office work is strongly emphasized in the Acts, a book dealing with the internal economy and external obligations of the church. If churches today were controlled by the Holy Spirit as in apostolic days, their life and work would be entirely revolutionized!

Imperfect views of His mission on the earth make for spiritual barrenness. Downer, in his enlightening volume *The Mission and Ministration of the Holy Spirit,* says, "The results of deficient attention to the study and preaching of the Third Person have appeared in dryness of spiritual experience, a low level of Christian life, formalism in worship, want of discipline in the Church, want of zeal in missionary enterprise."

He is personal, not impersonal.

The error of treating the Spirit in an impersonal way can be traced back to the third century, when the theory was first advanced that the Holy Spirit is a mere influence, an exertion of divine energy and power, and an emanation from God. Such an error has continued with the church and is the position of modernists, as well as a few professedly orthodox branches of the Christian church.

It is conceded that the present usage of the impersonal pronoun by many is attributable to the rendering of Romans 8:16,26 in the King James Version, where the Spirit is mentioned as "it." Such, however, is happily corrected in the modern translations. Surely, there is nothing more dishonoring and displeasing to the Spirit than lack of recognition.

In passages like John 14:16,17; 15:26; 16:7,8, the Spirit is revealed to us as *Him* not *it;* as the living and conscious Exerciser of true personal will and love, as truly and fully as the first "Paraclete," the Lord Jesus Christ Himself (1 John 2:1).

Although He is neither an "influence" nor a sum or series of influences, He yet possesses divine influence. As Harriet Auber expresses it in her renowned hymn on the Spirit,

He comes, sweet influence to impart,
A gracious, willing Guest.

Our fellowship then, as Dr. Jowett reminds us "is not with a 'something' but with a 'Somebody'; not with a 'force' but with a 'Spirit'; not with an 'it' but with 'Him.' " And this leads us to affirm that we must equally honor each of the three equal persons forming the blessed Trinity.

True spiritual worship is dependent upon belief in the Spirit's personality. "It is of the highest importance from the standpoint of worship that we decide whether the Holy Spirit is a Divine Person," says R. A. Torrey, "worthy to receive our adoration, our faith, our love, and our entire surrender to Himself, or whether it is simply an influence emanating from God or a power or an illumination God imparts to us. If the Holy Spirit is a Person, and a Divine Person, and we do not know Him as such, then we are robbing a Divine Being of the worship and the faith and the love and the surrender to Himself which are His due."

Our conception of the Spirit likewise determines our attitude toward Him. If we think of Him merely as an influence then our attitude will be an active one—how can we get more of this power? But if we believe Him to be a person then our attitude will be a passive one. Yielded and still, our daily desires will be, how can He have more of us?

He is represented in important terms.

Almost one hundred times we have the designation "The Holy Spirit." Let us therefore examine the words forming this general title.

The

This simple word may be thought unworthy of notice; yet in view of liberal teaching regarding the Spirit, it is imperative to give some attention to such an unpretentious, definite article. While there are passages where "the" is omitted, there is the

23

tendency to drop it altogether by those denying the Spirit's personality. To state the liberal view, the term *Spirit of God* is not to be interpreted through later theological usage and identified with the Holy Spirit. More probably it is an expression for the life-giving energy of God.

Such a deduction infers that we are not to call Him *the* Holy Spirit but "Holy Spirit," that is, a holy influence or energy. It is to be used in the same sense as the Catholics speak of "holy water." But although the article is missing in some passages relevant to the Spirit, the fact of His personality is not obliterated. Dealing with the question of the missing article, Handley G. Moule says, "In the general light of Scripture teaching on divine influence we are abundantly secure in saying that this means nothing less than the divine Person at work."

We are not to be disturbed if we discover some commentators reminding us that the article "the" is not in the original. The Spirit Himself is still meant, although not expressly named. When the article is used, attention is focused upon the person Himself. "They were all filled with the Holy Spirit" (Acts 2:4, ASV). When the article is omitted as in Acts 19:2, attention is drawn to the power of the person. Thus, it is essential to remember that when the Bible speaks of the Spirit rather than His person both are being emphasized.

Holy

There must be a reason for the use of this adjective some one hundred times. Why is the Spirit thus described? Here are a few reasons:

He is essentially holy in character. Holiness is not only one of His attributes as a member of the Godhead; it is a part of His being. He is holy.

He came from a holy God. And all representatives of such an august, holy One must bear His image (see John 14:26; 17:11; 1 Pet. 1:12,16).

He is in the world to represent the holy Savior. "He shall glorify Me" (John 16:7–15; Heb. 7:26).

He strives to transform us into holy people and advances all

24

holy living through His indwelling and dominion. It is thus that He is called "the Spirit of holiness" (Rom. 1:4), for He is the One who sanctifies the believer (15:16).

> Every virtue we possess
>   And every victory won
> And every thought of holiness
>   Are His alone.

Spirit

The Paraclete is called "Spirit" or "Ghost," the old English word for "spirit," not because He is the only "Spirit" in the Godhead. "God is spirit" (John 4:24 ASV). Christ corrected His disciples for imagining Him to be a "spirit" (Luke 24:37–39). The Holy Spirit carries this designation simply as One who does not have a visible body such as Jesus possessed.

Relation with the Father and the Son is expressed by "Spirit." He is named "the Spirit of God" and "the Spirit of Christ," since he proceeds from both. As human "breath," which is the word used for "spirit," is an invisible part of man and represents his vitality and his life, so the Spirit of God and of Christ is so designated because He is "breathed forth" or given by both for the accomplishment of their mutual purpose in and through man. The Spirit is "the breath of God."

The term also indicates what He is in contrast to what is material. The Spirit is opposite to all that is of the flesh and that is seen. Alexander Cruden has this illuminating comment: "The Holy Ghost is called Spirit, being, as it were, breathed, and proceeding from the Father and Son, who inspire and move our hearts by him ... stirring up spiritual motions in the hearts of believers, purifying and quickening them; or because he is spiritual, invisible, and incorporeal essence."

Again, "Spirit" indicates the particular work of Him who is the Breath of God.

As the thoughts of my mind are articulated through the action of my breath upon the vocal cords, and are transmitted

25

in the shape of words from the inner world of my being to the outer world, so the Spirit, the Breath of God, takes the thoughts of God and the inexpressible yearnings of the believer and articulates them (Rom. 8:26,27).

As "Spirit," the Third Person is the atmosphere in which we live. Like the air we breathe, He comes into continual and indispensable contact with our inner man, supplying our souls with the life and spirit which were in Christ (Ezek. 37:5–10). The name *Holy Spirit* carries with it the idea of a holy, moving, vitalizing breath. At Pentecost, this mighty breath came down like a rushing wind, bringing the soul-bracing atmosphere of the very presence of God in and around the waiting disciples (Acts 2:1–4). He is the One, who, as the wind, makes possible regeneration, and then becomes the atmosphere in which the regenerated one lives, moves, and has his being (John 3:8). The Spirit also visits us like the fragrant breath from some beautiful and fruitful garden, that causes us to feel the reality of that which is yet unseen, and so through hope satisfies every spiritual sense in the new nature, giving us days of heaven upon earth.

Third Person of the Trinity

This oft-quoted expression is not a biblical one but comes from an ancient creed. "The third person of the Trinity, proceeding from the Father and the Son, of the same substance and equal in power and glory, and is, together with the Father and the Son to be believed in, obeyed, and worshipped throughout all ages."

The term *Trinity* is likewise a nonspiritual one. It was first formally used at the Synod of Alexandria in 317 A.D. and was coined to express the doctrine tersely. It signifies threefoldness and is not, as sometimes stated, an abbreviation of "tri-unity." One must hasten to say that this threefoldness of Father, Son, and Spirit or the grouping together of the three persons of the Godhead is clearly taught in Scripture (see Gen. 1:26; 11:7; Matt. 28:19).

The Spirit is spoken of as being "third" not in any sense of inferiority, for no one person in the Trinity is inferior to another. All three are coequal and coeternal as we shall presently see. He is spoken of as being "third" because of His manifestation and work.

The relative functions of Father, Son, and Spirit can be expressed thus: God the Father is the original source of everything (Gen. 1:1). God the Son follows in the order of revelation (John 5:22–27). God the Spirit is the channel through which the blessings of heaven reach us (Eph. 2:18). Thus, the order of divine performance is from the Father, through the Son, by the Holy Spirit.

As the flowers or fruit form the last revealed part of the tree, so the Spirit is "third," since He is the last revealed personality of the trinity. "He is 'third,' not in order of time, or dignity of nature, but in order and manner of subsisting."

Therefore, "there is but one source of deity, the Father, from whom the Holy Spirit issues through the Son, whose image He is, and in whom He rests. The Holy Spirit is the link between the Father and the Son, and is linked to the Father by the Son."

> So God the Father, God the Son,
> And God the Spirit we adore,
> A sea of life and love unknown
> Without a bottom or a shore.

Proofs of Personality

We now come to elaborate the truth that the Spirit is not a mere "something," but a divine "Someone." If He were only a mere influence or force, the way Scripture describes Him would be contradictory and unintelligible.

Once the truth of the Spirit's personality and work are realized, there opens up to one a life of blessedness and power. Handley Moule's testimony is: "Never shall I forget the gain to conscious faith and peace which came to my own soul not long after a first decisive and appropriating view of the crucified Lord as the sinner's sacrifice of peace, from a more intelligent and conscious hold upon the living and most gracious personality of that Holy Spirit, through whose mercy the soul had got that blessed view. It was a new development of insight into the love of God."

Of course, our reach can exceed our grasp. Even the way of the eagle in the air is beyond us. Hence, our interpretation of who and what the Spirit is, is inadequate because of our inability to read or to describe our own experiences fully.

Of this we can be certain, however: Every believer may know without any doubt whatever the fact of the Spirit's indwelling presence, life-giving energy, and sanctifying power. Opinion may differ as to the origin and theory of the Spirit's presence in the soul. But we can be in perfect agreement as to the fact and power of His indwelling.

The Spirit possesses the true elements of personality.

As we usually associate personality with a body, it is somewhat difficult to comprehend the Spirit's personality, seeing He does not have a material form composed of hands, feet, eyes, and mouth. What we are apt to forget is that these parts of the human frame are not characteristics of personality, although they are channels of such; they simply belong entirely to the body.

True personality, then, is not the outward building but the tenant within. Personality is made up of distinctive features or elements known as heart, mind, and will. "Personality," it has been said, "is capacity for fellowship. The very quality which was most singularly characteristic of Jesus manifests itself in the Spirit, only more universally, more intimately, more surely." Being able to think, feel, and will, the Spirit has the capacity for fellowship, which is not possible without personality.

The heart of the Spirit

The heart is the seat of affection. With it, we love or hate persons and things. Paul speaks of "the love of the Spirit" (Rom. 15:30) and as we have elsewhere proved, He is indeed the Spirit of love. Without a heart, comfort is not possible. Early saints could walk "in the comfort of the Holy Spirit" (Acts 9:31 ASV). Grief is also an element of the heart. Where there is no love, there is no grief. The Spirit can be grieved (Eph. 4:30). And how careful we have to be, lest we cause such a loving heart unnecessary pain!

The mind of the Spirit

The mind is the source of intelligence, reason, and knowledge. With our minds we think, plan, devise, comprehend. That the Spirit has a mind is evident from a study of His activities. There is a beautiful precision and order and intelligence in all His works. The incomparable Scriptures, for example, prove His perfect mind. Paul refers to the "mind of the Spirit" (Rom. 8:27), and what a mind He has as "the Spirit of wisdom"! Well, the Spirit has a mind of His own, indicating thought, purpose, and decision (1 Cor. 2:10,11).

The will of the Spirit

With our wills we decide, giving expression to our thoughts and feelings. And true personality consists in preserving the balance between the heart, mind, and will.

Turning to Acts it would seem as if the will of the Spirit more than any other phase of His personality is emphasized. For example, the Spirit commanded and removed Philip (8:29,39). The same Spirit exercised authority over Peter (10:19,20). This Spirit restrained and constrained Paul (16:6,7).

This same person of sovereign majesty uses us just as He determines by His own will (1 Cor. 12:11).

Personality, then, is essential to our conception of the Spirit, as it is of those of the Father and the Son. And so, personality, implying the possession of the qualities of reason, will, and love, is attributable to the Spirit, seeing He is found acting, feeling, knowing, and speaking.

Because He is a Person, all relationships are personal. A man is known by the company he keeps. If, then, we live in His company and maintain a personal, unbroken relationship with Him, we shall become like Him in purpose, desires, thoughts, spiritual ideals, and ambition.

He has a heart, and loves me. Let me therefore love Him and ever strive to please Him!

He has a mind, and constantly thinks and plans for me. Let me learn, and take His plan for my life!

He has a will, so mighty to carry into effect all His loving plans. May I never cross His will, but have a personality completely dominated by Him!

The Spirit was accepted as a person by Christ.

Language has no meaning if the Spirit is not a person, seeing that Jesus repeatedly employed the masculine pronoun when speaking of Him. Thirteen times over, in John 16, for example, He refers to the Spirit as He, Him, Himself. As the Advocate He holds an office only possible to a person. " [I will send] you another Comforter" (John 14:16). Here our Lord speaks of another like Himself who would be able to intercede, help, and console.

The Spirit's mistreatment proves His personality.

Our meditation later in this book testifies to His gracious personality. He can be grieved, blasphemed against, insulted, lied to (Is. 63:10; Eph. 4:30; Matt. 12:31,32; Heb. 10:29; Acts 5:3).

If the Spirit of God is simply an influence, there is no need to concern ourselves about man's treatment of Him, for influence is incapable of recognition, feeling, or action. But believing Him to be one of the persons in the Godhead, "we must treat Him as a Person," says Thomas Goodwin, "apply ourselves to Him as a Person, glorify Him in our hearts as a Person, dart forth beams of special and peculiar love to, and converse with Him as a Person. Let us fear to grieve Him, and also believe Him as a Person." To which we can add the sentiment of Bishop Moule, "May He, the Lord, the Life Giver, personal, sovereign, loving, mighty, preserve us from unfaithfulness of regard toward His blessed person, from untruth of view of His divine work!"

The Spirit's actions could only be performed by a person.

In all, some 160 passages in the Old and New Testaments touch upon the actions of the Spirit. To deny personality to Him is to make these references meaningless and absurd. Here, for example, are some things the Holy Spirit can do:

He can search (1 Cor. 2:10). And what a Searcher! No province is beyond Him. "All things"—things of God, of Christ, of Scripture, of the human heart—He searches, then reveals His discoveries, precious or pernicious, as the case may be.

He can speak (Rev. 2:7; 1 Tim. 4:1). Seven times over we read, "The Spirit saith unto the churches." And His messages are reduced to the individual—"If any man hear." He is thus depicted as whispering into the ear of the saint.

> And His that gentle voice we hear,
> Soft as the breath of even.

He can cry (Gal. 4:6). "No language but a cry." It is in this way that He reminds us of a blessed relationship—a relationship made possible through His own regenerating work.

He can pray (Rom. 8:26). Prayer is only possible for a person. The Spirit then, must be a Person, seeing He can articulate prayer. He is thus identified with Christ as an intercessor (Rom. 8:34; Heb. 7:25; 1 John 2:1).

He can testify (John 15:26,27). It is clearly evident from these passages that if the Spirit is not a person, neither are we endowed with personality, seeing the same ability to witness is applied to Him and ourselves. The Spirit bears witness to us, then through us, to the world.

He can teach (John 14:26; 16:12–14, Neh. 9:20). If the Spirit is only a divine emanation or spiritual influence, then how can a mere "it" teach? The teaching of the Spirit is denied the believer and Christ proven a liar if He is not able to lead us into all truth.

He can lead (Rom. 8:14). Impersonal influence has no power of direct guidance. The Spirit, however, can gently lead into the paths of God. He is able to direct our footsteps and must therefore have life.

He can command (Acts 16:6,7). If we accept the theory of liberalism that the Spirit is only "a divine dynamic energy," how can we account for Paul's recognition of the Spirit's authority over the affairs of service? To the apostle, the Spirit was the dominating personality within the church and had to be implicitly obeyed. Acts presents the presence and presidency of the Holy Spirit of God. In this age, it is only as we recognize, revere, and reckon upon His person and power that we, too, can know what it is to turn the world upside down.

The Spirit's titles are a further evidence of personality.

The Scriptures present us with a remarkable array of titles and names applied to the Spirit, and patient consideration of them is most profitable. F. E. Marsh, in his *Structure of Scripture,* has given us a valuable exposition of many of these titles.

Perhaps one of the most exhaustive classifications of the Spirit's designation is that to be found in *Things of the Spirit,* by C. H. MacGregor, a saintly British scholar of a past generation. Introducing his outline, which we have adapted slightly and here present, MacGregor says that "in the Scriptures we do not find that distinction between nominal and real, which is so familiar to us in the usage of ordinary life. What anything is in name, that it is in reality. The supreme example of this is found in the name of God. What God calls Himself is a revelation of what he is. Therefore, in the names of the Holy Spirit we have a rich revelation of His character and work."

Old Testament names and titles

Within the Old Testament are some ninety direct references

THE PERSONALITY OF THE SPIRIT

to the Spirit, in which He receives eighteen different titles, falling into three groups.

A.   Those expressing His relation to God.

1. The Spirit of God	13 times
2. The Spirit of the Lord	23 times
3. The Spirit of the Lord God	1 time
4. The Spirit	14 times
5. My Spirit	13 times
6. Thy Spirit	4 times
7. His Spirit	6 times

B.   Those expressing His character.

1. Thy Good Spirit	1 time
2. A Free Spirit	1 time
3. Thy Holy Spirit	1 time
4. His Holy Spirit	2 times
5. A New Spirit	2 times

C.   Those expressing His operations upon men.

1. The Spirit of Wisdom	3 times
2. The Spirit that was on Moses	2 times
3. The Spirit of Understanding	1 time
4. The Spirit of Counsel and Might	1 time
5. The Spirit of Knowledge and of the Fear of the Lord	1 time
6. The Spirit of Grace and Supplication	1 time
7. The Spirit of Burning	1 time
8. The Voice of the Almighty	1 time
9. The Voice of the Lord	1 time
10. The Breath of the Almighty	1 time

New Testament names and titles

According to MacGregor's classification 263 passages in the New Testament directly refer to the Holy Spirit. Thirty-nine different designations are applied to the selfsame Spirit, falling into five separate groups.

A. Names expressing His relation to God the Father.

1. The Spirit of God	12 times
2. The Spirit of the Lord	15 times
3. My Spirit	3 times
4. His Spirit	3 times
5. The Promise of the Father	1 time
6. The Promise of My Father	1 time
7. The Gift of God	1 time
8. The Spirit of Him who raised up Jesus	1 time
9. The Spirit which is of God	1 time
10. The Spirit of our God	1 time
11. The Spirit of the Living God	1 time
12. The Holy Spirit of God	1 time
13. The Spirit which He gave us	1 time
14. The Spirit of Your Father	1 time
15. The Power of the Highest	1 time

B. Names expressing His relation to God the Son.

1. The Spirit of Christ	2 times
2. The Spirit of Jesus	1 time
3. The Spirit of Jesus Christ	1 time
4. The Spirit of His Son	1 time
5. Another Comforter	1 time

C. Names expressing His own essential deity.

1. The Spirit	99 times
2. The Same Spirit	6 times
3. The One Spirit	5 times
4. The Eternal Spirit	1 time
5. The Seven Spirits	4 times

D.   Names setting forth His own essential character.

1. The Holy Ghost		73	times
2. The Holy Spirit		17	times
3. The Holy One		1	time

E.   Names setting forth His relation to the people of God.

1. The Spirit of Truth		4	times
2. The Comforter		3	times
3. The Spirit of Holiness		1	time
4. The Spirit of Life		1	time
5. The Spirit of Adoption		1	time
6. The Spirit of Faith		1	time
7. The Spirit of Praise		1	time
8. The Spirit of Wisdom and Revelation		1	time
9. The Spirit of Power and Discipline		1	time
10. The Spirit of Grace		1	time
11. The Spirit whom He made to dwell in us		1	time
12. The Spirit of Glory		1	time
13. The Anointing		2	times

What a magnificent array of titles and designations! Truly, the Spirit can say of Himself, "In the volume of the book it is written of me" (Ps. 40:7). That is as true of Him, as of the Christ He glorifies. If our lives were as full of the Spirit as the Bible is, what different Christians we would be!

CHAPTER THREE

The Deity
of the Spirit

The Scriptures do not stop to prove either the personality or deity of the Holy Spirit. Everywhere, such truth is so clearly expressed and constantly implied that men must be blind to miss or deny it. Quite confidently, Bible writers speak of the Spirit as God, know Him as God, and give Him the position of equality with the Father and the Son.

Paul's description of the Antichrist can be rightfully used of the Holy Spirit, who is, as we are now to see, "as God [sitting] in the temple of God, showing himself that he is God" (2 Thess. 2:4 NKJB-NT).

The Spirit is acclaimed as God.

Often a combination of passages emphasizes the equality of the persons within the Godhead. Here, for example, is a combination covering Father, Son, and Spirit:

"I heard the voice of the Lord" (Is. 6:8–10).

"These things Isaiah said when he saw His glory . . ." (John 12:39–41 NKJB-NT).

"The Holy Spirit spoke rightly by Isaiah" (Acts 28:25-27 NKJB-NT).

In the threefold "holy" of Isaiah 6:3, there is a distinct suggestion of the tripersonality of Jehovah. Plurality is also dominant (v. 8).

Further evidences of equality can be traced by comparing Jeremiah 31:31–34 with Hebrews 10:15,16; Exodus 16:7 with Hebrews 3:7–9; Exodus 16:7 with 2 Corinthians 3:17,18. Where the word LORD is printed in capitals it means "Jehovah"

(Lev. 1:1). In Exodus 17:7 (ASV) the people tempted Jehovah saying, "Is Jehovah among us, or not?" This is referred to in Hebrews 3:7-9. (See also Ps. 78:17,21 and Acts 7:51.)

The early church had no doubt regarding the deity of the Spirit. Without hesitation, they applied divine names to Him. In Acts 5:3,4 Peter faces Ananias and Sapphira with their partial dedication and uses the two phrases "lied unto . . . God" and "lie to the Holy Spirit" interchangeably. The clear implication is that Peter believed the Spirit to be God.

The Spirit shares the attributes of the Father and the Son.

By *attributes* we mean those qualities and properties so conspicuous to deity. Let us briefly consider a few of these divine possessions.

Eternity. "The eternal Spirit" (Heb. 9:14). As the eternal One He is uncreated, and as uncreated is divine. "Eternal" means without beginning or ending of existence. Thus, "the Spirit proceeds timelessly from the Father and is coeternal with the Father and the Son."

Omnipresence. The prefix *omni* signifies "all." An omnibus is a vehicle for all kinds of persons. This quality indicates that the possessor has power to be present everywhere at the same time. Being human, we can only be in one place at a given time. The Spirit, however, is in all believers everywhere. "Whither shall I go from thy [Spirit]?" (Ps. 139:7-10).

Omniscience. There is nothing in and about God that the Spirit cannot know. Only God can search the depths of God. All that pertains to God, Christ, Satan, man, heaven, and earth is known to the Spirit. "The Spirit searcheth all things" (1 Cor. 2:10,11; cf. Is. 40:13,14; Rom. 8:26,27).

Omnipotence. Only God can do all possible things. The power of the Spirit is the power of God, who is the omnipotent One (Rev. 19:6). Christ cast out demons by the Spirit of God (Matt. 12:28). Notice the parallel reference in Luke 11:20 to the "finger" of God. The arm, hand, or finger of God are figures of speech descriptive of the Spirit's unlimited power (Mic. 3:8; Rom. 15:13,19).

Holiness. Holiness, an emphatic mark of deity, is a quality attributed to the Spirit some one hundred times in Scripture; for example, "the holy Spirit of God" (Eph. 4:30). And, as the holy One, He alone can make us the recipients of divine holiness.

Foreknowledge. Deity only can know the end from the beginning or possess the knowledge of a thing before it happens. And that the Spirit has "foreknowledge" is proved by Peter's declaration, "The holy [Spirit] by the mouth of David spake before concerning Judas" (Acts 1:16). Some one thousand years before Judas lived, the Spirit led David to make his prophecy. Another evidence of His foreknowledge, which is a phase of omniscience, is given in Acts 11:27,28.

Sovereignty. By sovereignty, or lordship, we infer complete power of dictation. The apostles recognized this prerogative of deity that the Spirit manifested: "the Lord the Spirit"; "The Spirit saith" (2 Cor. 3:17,18 ASV; Rev. 2:7). "The Holy Spirit said, Separate me Barnabas and Saul for the work whereunto I [the Spirit] have called them" (Acts 13:2-4).

The Spirit performs tasks only possible to deity.

Divine works accomplished by the Spirit are of a varied nature. As the executive of the Godhead, the Spirit is God in action. Among His many works are:

Creation. Man can make; only God can create. Creative power being a divine prerogative, it was exercised by the Spirit at creation. As a mother bird, He brooded over a chaotic condition and produced this beautiful world of ours (Gen. 1:2). As the result of the Spirit's energy, the beauty of the earth, the glory of the sky, and the wonders of oceans came into being. Thus, Cowper in "The Task" expresses it:

> One Spirit—His
> Who wore the platted thorns with bleeding brow,

Rules universal nature. Not a flower
But shares some touch, in freckle, streak or stain,
Of His unrivaled pencil.

Inscribed upon Ruskin's Memorial at Friar's Crag, Keswick, England, are the words, "The Spirit of God is around you in the air you breathe. His glory in the light that you see, and in the fruitfulness of the earth and joy of His creatures. He has written for you day by day His revelation, as He has granted you day by day your daily bread."

The Spirit created the world (Ps. 33:6; Gen. 1:2), created man (Job 33:4), and beautified the heavens (Job 26:13). He brings death upon it (Is. 40:7) and brings life into it (Ps. 104:30).

Inspiration. In biblical usage "inspire" means one who is instructed by divine influence. When Bible writers are spoken of as being borne along by the Spirit, we are to understand them as having minds and pens controlled by the Spirit. The word *inspiration* is made up of two Latin words; *in* or "unto," and *spirare,* meaning "to breathe." To be inspired by the Spirit means that the Spirit has breathed into an individual certain truths He desires for that person to know and declare.

The Spirit came upon individuals both in the Old and New Testaments, causing them to deliver inspired messages (2 Sam. 23:1–3).

The Spirit inspired prophecy in general (1 Tim. 4:1).

The Spirit inspired Scriptures as a whole (2 Tim. 3:16; 2 Pet. 1:21).

Regeneration. As the Spirit of life is able to give life, He generated material and physical life at creation. He brought into being the God-Man, a life unique and marvelous, and now produces spiritual life in all who believe (2 Cor. 3:6; Rom. 8:11).

The Holy Spirit is the personal agent in the new birth, and the instrument He uses is the Word of truth (John 3:1–8). We enter and see the kingdom of God, not by any material process, not by any ceremonial act, not by any self-determination, but by the power of the Spirit of God (1:13).

After quickening and giving life, He indwells those whom

He quickens (1 Cor. 3:16) and then endeavors to indwell them fully (Eph. 5:18). The Spirit abides in those He regenerates as the seal and earnest of their final redemption and future blessedness. Through His indwelling, the Spirit sanctifies (Rom. 15:16; Titus 3:5; 1 Peter 1:2).

Resurrection. Man can bury, but only God can resurrect: "God which raiseth the dead" (2 Cor. 1:9). Deity is evident in all acts of resurrection. As the Spirit has a share in the resurrection of Christ, He must be God—"the Spirit of him that raised up Jesus from the dead . . ." (Rom. 8:11). And the same Spirit will aid in our translation at the Rapture of the church. "The Spirit lifted me up between the earth and the heaven" (Ezek. 8:3) can be linked with the meeting of the Lord in the air (1 Thess. 4:17).

The Spirit is identified with the Father and the Son.

C. I. Scofield says, "There is no biblical reason for believing in the deity and personality of the Father and the Son, which does not equally establish that of the Spirit." How profitable it is to trace the blessed partnership of the Trinity.

The work of the Cross

Because it is a divine work, the redemption of the soul is precious (see Ps. 49:8). None can redeem his brother (v. 7); therefore, Christ was "made unto us . . . redemption" (1 Cor. 1:30). As redemption is the work of deity, and not of man, all associated with it must bear the same nature.

It is easy to prove that the holy three—Father, Son, and Spirit—were associated in the work of the Cross. One key verse is Hebrews 9:14.

There is the Godward aspect—"without spot to God."

There is the Christward aspect—"the Blood of Christ."

There is the Spiritward aspect—"through the eternal Spirit."

There is the manward aspect—"Purge your conscience from dead works to serve the living God."

The three parables of Luke 15—the lost son, the lost sheep, the lost silver—fittingly illustrate the respective work of the Father, the Son, and the Spirit in salvation.

The baptismal formula

In our Lord's great commission (Matt. 28:16-20), He instructs His disciples to baptize all who believe in "the name of the Father and of the Son and of the Holy Spirit" (ASV). Note, it is not in the names, but "name." All three, then, are one—one in deity and accomplishment. The singular here presents one God in three Persons.

The apostolic benediction

The much loved benediction of the church, with which Paul closes his second Epistle to the Corinthians, is also eloquent with the truth of the Trinity. Not only does this benediction teach us the invocation and adoration of Father, Son, and Spirit, it likewise ascribes to each their understanding quality: "The grace of the Lord Jesus Christ," medium of all blessing; "the love of God," source of all blessing; and "the fellowship of the Holy Spirit," dispenser of all blessing.

The heavenly witness

Scholars are agreed that John's word relative to the threefold heavenly witness is not authoritative but has crept into the text; yet the implied truth is nevertheless precious. "There are three that bear record in heaven, the Father, the Word, and the Holy [Spirit]: and these three are one. And there are three that bear witness in earth, the spirit, and the water, and the blood: and these three agree in one" (1 John 5:7,8).

The united access

In emphasizing that Jews and Gentiles are one body in Christ, Paul unites the persons of the Trinity. "For through him (Christ Jesus) we both (Jew and Gentile) have access by one Spirit unto the Father" (Eph. 2:18). Thus, whether it be for

41

salvation or worship, we come to God, through the Son, by the Holy Spirit.

Concluding this meditation on the Spirit's deity, in which we have sought to prove His equality with the Father and the Son, it may be necessary to indicate evidences of subordination on His part. The Scriptures draw the clearest possible distinction between the Father, Son, and Spirit. Giving to each their separate personalities, and outlining their mutual relations as they act upon one another, they apply pronouns of the second and third persons to one another. The same Scriptures also teach the Spirit is subordinate to God and to Christ.

One of the mysteries of our faith is that Christ, who thought it not robbery to be equal with God (Phil. 2:6), was yet subordinate to the will of His Father (John 6:29; 8:29,42; 9:4; 17:8). The subordination of the Spirit to the Son is brought out in that He does not glorify Himself but Christ, even as Christ Himself sought not His own glory, but the Father's (7:18; cf. 16:13–15). Thus, as Bengel expresses it, "The Son glorifies the Father, the Spirit glorifies the Son." And, if any addition is allowed, the believer glorifies all three.

The practical application of the Spirit's subordination is not far to seek. We must be as subordinate to Him as He Himself was, and is, to the Father and the Son. And in our continual subordination to the Spirit, we are inspired by the example of the Master, who, as it has been stated, "is the one perfect manifestation in history of the complete work of the Holy Spirit in man." As He is our pattern, and "the firstborn among many brethren" (1 John 2:6; Rom. 8:29), then whatever He realized through the Spirit is for us to realize in our daily lives.

During a preaching mission in Minneapolis, D. L. Moody gave his remarkable sermon on "The Holy Spirit." At the close of the service a man came up to the evangelist and said, "Mr. Moody, you speak as if you had a monopoly on the Holy Spirit." Moody's reply was, "No, decidedly, no! But I do trust the Holy Spirit has a monopoly on me."

CHAPTER FOUR

The Attributes of the Spirit

A close study of Scripture reveals three great dispensations or ages in which one of the three persons in the Godhead is prominent.

The Old Testament is the dispensation of the Father. In it He is at work for us. His promises are scattered everywhere, and they must be realized in experience.

In the Gospels we have the dispensation or age of God the Son, during which He lives with us, promising to send us the Spirit. No one before Pentecost could become a partaker of the life and fullness of the risen Savior.

In the Acts and the Epistles is found the dispensation of God the Spirit, who carries on the work of Christ in and through us. Note the progressive development: God is *for* us, *with* us, *in* us. And the Holy Three are vitally connected. The relation of the dispensation of the Spirit to that of the Father and of the Son is one of fulfillment and promise.

Such a threefold division is clearly distinct, outlining as it does the time and ministry of each person of the Trinity. Yet because the Bible gives to us a gradual, progressive revelation of the Spirit's person and power, I think it necessary to study the activities of the Spirit from our first glimpses of Him in Genesis to His full manifestation in Revelation.

Old Testament Activities

Association in creation

From the first reference to the Spirit (Gen. 1:2) to the last mention of Him in the Old Testament (Mal. 2:15), we have in twenty-two of the thirty-nine books comprising this section of the Bible a wonderful insight into the power and prerogatives of the Spirit.

Of such a limited manifestation Dr. Downer writes,

> His separate personality, although indicated, was not clearly set forth. Mankind was not prepared for the intense interest belonging to a new personality in the divine nature. They had not yet learned to know the Father perfectly. Nor again, had there yet appeared the divine Man, in whom alone the blessed Spirit could dwell without measure or hindrance, could put forth His noblest powers, could exhibit and unfold God's purpose, not made known previously to the Incarnation, by means of the mediator's cross and resurrection.
>
> The true abode of the Spirit was, and ever must be, the God-Man, crucified, risen, ascended, coming again. ... In its relation to New Testament days, the Old Testament revelation of the Spirit must be regarded as an earnest, the Pentecostal revelation being the fullness. Yet, the work He did in the souls of men before Christ came, He still continues to do, but more perfectly, inasmuch as it is done now in closest connection with the Son of God, incarnate, crucified, ascended and glorified.

Consider the Spirit's work in creation. Bishop Handley Moule reminds us that He is mysteriously yet distinctly revealed as the immediate divine agent in the making and manipulation, so to speak, of material things.

Strange, is it not, that although the Holy Spirit is thus named partly because of the contrast of His substance with that which is material, He is most definitely connected with a world of matter. Biblical writers scarcely took into their thinking the idea of second causes, as many modern writers do in seeking a rational reason for all that is seen. To holy men of old the phenomena of nature were the results of God's direct action through His eternal Spirit.

He is co-Creator of the world.

There are at least three key passages proving the Spirit's

share in the creation of the universe. "The Spirit of God moved upon the face of the waters" (Gen. 1:2); "By his spirit he hath garnished the heavens" (Job 26:13); "Thou sendest forth thy Spirit, they are created" (Ps. 104:30; 147:14–18). (In the latter passages the psalmist refers to all aspects of creation.)

Recognizing what A. T. Pierson called "the law of first mention," our first glimpse of the Spirit in Scripture is that of a Creator (Gen. 1:2). And this is as it should be, seeing that creative power is a dominant feature of His activities.

Before God said, "Let there be light," He said, "Let there be Spirit," comments George Matheson. "It was the keynote of all His voices to the human soul. It is no use to bring light until you have brought the Spirit. Light will not make the waters of life glad unless the Spirit of joy has already moved them. . . . It is well that the Spirit should come before all His gifts—before the light, before the firmament, before the herb of the field."

But we are guilty of inverting the order of the Spirit's work, and crave for gifts rather than the Giver! What we cry for is light, sun, moon, and stars; for the green herb, for the birds of heaven, forgetting that without the Giver Himself there could not be light to charm, grass to grow, birds to sing. As Matheson prayed, "Without Thee the days of my creation are evenings without mornings: the nightless Sabbath shall have dawned when Thou shalt move upon the waters."

He is co-Creator of man.

In the Nicene Creed the Spirit is spoken of as "The Lord, the life-giver." A combination of further passages describes Him as the direct agent in the creation of man, just as He is responsible for His re-creation. As "the breath of the Almighty," He imparts life to nature and man. Generation and regeneration are among His activities. "Let us make man in our image, after our likeness," He says in Genesis 1:26. "(He) breathed into his nostrils the breath [spirit] of life" says Genesis 2:7. "The Spirit of God hath made me, and the breath of the Almighty has given me life," says Job (33:4).

Man likes to have an honorable pedigree. He is proud of a good ancestry, an ancestry whose character was goodness.

> We have an ancestry which goes back beyond nature, beyond maternity, beyond the flesh. We have a pedigree which is older than the mountains, older than the stars, older than the universe. We are come from a good stock; we are branches of a high family tree; we are scions of a noble house, a house not made with hands, eternal in the heavens. Nature is the parent of our flesh, but the divine is the Father of our spirits, the Spirit of God hath made us, and the breath of the Almighty has given us life.

This poetic description of our heritage, taken from George Matheson's *Voices of the Spirit,* proves the divinity of our origin. We did not gradually evolve from lower forms of creation. God the Spirit was responsible for our being.

He is co-Creator of the animal world.

It is no degradation of our nature to declare that the same Spirit responsible for our creation fashioned all that has breath. "To believe that God's Spirit is the missing link between ourselves and the animal world," says one writer, "is to reach a Darwinism where there is nothing to degrade. We did not come from them, but we and they together are the offspring of God."

"Thou sendest forth thy Spirit, they are created . . ." (Ps. 104:30). It is evident from the immediate context that the "all" and the "they" refer to the living creatures of the whole world, and to beasts, birds, and fish in particular (104:25,26; Gen. 1:21).

Two thoughts emerge from this aspect of the Spirit's creative work. First of all, seeing we are bound together with the animal world by one Spirit of creation, we cannot be cruel to those creatures sharing our natural life. Here is the greatest argument in favor of the prevention of cruelty to animals.

In the second place, seeing we sit at "the one communion table of nature" (cf. Is. 65:24,25) the animal world will also share in the fruits of Christ's redemption and experience a mighty deliverance when He comes to reign as the Prince of the kings of the earth (see Rom. 8:19–22).

He is the co-Creator of beauty.

Job tells us that it was the Holy Spirit who made splendid the heavens (Job 26:13). Paul discourses on the respective glory of the sun, moon, and stars and staggers us with the thought that "one star differeth from another star in glory" (1 Cor. 15:41). Truly, "the heavens declare the glory of God" (Ps. 19:1).

Matthew Henry, one of the most thought-provoking of Bible commentators, has this expressive comment.

The Spirit not only made the heavens, but beautified them: has curiously bespangled them with stars by night, and painted them with the light of the sun by day. God, having made man to look upward (to man he gave an erect countenance) has therefore garnished the heavens, to invite him to look upward, that by pleasing his eye with the dazzling light of the sun, and the sparkling light of the stars, their number, order and various magnitudes, which as so many golden studs, beautify the canopy drawn over our heads, he may be led to admire the greater Creator, the Father and Fountain of Lights, and to say, "If the pavement be so richly inlaid, what must the palace be!" If the visible heavens be so glorious, what are those that are out of sight! From the beauteous garniture of the antechambers, we may infer the precious furniture of the presence chamber. If stars are so bright, what are angels!

But while the Spirit is the Creator of all beauty above, He is likewise responsible for beauty all around us in a world "where every prospect pleases." What a wealth of loveliness, richness of variety, color, and form nature presents! It is here that we can appreciate Psalm 29, especially when we remember that the creative voice spoken of therein is the Holy Spirit Himself, whom Ezekiel describes as "the voice of the Almighty" (Ezek. 10:5).

THE HOLY SPIRIT OF GOD

He is co-Creator of substance.

Few of us realize that the continual harvests of the fields are made possible by the Holy Spirit. Combining the following passages we come to praise the Spirit as our daily Provider and Benefactor.

"Until the Spirit be poured upon us from on high, and the wilderness be a fruitful field, and the fruitful field be counted for a forest" (Is. 32:15). "These wait all upon thee; that thou mayest give them their meat in due season" (Ps. 104:27; cf. 136:25; 145:15,16; 147:9).

And what the blessed Spirit is within the realm of nature, He is also within the realm of grace. Spiritual harvests and renewals are dependent upon His gracious visitations. Food for the maintenance of our spiritual lives is likewise derived from such a bountiful Source. He it is who feeds our hungry souls with the Bread of Life.

> Bounteous Spirit ever shedding
>   Life the world to fill!
> Swarms the fruitful globe o'erspreading,
> Shoals their ocean pathway threading,
>   Own Thy quickening thrill:
> Author of each creature's birth,
> Life of life beneath the earth,
> Everywhere, O Spirit Blest,
> Thou art motion, Thou art rest.
>
> Come, Creator! grace bestowing,
>   All Thy sevenfold dower!
> Come, Thy peace and bounty strowing,
> Earth's Renewer! Thine the sowing,
>   Thine the gladd'ning shower.
> Comforter! what joy Thou art
> To the blest, and faithful heart;
> But to man's primeval foe
> Uttermost despair and woe.
>
> O'er the waters of creation
>   Moved Thy wings Divine:

48

When the world to animation
Walking 'neath Thy visitation,
    Teem'd with powers benign:
Thou didst man to being call
Didst restore him from his fall;
Pouring, like the latter rain
Grace to quicken him again.
                        —Author unknown

He is the co-Creator of rest.

What a tender, considerate Holy Spirit we have! Who would ever think of associating the sweet, refreshing sleep of hard-worked animals with the gracious Spirit! Yet it is so, for as the Spirit of life He renews both man and beast alike with the priceless boon of rest (Ps.127:2). "As the cattle that go down into the valley, the Spirit of Jehovah caused them to rest" (Is. 63:14 ASV).

And as the gentle Dove, He can put to sleep those fears, doubts, and turbulent forces within our hearts making for disquiet and unrest. "Thou art motion, Thou art rest," says one lyricist.

Such a spiritual application is beautifully emphasized in these unforgettable words taken from George Matheson's cameos of the third person.

The Spirit gives us rest by abasing our animal nature, "as the beast goeth down into the valley." The process by which the cattle go down into the valley is not restful; it is the descent of a steep. Their rest is reached by unrest—by movement downward. Even so it is with the spiritual rest. It is only in the valley of humiliation that thou canst find it. By nature thou art in the mountains. Thou art standing on the hilltop of vanity: thou seest nothing above thee: thou art low unto thyself. . . . God's Spirit must lead thee down as the cattle are led down. Thou must be brought down into a lowly place where thy pride shall die. . . . O glorious shadows that hide me from my own shadow, O gentle valley that divides me from the mountains of my pride, O wondrous evening that shelters me from the burden and heart of my selfish care, O

49

rest of love that means the awakening of all that is noble, it is worth while to be brought down that I may repose in Thee.

He is co-Creator of death.

The Holy Spirit, as the life giver, able to make alive and continually quicken the body, is also able to take life away. At the command of God, the Spirit looses "the silver cord," breaks "the golden bowl" (Eccl. 12:6,7). Look at these further passages: "My Spirit shall not always strive with man, for that he also is flesh" (Gen. 6:3; 7:22). "The grass withereth, the flower fadeth: because the Spirit of the Lord bloweth upon it: surely the people is grass" (Is. 40:7; cf. Ps. 104:29; 147:16,17). Turning to Acts 5:1–4 we find that the same Spirit can also produce sudden death.

He is co-Creator of Christ's human body.

As the Spirit formed the first Adam without natural agency, so He fashioned the body of the last Adam apart from the ordinary course of nature. Christ's birth was miraculous, not in the forming of His body within the womb of Mary, but in the manner of its begetting. Our Lord's birth was supernatural in that He was created as the result of a divine creative act apart from natural generation. He was conceived of the Holy Spirit (Matt. 1:20).

Further, this direct act of the Spirit within the body of Mary produced not only a human body for Christ, but also a sinless one (Luke 1:35). Christ's body in which He lived, toiled, suffered, and died, was glorified and taken up to heaven. And, as Rabbi Duncan expressed it, "The dust of the earth is on the throne of the Majesty on high."

Such a body, however, was composed of flesh and blood received from Mary, who although a virgin was tainted with original sin. Job asks how anyone can be clean: "Who can bring a clean thing out of an unclean? not one" (Job 14:4). How can we account for Christ's sinlessness? The mystery is solved by the phrase, "The Holy Spirit shall overshadow thee" (ASV). The Spirit of holiness consecrated and purified that part of the virgin's flesh whereof Christ, according to the flesh, was fashioned. A writer of a past generation put it thus, "As the alchemist extracts and draws away the dross from the gold, so the Holy Ghost refines and clarifies that part of the virgin's flesh, separating it from sin. Though Mary herself had sin, yet that part of her flesh, whereof Christ was made, was without sin, otherwise it must have been an impure conception."

Thus, what happened from the divine side was "a divine, created miracle wrought in the production of this new humanity which secured from its earliest germinal beginning, freedom from the slightest taint of sin." No wonder one of the old divines exclaims, "I can scarce get past His cradle in my wondering to wonder at His Cross. The infant Jesus is in some views a greater marvel than Jesus with the purple robe and the crown of thorns."

He is co-Creator of the new nature.

Our Lord's birth by the Spirit is a type of our new birth or rebirth. It is "that which is born of the Spirit" (John 3:6); "born . . . of God" (1:3); "Through the Spirit . . . being born again" (1 Pet. 1:22,23); "A new creation" (2 Cor. 5:17 NKJB-NT).

The notable difference between the creation of our Lord's physical nature, and the creation of our spiritual nature by the same Spirit can be expressed this way: At the Virgin Birth of Christ there was added to His already existing divine nature, a human nature, while at our rebirth the Spirit adds a divine nature to an already existing human nature.

Regeneration does not make a sinner a better man, but brings in a new man. By faith the believing one is made a partaker of the divine nature.

He is co-Creator of the church.

Pentecost marks the birthday of the church of Jesus Christ. Previously, the disciples existed as units but through the coming of the Spirit they were fused together into the mystic fabric Paul called "the church of God" (Acts 20:28).

Responsible for the Lord's physical body, the Spirit produces

51

His mystical body of which Christ is the head. Having brought the church into being, the Creator-Spirit graciously condescends to indwell such a holy creation (see Eph. 2:19–22).

He is co-Creator of the Scriptures.

While over forty writers were employed in the compilation of Scripture, it possessed only one divine Author. "Holy men of God spake as they were moved by the Holy [Spirit]" (2 Pet. 1:21; cf. 1 Pet. 1:10,11; 2 Tim. 3:16; 2 Sam. 23:2,3).

And having inspired the Scriptures, the Spirit alone is able to unfold their treasures to obedient hearts. He it is who guides us into all truth and grants us spiritual discernment (John 16:13–15; 1 Cor. 2:10–14). Proud man, exalting his acquired knowledge and culture, endeavors to understand the Word of God by the light of his own natural reason, but remains totally ignorant of its spiritual content. Truth is revelation, and such revelation can only come from the Spirit of wisdom and revelation.

He is the co-Creator of the new creation.

While there are no direct Scriptures linking the Spirit to the new creation as His express work, the inference is that having been commissioned by God to act in a creative capacity, He will have a share in the last creation, magnificent beyond degree. The new heavens and a new earth will form the climax of His creations. They will form His masterpiece (Is. 65:17; 66:22; 2 Pet. 3:12,13; Rev. 21:1).

With this aspect of the Spirit's activities before us we can understand the holy joy and exaltation possessing such a Creator as He carried John to a great and high mountain and unfolded to his adoring gaze "that great city, the holy Jerusalem, descending out of heaven from God" (Rev. 21:10). And believing that the holy city is "the bride, the Lamb's wife," that is, the church in government and millennial splendor, we can detect a beautiful combination in such a fact. The church is not yet without spot and wrinkle. Here below she has many blemishes, living as she does in a corrupt and hostile world. But when she is glorified and made entirely holy she is to have a world akin to her perfect nature. Thus, the last creative act of the Spirit is to prepare an absolutely holy home for an absolutely holy bride and bridegroom.

Association with Old Testament characters

Classifying the manifold operation of the Holy Spirit in, through, and upon certain biblical characters is indeed a most profitable study.

Before attempting such an analysis, however, it must be made clear that in the Old Testament the Spirit is found working in an *external* way. He came upon different men endowing them for different purposes with different kinds of power.

While it is true that He did enter several individuals (Gen. 41:38; Ex. 31:3; Num. 27:18; Neh. 9:30; Dan. 4:8,9; 1 Pet. 1:10,11), His incoming was more of an inworking than an indwelling. Remaining among men, He did not abide with them (cf. Ps. 51:11 with Hag. 2:5).

In the New Testament, where we have the fuller and final revelation of the Spirit's activities, His *internal* work is strongly emphasized. He now comes, not merely upon men, but into their hearts, there to remain until death or translation at Christ's return (John 14:16). His coming in the Old Testament was intermittent, but in the New Testament the glorified Christ sent Him as the permanent gift to His own.

In the Old Testament the Spirit of God comes upon men and works on them in special times and ways, working from above and without, inward. In the New, the Holy Spirit enters and dwells within them, working from within, outward and upward. Let us then trace His footsteps in Old Testament Scriptures.

As seen in rulers and kings

The Spirit, as the executive of the Godhead, bestowed administrative, governmental, and legislative abilities. He inspired leadership and military efficiency and all functions of government legislation, the direction of troops and the defense of the country.

Joseph received administrative and governmental power (Gen. 41:39). By the Spirit Joseph was given political wisdom and ruled wisely and well for Pharaoh. Many national problems would cease if rulers today would choose Spirit-filled men with administrative ability as Pharaoh did.

Moses and the seventy elders were endued with the power of leadership (Num. 11:17-29). The Spirit divided the burden of the people among Moses and the chosen elders.

Joshua was prepared by the Spirit as the successor of Moses (Num. 27:18; Deut. 34:9). Filled with the Spirit of wisdom, Joshua became famous as the leader and guide of Israel. It is ever good when one Spirit-endowed leader follows another.

Saul was associated with the Spirit in a threefold way. By the Spirit he was given another heart in order to prophesy (1 Sam. 10:7-10). By the Spirit he manifested holy righteous anger (1 Sam. 11:6). By the Spirit he was given over to an evil spirit (1 Sam. 16:14).

David was empowered by the Spirit to reign and write. By the Spirit he was anointed king (1 Sam. 16:13-18). By the Spirit he wrote his last message (2 Sam. 23:1-3). By the Spirit he composed all his Psalms (Matt. 22:43; Acts 1:16; Heb. 3:7; 4:3-7).

Amasai was given physical and moral courage (1 Chr. 12:18). In these apostate days we certainly need men of Amasai's caliber, who can say to Christ what Amasai said to David, "Thine are we . . . and on thy side. . . ."

Daniel was empowered as an interpreter and ruler. This prime minister of Babylon was helped by the Spirit in a twofold way. The Lord gave him power to interpret dreams (Dan. 4:8-18; 5:11), and He gave him political and administrative wisdom (Dan. 5:14; 6:2,3).

Even ungodly rulers, destitute of the Spirit themselves, recognized the presence of spiritual enduement in those who were Spirit-possessed (see Gen. 41:38).

As seen in the power conferred upon judges

Approaching the Book of Judges for the purpose of outlining the presence and plan of the Spirit, we are somewhat amazed to find that He sometimes imparted His power to people without regard to their moral qualifications. God's purpose concerned the theocratic kingdom and implied the covenant between Him and Israel, not just the individuals upon whom the Spirit came.

Othniel was blessed to judge and deliver Israel (Judg. 3:10). Gideon was empowered to conquer his nation's foes (Judg. 6:34). Jephthah, by the Spirit, judged and delivered Israel (Judg. 11:29). Samson received his Herculean strength from the Spirit for his journeying (Judg. 13:25); to slay a lion (Judg. 14:6); to slay thirty men (Judg. 14:19); and to slay one thousand Philistines (Judg. 15:14,15).

As seen in the ministry of prophets

Without doubt the most distinctive and important manifestation of the Spirit's activity in the Old Testament was in the sphere of prophecy. True prophets were especially distinguished from others as those who were related to the Spirit of God (Hos. 9:7). These prophets ascribed their messages directly to Him (Ezek. 2:2; 8:3; 11:1,24; cf. 13:3; 1 Pet. 1:11; 3:19; 2 Pet. 1:21). He it was who gave them spiritual insight and foresight, and made them both forthtellers and foretellers.

By the Spirit Moses and the elders prophesied (Num. 11:17–29). And by the Spirit Balaam proclaimed the glory of Israel (Num. 24:2).

"The case of Balaam," says Professor E. Mullins, "presents difficulties. He does not seem to have been a genuine prophet; but rather a diviner, although it is declared that the Spirit of God came upon him. Balaam serves, however, to illustrate the Old Testament point of view. The chief interest was the national or theocratic or covenant ideal, not that of the individual." Saul presents a similar example. He was God's messenger speaking God's message by the Spirit. His message was not his own. It came directly from God, and at times it overpowered the prophet with its urgency, as in the case of Jeremiah (see Jer. 1:4–10).

God sometimes uses bad men and disobedient believers (Num. 20:11–13; 23:5; 1 Sam. 10:10), not because they are bad or disobedient, but because they are the best material at hand for the accomplishment of His purpose. Balaam, for example, was resistant to being used by the Spirit and therefore will receive no reward for his work. May we covet to be used by the Spirit because we are worthy of being used!

In order, we have other prophets associated with the Spirit.

> Saul and his messengers (1 Sam. 9:19–24)
> Elijah (1 Kin. 18:12; 2 Kin. 2:16)
> Elisha (2 Kin. 2:15)
> Zedekiah (false prophet) (1 Kin. 22:21,24; 2 Chr. 18:23)
> Azariah (2 Chr. 15:1)
> Isaiah (Acts 28:25)
> Jeremiah (Jer. 1:9; 30:1,2)
> Ezekiel (Ezek. 2:2; 3:12,14; 8:3; 36:26,27; 37:1,14; 39:29)
> Daniel (Dan. 4:8,9)
> Joel (Joel 2:28; Acts 2:16,17)
> Micah (Mic. 3:8; cf. 2:7)
> All the prophets (Neh. 9:20; Prov. 1:23; Zech. 7:12; Acts 11:28; 1 Pet. 1:11; 3:19; 2 Pet. 1:21)

As seen in the service of priests

Closely allied with the ministry of the prophet was that of the priest. The prophet went out to speak to man from God; the priest went before God for man's sake. Believers are both prophets and priests. Samuel exercised both offices, being Israel's prophet–priest while the nation was a theocracy.

Among the priests operated upon by the Spirit, mention can be made of the following:

> Jahaziel encouraged those to whom he was sent (2 Chr. 20:14).

Zechariah rebuked Israel (2 Chr. 24:20).
Zechariah received the announcement of John's birth (Luke 1:5,67).
Priestly work foreshadowed Calvary (Heb. 9:6–8).

Association with institutions

Two prominent institutions were associated with the life of Israel from Moses to Christ, namely the tabernacle and the temple, the latter being the most permanent structure for religious exercises. In the erection of these dwelling places of God, certain individuals possessing natural talent and skill received a special endowment of the Holy Spirit of a constructive and artistic nature.

The tabernacle

Bezaleel and others received artistic talents and practical skill to work in all manner of crafts (Ex. 31:1–6; 35:30–32; cf. 28:3).

The Spirit gave wisdom to make priestly garments (Ex. 28:3; 31:3). He also inspired the people to give liberally (Ex. 35:21,22). The same Spirit revealed that the tabernacle was only temporary and typical (Heb. 9:8).

The temple

The Spirit was also related to the more glorious permanent shrine prepared for by David and built by Solomon. All plans for the building of the temple came from the Spirit (1 Chr. 28:12).

He also inspired the prophecy of its rebuilding in the latter days (Zech. 4:6). This promise seems to indicate that where man's power and wisdom proved insufficient, the Spirit of the Lord would enable the rebuilding of the temple.

Association with nations

The first indication in Scripture of the Spirit's ministry in respect to national affairs is in Genesis 6, where it is said that He would not always strive with men. It may be that He was the direct agent in the destruction overtaking the antediluvians.

In the following outline it will be found that the Spirit was not only associated with the nation Israel. Through her, the Spirit touched the surrounding nations. Israel was chosen by God from among the nations, not that He might regard her as a favorite, but that through the chosen race He might gather a vast multitude unto Himself out of every tribe, tongue, and nation. Here, then, is a summary of the Spirit's association with Israel.

He foretold her beauty and order (Num. 24:1–9).
He was her companion (Hag. 2:5).
He was her teacher (Neh. 9:20).
He revealed her failure (2 Chr. 24:20).
He was grievously sinned against by her (Is. 63:10; Mic. 2:7; Acts 7:51).
He witnessed against her (Neh. 9:30).
He denied her blessing (Ps. 95:7–11; Heb. 3:7–19).
He predicts her judgment (Mic. 3:8).
He promises fullness to her King (Is. 11:1–3; 42:1; 48:16; 61:1).
He proclaims her restored fruitfulness (Is. 32:15,16; 44:3).
He guards her interest (Is. 59:19).
He equips her Messiah to establish her (Is. 61:1–11).
He prophesies wonderful times for her (Ezek. 2:2; 3:12–14; 8:3; cf. Joel 2:28,29; Zech. 12:10).

In some old Bibles the headnotes indicate that all the blessings spoken of in the Old Testament were for the church, and all the curses for the Jews. It is, of course, superfluous to say that such introductions are not part of original Scripture, but simply the additions of men. The church is not revealed in the Old Testament, as Paul clearly teaches (Eph. 3:1–5). Thus, all the blessings are primarily for those to whom they were given, namely Israel.

But while all the above is true, the church has the "life-rent" of many of the foregoing Spirit-inspired promises given to the Jew. Although given to Israel and partially fulfilled on her behalf, their complete fulfillment is in abeyance because of her disobedience. And now, since the Spirit's outpouring at Pentecost, the church has every right to enjoy the "life-rent" of such promises. Israel's time of full possession is coming.

The equipment of the saints

Thus, while all the Bible is not about us, it is all for us. For example, take what the prophet has to say about the enemy coming in like a flood and the Spirit lifting up a standard against him (Is. 59:19). The promise was given to Israel and refers to her coming, final deliverance. Yet we can take it and live upon it. The enemy is the Devil and all his forces; the standard is the Cross and Calvary's finished work is ever the Spirit's weapon of victory over all satanic powers.

> He is the embodiment of goodness (Neh. 9:20; Ps. 143:10).
> He inspires fear of the Lord (Is. 11:2–5).
> He represents judgment and righteousness (Is. 32:15–17).
> He prompts devotion to the Lord (Is. 44:3–5).
> He begets hearty obedience and a new heart (Ezek. 36:26).
> He leads the soul to repentance and prayer (Zech. 12:10–14).

An examination of the foregoing outlines, then, recognizes the Holy Spirit as the source of inward, moral purity, even though such a work is not so fully revealed or developed as in the New Testament. Already, under remarks on Balaam, we have noted in Old Testament times the Spirit came upon people irrespective of moral character. But in this dispensation of grace, things are totally different. Now He enters and abides within believers, and constantly endeavors to transform them into the holiness God commands: "Be ye holy."

Our possession of the Spirit depends upon our acceptance of Christ as Savior. His entire possession of us depends upon our entire submission to His control and of the continual application of Christ's blood to our sins.

Such, then, is a glimpse of the varied work of the Spirit in Old Testament Scripture. Among His many varied gifts, we have taken note of physical strength, mental power, practical skill, prophetic foresight, political wisdom, moral courage, and spiritual insight. What a mighty Spirit the third person of the Trinity is—the Spirit of God!

Yet He is mightier now, for He is not only "the Spirit of God" but "the Spirit of Christ," which means that all included in our Lord's incarnation, death, resurrection, ascension, and intercession is added to His bestowals. And this is the great One who condescends to indwell us. What grace!

As we end our discussion of the Spirit's activities in the Old Testament, we may find it profitable to catalog how he equips certain individuals for their specific tasks.

The Spirit "comes" upon men.

The word for "come" literally means "clothes Himself with men" and is used in three instances:

Gideon. "The Spirit of the Lord came upon Gideon" (Judg. 6:34). Gideon's name means "he that bruises and cuts off iniquity." With Gideon, the Spirit became the mantle of exhortation.

Amasai. "The Spirit came upon Amasai" (1 Chr. 12:18). His name signifies "burden of the Lord," and with Amasai the Spirit became the mantle of courage.

Zechariah. "The Spirit of God came upon Zechariah" (2 Chr. 24:20). A suggestive name this, it means "remembrance or man of the Lord." The Spirit came upon Zechariah as the mantle of rebuke.

The Spirit "comes mightily upon" men.

The phrase "comes mightily upon" literally implies that He attacked men; as a greater force He compelled them to accomplish His task. It was thus He came upon:

Samson. "The Spirit of the Lord came mightily upon him" (Judg. 14:6,19; 15:14).

Saul. "The Spirit of God came mightily upon Saul" (cf. 1 Sam. 10:6,10).

David. "The Spirit of the Lord came upon David" (1 Sam. 16:13).

The Spirit is "upon" men.

"Was upon" is a milder phrase and expresses a divine endowment for the time being. For illustrations of this action turn to Numbers 11:17; 24:2; Judges 3:10; 11:29; 1 Samuel 19:20,23; 2 Chronicles 15:1; 20:14; Isaiah 59:21; 61:1.

The Spirit is "in" men.

Such an incoming was not an indwelling. Entering a person, He inspired them to act under His internal promptings. Such people were:

Joseph—"a man in whom the Spirit of God is" (Gen. 41:38).

Joshua—"a man in whom is the spirit" (Num. 27:18).

Daniel—"[a man] in whom is the Spirit" (Dan. 4:8,9).

Prophets—"The Spirit of Christ . . . in them" (1 Pet. 1:10,11; Neh. 9:30).

Israel restored—"I will put a new spirit within you" (Ezek. 11:19; 36:26).

The Spirit "rests" upon men.

"Rests" is a gentle word suggesting the dove-like character of the Holy Spirit. It signifies "to be at rest" as in Isaiah 57:2: "They shall rest in their beds." Some examples are:

Seventy elders. "The Spirit rested upon them" (Num. 11:25,26).

Elisha. "The Spirit of Elijah doth rest on Elisha" (2 Kin. 2:15).

The Messiah. "The Spirit of the Lord shall rest upon Him" (Is. 11:2).

The Spirit "enters" into men.

As the Creator-Spirit (Job 33:4; Ps. 104:30), He has the right of entry into His own creation. He has the prerogative of doing what he likes with His own. "The Spirit entered into me" (Ezek. 2:2; 3:24).

The Spirit "moves" men.

The word "moves" can be taken to mean "cause to step," and, let it be said, the Spirit can cause us to "stop" as well as "step." When we read that "the Spirit of the Lord began to move [Samson]" (Judg. 13:25) we have the thought of His constraining, impelling power over men.

The Spirit "lifts" men up bodily.

Being the superior power, the Spirit can operate upon men at will and remove them to where He wants them (cf. 1 Kin. 18:12; 2 Kin. 2:16; Ezek. 3:12–14; 8:3; 11:1,24; 37:1).

The Spirit "fell" upon men.

Such an action seems to imply a sudden mantling with the Spirit for some immediate, specific task. "The Spirit of the Lord fell upon me" (Ezek. 11:5).

The Spirit "filled" men.

Old Testament "fillings" were of a temporary nature, and must not be confused with the filling of the Spirit Paul speaks of in Ephesians 5:18. Certain men were filled with some particular aspect of the Spirit's power in order to accomplish a definite piece of work. When such was completed, the inference is that the Spirit withdrew His gift. It was in this way He dealt with the wise-hearted and with Bezaleel (Ex. 28:3; 31:3; 35:31). A similar action is found in 1 Kings 22:24 and 2 Chronicles 18:23 where the Spirit leaving Zedekiah, whom He possessed for a purpose, passed into Micaiah.

New Testament Activities

Because of the generally-accepted uninspired character of the Apocrypha books we have not troubled to trace the movements of the Spirit within such dubious literature. It echoes no new and living voices. As for the inter-Testamental period, known as the "four hundred silent years," the Spirit is as a stream flowing underground, only to emerge in the fullness of our Lord's teaching.

Studying the New Testament's fuller revelation of the Spirit we are impressed with the clearer view of His person and of His relations, essential and economical, with the other persons of the Trinity. We cannot escape the ever-expanding exposition of His functions and operations. This study takes on an intensely personal nature as we learn of His relations with Christ and His perpetual indwelling in the church. He is revealed as being infinitely nearer to us. And gradually we see in Him the One who slowly but certainly brings back a lapsed world under the divine sway, thereby realizing the purpose of that creation in which he appeared as the foremost agent.

It is only as we take the New Testament in our hands and diligently pursue our journey through its sacred pages that we realize how full it is of "the things of the Spirit." Elder Cumming, whose work *Through the Eternal Spirit*, in one of the most helpful studies on the subject, affirms that "there are in all 261 passages in which the Holy Spirit is specially and directly mentioned. A few of these no doubt may be questioned, but these can make little difference.

The Gospels contain	56 passages
The Acts of the Apostles	57 passages
Paul's Epistles	112 passages
Other Books	36 passages

"Philemon and the Second and Third Epistles of John are the only books in which the Spirit is not named."

That the blessed Spirit was known and believed in at the

dawn of the New Testament era is evident by the fact that those to whom He came clearly understood His words and works. Along with John the Baptist, the Holy Spirit can be counted as a forerunner, for while John prepared the way for Jesus, it was the Spirit who prepared the way for both John and Jesus.

Pre-messianic operations

By the pre-messianic operations of the Spirit we mean His movements preliminary to Christ's appearance. As our Lord was about to enter the world, the Spirit began to stir devout souls who had been waiting for the consolation of Israel. New and strange influences directed their thoughts toward the Coming One.

Zechariah and Elisabeth

These two priestly souls, "both righteous before God, walking in all the commandments and ordinances of the Lord blameless," had a unique experience of the Spirit's miraculous creative power. Zechariah learned that John, his coming son, was to be filled with the Holy Spirit from the womb (Luke 1:15). Elisabeth was filled with the Spirit as John was about to be born (Luke 1:41). Zechariah was filled with the Spirit to declare the prophecy regarding the mission of the Baptist (Luke 1:67).

Joseph and Mary

With Mary, the Virgin, and her husband-to-be Joseph, the Holy Spirit had very delicate, sacred associations. Analyzing the "birth narratives" of our Lord we have this summary: Joseph was informed that Mary's child would be conceived by the Holy Spirit (Matt. 1:20). Mary's pregnant condition, disturbing to Joseph, was fully explained by revelation (Matt. 1:18–23). Mary received the secret of our Lord's conception apart from human agency, and was elevated as one blessed above all women as the mother of the Messiah (Luke 1:35).

Simeon

This aged saint of Jerusalem, "just and devout," lived in constant expectation of Christ's coming. He waited "for the consolation of Israel" and was given the assurance that he would live to see the Messiah. Simeon's name means "one who hears and obeys."

The Spirit was upon him (Luke 2:25) and revealed unto him the fulfillment of his desire (v. 26). The Spirit also led him into the temple to see Jesus when He was brought to the temple to be given to Jehovah as the first-born and to be redeemed by payment of a ransom (Ex. 13:12; Luke 2:23,26,27).

John the Baptist

Our Lord's forerunner was likewise subject to the multiple operations of the Spirit of God. For example, John was filled with the Spirit from his birth (Luke 1:15) and born of a Spirit-filled mother (v. 41). He exercised his ministry in the power of the Spirit (v. 17; Mark 6:20). John prophesied the baptism with the Spirit and witnessed the descent of the Spirit upon Christ (Matt. 3:11; Mark 1:8; Luke 3:16; John 1:33).

Although it is not expressly mentioned, we are at liberty to infer that the Spirit, acting upon the foregoing, was also associated with the search and joy of the wise men from the East, and with the adoration and testimony of the shepherds. Thus, the Spirit bridged the transition period between the two Testaments by permeating the lives of those godly souls grouped around our Lord's entrance into our humanity, with His own holy presence and power.

Messianic ministrations and teaching

We have now come to one of the most profitable aspects of our study, namely the blessed and wonderful relationship existing between the Holy Son and the Holy Spirit. Peter informs us that our Lord left us an example, that we should follow his steps (1 Pet. 2:21). In Christ's association with the Spirit we have an example it is imperative to follow, if we would be victorious in life and fruitful in service.

Jesus declared that "the disciple is not above his master, nor the servant above his Lord" (Matt. 10:24). One application of such a declaration is that if He had needs which the Holy Spirit could meet, and which He brought to the Spirit in humble dependence, we too must be as equally dependent upon the Third Person.

We can gather material on the theme before us by considering the Spirit in our Lord's teaching and types, and the Spirit in our Lord's life and labors.

The Spirit in our Lord's teaching

The teaching of Christ on the Spirit is full and varied, especially near the close of His earthly ministry. And, as we will demonstrate, He never referred to the Paraclete in any impersonal way.

As Scripture presents a progressive unfolding of the truth about God, we expect to find as we reach our Lord's teaching a clearer and fuller revelation of the Spirit's person and work. While wonderful expansions of the truth of the Spirit can be traced after our Lord's ascension, this must be borne in mind. With all the full blaze of a noonday revelation, such as the Acts and the Epistles contain of the Spirit's operations, after Christ's testimony no new truth appears. All that the apostles taught regarding the Spirit can be found in germ within Christ's teaching.

Concerning the work of the Spirit as revealed in the New Testament, we can classify the truth in this manner. Who the Spirit is, and what He does, is unfolded:

> Historically in the Gospels.
> Experimentally in the Acts.
> Doctrinally in the Epistles.
> Governmentally in the Revelation.

The Spirit prayed for by Christ

Several salient features of Christ's revelation of the Spirit are inescapable as we ponder the four Gospels. The first is that the Spirit came in answer to Christ's prayer, "I will pray the Father, and he shall give you another Comforter . . ." (John 14:16). The experiences of the apostles throughout Acts constitute an answer to Christ's prayer.

Christ also encouraged His disciples to pray for the Spirit: "How much more shall your heavenly Father give the Holy Spirit to them that ask Him?" (Luke 11:13). Such a request forms the burden of His high-priestly petition (John 17), seeing it is only through the gift of the Spirit that His desires for His own can be fully realized.

As believers, then, we have the Spirit through the joint prayers of the Lord and ourselves.

The Spirit prophesied by Christ

On the last day, that great day of the holiest and greatest of all feasts, the feast of tabernacles (Lev. 23:39), Jesus gave a telescopic view of the Spirit's ministry. He said the Holy Spirit is to flow out of a believer's life as rivers of water (John 7:37-39). This word "flow," occurring nowhere else in the New Testament, implies the continual movement of the Spirit. Flowing into the believer, He flows through, then flows out, bringing spiritual refreshment to the dry, barren wilderness around.

The Spirit, here symbolized as "rivers of water," was not yet given, for Jesus had not yet been glorified. Such a fact was true dispensationally. The Holy Spirit could not come as the gift of Christ until His entrance into heaven. Thus, the presence of the Spirit now is an evidence of the ascended, glorified Lord. It is likewise true experientially. No believer can realize the fullness of the Spirit in life and service unless he is willing to glorify Jesus. As the Spirit loves to glorify the Lord, He cannot bless and use those who are self-confident, boastful, and self-glorifying.

The Spirit given by Christ

As Christ is God's love-gift to "a world of sinners lost and ruined by the Fall," so the Spirit is Christ's love-gift to His

67

blood-bought ones. It is clearly evident, however, that the gift of the Spirit was a donation that neither the Father nor the Son could give alone. The procession of the Spirit is from the Father through the Son. The bestowal of this blessed gift can be set forth in three steps.

The Spirit was given by the Father (John 14:16,26; Acts 1:4). As Christ is the gift of God (Rom. 6:23), who, as the absolute possessor of all things, possesses Christ (1 Cor. 3:23), so the Spirit of God's gift and therefore His possession (Gen. 6:3; Zech. 4:6).

The Spirit was given by Christ (John 15:26). In response to Christ's own express declaration to send the Spirit, He came upon the disciples on the day of Pentecost as the promised, empowering gift of the ascended Lord.

The Spirit came on His own initiative. "When he . . . is come" (John 16:13). Behind this affirmation is the willing, voluntary service the Third Person gave and still gives. God and Christ had no need to press Him into the ministry He represents. All His operations, like the incarnation and death of the Savior, are willing and without coercion.

The Father was willing to give His Son as the sinner's substitute. The Son was willing to die in the sinner's stead. The Spirit was willing to enter and remain in the world from Pentecost until the translation of the church, and by His long ministry complete such a church, which is the Lord's body.

The Spirit prepared for by Christ

As our Lord was about to ascend on high "He breathed on [His disciples], and saith unto them, Receive ye the Holy Spirit" (John 20:22 ASV). Did the disciples actually receive the Spirit at this time or later on, at Pentecost? It would seem as if the experience was prophetic, a foretaste of Pentecost.

By the acted parable of breathing audibly, Christ created an atmosphere, preparing His own to receive the Spirit. Knowing that a right attitude and atmosphere are necessary for the definite reception of the Spirit, Christ seems to be saying, "Get ready to receive the Spirit." Bishop Moule, discussing whether the Spirit was given in "act" or "prospect" at this point, says, "The risen Lord's action of breathing was the sacrament, so to speak . . . of a coming gift of the Spirit."

We must not lose sight of the fact that there must ever be on our part the active receptivity to the Spirit, whom the Lord out-breathes.

The Spirit received by Christ for us

Both Peter and Paul emphasize this aspect of our theme. "Having received of the Father the promise of the Holy [Spirit], he hath shed forth this, which ye now see and hear" (Acts 2:33). Paul reminds us that on His ascension, Christ "gave gifts unto men" (Eph. 4:8). As the greater included the lesser, the Spirit—the greatest gift from Christ—is the dispenser of all gifts to the church (1 Cor. 12; Ps. 68:18).

As the Spirit indwelt our Lord's human body, so the Father gives the Spirit to us in order that He might indwell us as those forming the Lord's mystical body, exhibiting in and through each believer those spiritual gifts necessary for "the perfecting of the saints, for the work of the ministry, for the edifying of the body of Christ" (Eph. 4:12).

The Spirit witnessed Christ's exaltation.

The disciples saw Christ ascend from the earth, but we are possessed by One who witnessed His arrival in heaven (Acts 5:30–32; John 7:39; 16:7). As Jesus, gloriously exalted, sat down on the right hand of the majesty on high, the Holy Spirit descended to undertake His advocacy of the Lord's people.

The Spirit being among us is not only an evidence of Christ's enthronement, but also the proof of His resurrection. If His body was stolen or dissolved into gases, then there could have been no manifestation to the disciples as recorded. If the resurrection of Christ is a myth, then there was no ascension after forty days, and consequently no descent of the Spirit as promised by Christ upon His return to glory. But the Spirit being here declares Jesus to be alive forevermore.

The Spirit testifies of Christ.

Referring to the ministry of the Spirit, Jesus said, "The Spirit of Truth . . . shall testify of me" (John 15:26). Note the title used here—"the Spirit of truth." As Christ Himself is "the truth" (14:6), it is imperative to have One sharing His nature to bear testimony to Him.

And the Spirit loves to make much of Christ. How He leads us to the Master and keeps Him warm in our heart! The center point of our evangelical faith is that Christ with His infinite resources, with all His love and grace, is near to the individual believer, and made part of His very being by the gift of the indwelling Spirit. Without the Spirit we have practically no Christ.

There is, of course, the twofold witness as indicated by Peter (Acts 5:32), the Spirit's testimony and our own (John 15:26). We give what we get; we reflect what we receive. The Spirit testifies to us; we testify unto the world. No man is Spirit-taught, if he fails to preach and exalt Christ.

The Spirit glorifies Christ.

Bengel's pregnant phrase has it, "The Son glorifies the Father, the Spirit glorifies the Son." And the blessed work of the Spirit is to make Christ grander in our estimation. "He shall glorify me" (John 16:14). Christ's virtues as the God-man, Savior, Friend, Companion, Lord, are extolled by the Spirit.

Bishop Moule expresses it,

There is no separate gospel of the Holy Spirit. The plan of God assuredly is not to teach us about Christ, as a first lesson, and then, as a more advanced lesson to lead us on into the truth about the Holy Spirit, apart from Christ. We do indeed, and to the last, need teaching about the blessed Spirit. But the more we learn about Him the more surely we shall learn this from Him, that His chosen and beloved work is just this—to glorify the Lord Jesus Christ. . . . He sheds an illuminating glory upon a heart, a face, an embrace—the beloved Jesus Christ, our Lord.

And such a chosen and beloved work is accomplished, let us remember, both in the character and through the confession of those who are the Lord's (John 17:1,5,10).

Relationship between Christ and the Spirit

The Spirit convicts the world about Christ.

The time mission of the Spirit began at Pentecost and will continue until the church is complete. With the translation of the church at the return of Christ, the Spirit's association with the world in the sense in which He came at Pentecost will cease. Presently, His work is in and with the world, and in, with, and through the church.

In His sermon dealing with the Spirit's activities, Christ declares the Spirit's first action is world-wide conviction in a threefold realm, namely, in sin, righteousness, and judgment (John 16:8). As the world is dead or spiritually insensible (v. 3), it greatly needs this preparative ministry of the Spirit. The tragedy is that such a work is so resisted as to frustrate the saving purpose of God. Or it is received in vain, for change of mind is not always followed by that godly sorrow which carries out the work begun by repentance to its completion in the acceptance of salvation (2 Cor. 7:10). Let us examine the threefold conviction the Spirit strives to produce.

Sin. "Of sin, because they believe not on me" (John 16:9). The world has come to deal with sin as if it had no real existence. In some quarters sin is treated simply as an offense against law or against the natural conscience, but not against God. Left to himself, man can never know truly and fully what the nature of sin is. The Spirit alone can reveal sin, as He does in many ways. By the law is the knowledge of sin (Rom. 7:7). The

71

character of sin, however, is best seen in the light of the holy life and the self-sacrificing love of the crucified Savior. In the light of the Cross, unbelief becomes the sin of sins. Unbelief is the very germ and root of all evil. Notice how conviction of sin was wrought in the minds and hearts of the hearers of Peter through the preaching of the Cross (Acts 2:36–37).

Righteousness. "Of righteousness, because I go to my Father, and ye see me no more" (John 16:10). Self-righteousness stands condemned. Christ is God's righteousness, the Spirit proclaims, and man's only covering for sin.

The world looked upon Christ as a blasphemer, numbering Him among transgressors, ultimately nailing Him to the cross as One accursed (Gal. 3:13). He was rejected as being the Righteous One, but because of what Christ had been, borne, and done, God raised and highly exalted Him. By accepting Christ as righteous, God reversed the judgment of man.

Judgment. "Of judgment, because the prince of this world is judged" (John 16:11). By the term *world* we understand human society apart from, and in opposition to, God. It is the God-hating and Christ-rejecting world animated by the spirit of disobedience, even Satan, the prince of this world and god of this age. Since the days of Adam and Eve, by his craft and power the Devil has led men in hostility to God.

Calvary, however, was Satan's Waterloo. Because of sin he had the power of death (Heb. 2:14); but by dying, Christ slew death. And His resurrection and ascension prove that Satan was defeated. Now the Spirit upholds the authority and power of Christ and denounces Satan as a usurper. Through the Word the Spirit assures the fully awakened sinner that the work of Calvary is perfect and final. The Devil is a defeated foe, and all who accept the Crucified are no longer under condemnation (Rom. 8:1).

The prince and kingdom of darkness, in which the world lies, are still evident. But the day is coming when the kingdom of this world shall become in fact what it is by right, the kingdom of our God and of Christ (Rev. 11:15).

Thus, the Holy Spirit convicts in a threefold way: Man in the realm of sin, Christ in the realm of righteousness, and Satan in the realm of judgment.

The Spirit transforms men into Christ's image.

Another precious phase of the Spirit's work is His creating of the image of the Master within willing, obedient lives. "The glory of the Lord . . . transformed into the same image . . . even as from the Lord the Spirit" (2 Cor. 3:18 ASV). As we possess four Gospels, presenting four different aspects of the one divine person, so the continuous ministry of the Spirit is to fill the world with men and women reproducing Christ.

In St. Peter's Cathedral in Cologne, Germany, are two pictures side by side, both of the crucifixion of the apostle Peter. In the eighteenth century only one such painting was there, and Napoleon took it to Paris when he conquered the city. In the absence of the original, an artist painted a copy of it, which was put in its place in the church. When the original was restored, and the two pictures were placed side by side, even experts failed to detect any difference between them. In the absence of the original, he had painted a perfect copy.

This is the glorious work in which the Spirit of God, that master artist, is engaged. However unworthy the canvas may be, His skill is such that He can make a perfect copy on earth of the original who has passed into the heavens. The Spirit is producing Christ in countless lives. His work shall one day be crowned when the original, who lived His life on earth by the Spirit, is glorified in those who by the same Spirit have been changed into the same image and who, in heaven, shall forever show forth the praises of Him who redeemed them.

What we must be careful to observe is that Paul is speaking of "transformation" not "imitation." Thomas à Kempis wrote his *Imitation of Christ,* a priceless book of devotion; but the life pleasing to God is not the one in which the ways of Christ are copied or imitated, as suggested by Sheldon in that popular religious novel, *In His Steps.* It is easy to sing, "Be like

Jesus, this my song," but imitation is the effort of the flesh; it is the ways of Christ we seek to produce.

Transformation, however, is the unique work of the Spirit, seeing that He alone possesses the power to reproduce the Savior in lives yielded to His control.

The Spirit named by Christ

As our Lord typifies the Spirit in various ways so there are distinct titles given to the Spirit by Christ. As all fullness dwells in Christ, and God has summed up all things in His Son (Col. 1:19), so all the deep things of the Spirit come from the same source of all knowledge.

The Spirit (John 3:5,6,8). This simplest and shortest name often used by Christ and others is of deep significance. It indicates the Spirit's spiritual, invisible, incorporeal essence. Coming to work within the spirit of man He bears the name similar to His sphere of operation. As the Spirit He is in contrast to that which is material. The term *Spirit* is the same translated "wind" (John 3:8) and implies the invisible force of God.

The Spirit of the Father (Matt. 10:20). Here we have an expressive title referring to the tender, filial relationship the Spirit Himself brings about through regeneration. Because we are God's children, the Spirit is able to administer grace in times of need.

The Spirit of God (Matt. 12:28). In this first title given the Spirit of the Bible (Gen. 1:2), we have the revelation of His origin. Coming from God, He functions for God. And having a divine origin and nature, the Spirit exerts divine power and exists to fulfill the divine will. *God* or *Elohim,* meaning "the strong one," is the creation name and covers the Trinity (Gen. 1:26).

The Holy Spirit (Luke 11:13). This frequently used title emphasizes the Spirit's essential, moral character. He not only

74

proceeds from a holy God; He not only inspired the Holy Scripture; He not only creates our holiness, He is holy in Himself. "Every thought of holiness is His alone." And, as the "holy" Spirit, He cannot condone anything in our lives alien to His holy mind and will.

The Spirit of the Lord (Luke 4:18). The word here used for "Lord" is *Jehovah,* the covenant-keeping One. As the Spirit-anointed One, Jesus acts in His official capacity as God's representative and as the fulfiller of all Old Testament predictions.

The Spirit of truth (John 14:17; 15:26). As "the Truth," Christ must have One who is akin to Him in this respect. And as "the Spirit of Truth," the Spirit is associated with truth in three ways: He inspires the truth (Matt. 22:43; Mark 12:36; 1 Pet. 1:11); He works with the truth (John 3:5; Eph. 6:17); and He imparts the truth (John 16:13).

Riding most triumphantly in His own chariot, the Spirit will only work alongside of, or through, the truth. Lectures, essays, and sermons, interesting and profitable in themselves, can be conceived and delivered without the least aid of the Spirit. But if the truth is to be preached and taught and if the message is to be quick and powerful, "sharper than a two-edged sword," it is imperative to have the illumination and power of the Spirit.

The Comforter (John 14:16,26; 16:7). As Jesus was so named by the angel before His birth (Matt. 1:21), so the Spirit was named "Comforter" by Christ before His advent. The title implies "one called to another to take his part," and is the same word used of Christ in 1 John 2:1, namely *advocate.* Thus, we have a stand-by within our hearts and in heaven. With such a blessed double advocacy how shameful is defeat in the life of a believer! If we desire to save Christ the sorrow of clearing us up in heaven when we do sin, let us learn to obey the Spirit within our hearts as He prompts us not to sin. "Walk in the Spirit, and ye shall not fulfill the lust of the flesh" (Gal. 5:16).

The Spirit's tasks outlined by Christ

The varied ministry of the Spirit, as outlined by our Lord, was of an anticipatory nature. From his revelation of the Spirit we are told who He would be, and what He would do after His coming at Pentecost. The tasks of the Spirit, as we have shown in other portions of this study, cover Christ's earthly life, the world, the church, and the believer.

The New Testament reveals a holy intimacy between the Holy Son and the Holy Spirit. A mystic union characterized them. Jesus could say, "I and My Father are One" (John 10:30). It was likewise true that Christ and the Spirit were one. "I . . . by the Spirit of God" (Matt. 12:28), covers our Lord's every action, as well as the casting out of demons.

One or two preliminary thoughts must claim our attention before we come to the absorbing theme before us.

The Gospels mark the transitional period of the Spirit. The four Gospels, with their life and teaching of Christ, form the bridge between the Old Testament and the Acts and Epistles. The rivers of the Old Testament run into Christ, gather greater volume in His life, then flow out after His ascension, with a more wonderful fullness.

Already we have thought of the varied operations of the Spirit of the Old Testament. He made possible for certain men political wisdom, power of leadership, physical strength, practical skill and artistic beauty, prophetic foresight, spiritual insight, moral courage; but all these virtues were never found in one person. All gifts, however, meet in Christ, for all the past rivers of the Spirit run into the sea of Christ (Eccl. 1:7). Upon Him came the promises of the sevenfold Spirit (Is. 11:2).

Samson had the power of the Spirit, but not His purity. Moses had the wisdom of the Spirit to lead, but not the skill to build. As then, so now, the Spirit distributes His gifts severally as He will. Christ, however, possessed the Spirit in His entirety, and through the Lord the Spirit manifested His manifold gifts.

The Holy Spirit exclusively occupied Christ. Until Christ's day, the Spirit had not yet a permanent home in human nature. But in Christ we have something different. The Spirit indwelt a human body for over thirty-three years. A somewhat striking feature of Christ's relationship with the Spirit is that after His birth by the Spirit there is no record of His being associated with any other individual until He came at Pentecost as heaven's love-gift for all. There had to come a man who was both able and willing to receive the fullness of the Spirit before that fullness could be bestowed upon others. And that first man, able and willing, was Christ.

In Old Testament days it was one measure of the Spirit for one man, but God gave not the Spirit by measure unto His Son (John 3:34). The Spirit was "not yet" (7:39), which means, He had not come to others. During our Lord's sojourn, the Spirit concentrated all His energies about Him, making Him the channel of constant blessing (Acts 10:38). Christ lived and labored in the Spirit. Do we?

The exact gift of Pentecost. What really constituted Christ's ascension-gift of the Spirit? Christ in His condescension became "the God-man." Within the womb of Mary, the Spirit fused deity and humanity into one; thus Christ appeared as God manifest in flesh. Therefore, because He produced the God-man and possessed Him, the Holy Spirit came as the Spirit of both God and man. He understands everything from the divine and human standpoints. Indwelling the Man, Christ Jesus, for so long, He knows all about human needs and emotions and is able to succor accordingly.

Let us look at some of the titles expressing the Spirit's relationship with the Son of God.

"The Spirit of Christ"

Paul's description of the third person of the Trinity (Rom. 8:9) does not mean a Christlike spirit, but the Spirit Himself who possessed Christ. He is so called because He came as Christ's gift, and He strives to reveal Christ to us, and form Christ within us. As "the Spirit of Christ," it is not an earthly

77

Christ He glorifies, so much as the Christ re-invested with all glory and power.

"The Spirit of Jesus"

"The Spirit of Jesus suffered them not" (Acts 16:7 ASV). *Jesus* is the earthly name, and is connected with all He endured in the days of His flesh. Does it not enhance our love for the Spirit as we realize that He had heart-fellowship with Jesus who willingly allowed Himself to be tempted or tested in all points as we are?

"The Spirit of Jesus Christ"

The combination of names here represents Christ as the human One, anointed and raised on high. Paul speaks of "the supply of the Spirit of Jesus Christ" (Phil. 1:19). Alas, many of us seem to exist on a meager supply! Yet there is no gauge checking the supply of the Spirit. All He has is at the disposal of the humblest saint.

"The Spirit of His Son"

St. Augustine called Pentecost, "the birthday of the Spirit," and a privilege coming with such a birthday gift was that of sonship. "Now are ye the sons of God." But this relationship was not possible until after Pentecost. Now through regeneration, the Spirit makes blessedly real the spirit of adoption "whereby we cry, Abba, Father." As the filial Spirit, His indwelling testifies to our sonship.

The self-abnegation of Christ. One of the mysteries of our faith is that of Christ's death to self. Although equal to God, as He came among men He elected to become subordinate to the will of the Father and dependent upon the Holy Spirit. "Not my will, but thine be done," and "I . . . by the Spirit of God" are the twin desires of Christ.

In this double way the Master is our pattern and exemplar. Says Pascal, "It is one of the great principles of Christianity that whatever happened to Jesus Christ should come to pass in the soul and body of every believer." If it was imperative for

Him to depend upon the Spirit as he did, then how great must our need be of the same holy Energizer?

The evident fact that Christ's earthly life became effectual as the result of His obedience to the will of God and through the ministry of the Spirit within Him, and not alone through the inherent virtue and power He brought with Him, is one that arrests us. Somehow, such a fact has become one of the commonplaces of theology. We do not realize its true import. Nor do we cultivate the humility and dependence of soul which should distinguish us if our Lord's self-denial was ever in view.

Our personal need of a life possessed by the Spirit, even as Christ's life was, is set forth in type in the anointing of Aaron and his sons (Ex. 30:30). Upon both, the oil came. Thus, all the Spirit accomplished for and through Christ, He is willing to accomplish for and through us. Every step of our pilgrim journey we can claim and use the Spirit's fullness, even as the Master did before us.

Reverently, then, let us trace the various aspects of the mystic union existing between Christ and the Spirit. As our meal offering, Christ was the "fine flour unleavened, mingled with oil" (Lev. 2:5). To change the figure, if Christ was the vine, the Holy Spirit was the sap permeating every phase of His life and work.

Christ prophesied by the Spirit

Concerning the whole of Old Testament Scripture, Christ could declare that such Scripture presented His character and ministry. "In the volume of the book it is written of me" (Heb. 10:7; Luke 24:26,27). And, as Peter reminds us that it was the Holy Spirit who was in the prophets of old, inspiring them to testify beforehand the sufferings of Christ and the glory that should follow (1 Pet. 1:11), the Spirit is before us in the role of Christ's divine forerunner. In prophecy, type, and symbol, the Spirit prepared the way for Christ.

As the time drew near for the prophesied Christ to appear, the Spirit became specially active, prompting devout minds who waited for the consolation of Israel to proclaim the fulfillment of God's promise to send His Son. Zechariah and his wife, as well as John the Baptist, were all alike filled with the Spirit and spoke of the coming Christ. The Spirit also comforted Simeon with the assurance that he should live to see the Lord's Christ. By the same Spirit Simeon recognized Christ as the salvation of God when He was brought into the temple as the first-born to be redeemed by payment of a ransom (Luke 1:15,41,67; 2:23,26; Ex. 13:12).

As in those far-off days the Spirit prepared the way for the First Advent, so in these last days He is preparing Christ's own and the world for the Second Advent. This fact, I believe, accounts for the unusual interest in prophecy.

Christ born of the Spirit

The consistent revelation of the New Testament is that the Spirit was the agent of the Father in the incarnation of the Son. It was long prophesied that, as the seed of the woman Jesus the Christ would become the Savior of man, and in the fullness of time He was born of a virgin (Gen. 3:15; Is. 9:6; Matt. 1:18).

As we approach the sublime truth of the Virgin Birth of our Lord, we find ourselves in the realm of mystery. To explain the Incarnation is to lose our reason; to deny it is to lose our soul. No one can be a Christian after the New Testament order who discredits and denies the Virgin Birth.

Matthew's explicit statement reads, "Mary . . . was found with child of the Holy Spirit" (Matt. 1:18 rsv). The Spirit of life, then, was the completer of the union of God and man. He was the love-knot between deity and humanity, producing the God-man. Within Mary, the Spirit added to Christ's already existing divine nature, a human nature; thus He came as the Man Christ Jesus. In our new birth the reverse takes place. The Spirit adds to our already existing human nature, a divine nature, making us partakers of the divine nature (2 Pet. 1:4).

Mysterious indeed is the fact that Jesus was born of a

woman, a woman who recognized her need of a Savior, for Mary sang, "My spirit hath rejoiced in God my Savior" (Luke 1:47)—yet He was clean. The questions of Job are, "How can he be clean that is born of a woman?" "Who can bring a clean thing out of an unclean? Not one" (Job 14:4; 25:4). Christ was born of a woman who, like all women, had been born "in sin and shapen in iniquity." Yet out of the unclean the Clean Thing came, as Gabriel announced to Mary, "Therefore also that Holy Thing which shall be born of thee shall be called the Son of God" (Luke 1:35).

Apart from the action of the Spirit at the conception we cannot account for our Lord's sinlessness. The miracle and mystery of the Spirit's work are seen in that he was able to lay hold of the Virgin's flesh out of which the body of Jesus was to be formed, and purify it, making possible the One who came among men "holy, harmless, undefiled, separate from sinners." As the Spirit of holiness he overshadowed Mary, and apart from natural generation produced a perfectly holy Being. The Spirit touched the springs of motherhood in the most blessed of women, and brooded in the germ cell out of which sprang an incomparably Holy Life.

And Christ's birth by the Spirit offers a twofold type. Christ was born of the Spirit, and we can only enter the world of grace through the same agency. The Virgin Birth of Christ and our new birth are alike in that neither can be explained by human reason. Both these works of the Spirit have to be received by faith.

It is also a type of our sanctification (Gal. 4:19). Paul used a delicate but daring simile when he told the Galatian believers that he was a travailing mother until Christ was formed in them. What is the application of Paul's mystic phrase? Why, as Mary surrendered her body to the Spirit saying, "Be it unto me according to thy Word," and willingly allowed Him to form Jesus within her, so we are to surrender our bodies to the same Spirit, allowing Him to fashion Christ within our hearts and lives. "Christ liveth in me" (Gal. 2:20; Rom. 12:1,2). We pray,

O Jesus Christ grow Thou in me,
And all things else recede
My heart be daily freed from sin,
And closer drawn to Thee!

Christ justified by the Spirit

It has been affirmed that there is no direct reference to the Spirit in our Lord's life from His birth to His baptism, and if we confine ourselves to the Gospels such an affirmation may be true. The manifestation of remarkable wisdom, however, at the early age of twelve, and the mark of humility in Christ's subjection to Joseph and Mary infer the work of the Spirit in Christ as prophesied by Isaiah (Luke 2:20,47,51,52; Is. 11:1,2).

Paul reminds us that Christ was "justified" or vindicated "by the Spirit," which is a phase of the Spirit's action covering not only the three and one-half years of ministry, but the first thirty silent years. In His humble home at Nazareth, Jesus found Himself misunderstood by those around. He was a stranger unto His brethren and an alien unto His mother's children (Ps. 69:8). But through all those years of rejection, Jesus had the constant attention of the Spirit. To all His claims to divine sonship, the Spirit could say, "Amen!" As Mary's Son, He did not occasion much pleasure, but turning aside from Nazareth and entering His brief but dynamic ministry there came the benediction, "This is My beloved Son, in whom I am well pleased" (Matt. 3:17; Acts 4:27,30).

As Christ's followers, we should know what it is to be dead to self-vindication, awaiting at all times the Spirit's vindication, which sooner or later is given, much to the confusion of those who misjudge us. Christ cared not about His reputation. He flung it to the winds, making Himself of no reputation (Phil. 2:7). He was ever careful, though, regarding His character. And, as D. L. Moody put it, character is what a man is in the dark.

82

Christ anointed with the Spirit

At the inauguration of Christ's official life the Holy Spirit was again active. In the form of a dove, a living symbol, the Spirit came upon Jesus as He emerged from His retirement for His mediatorial work as Prophet, Priest, and King. As it has been stated, "At last, the time had arrived when the bud should break into flower."

Basic passages shedding light upon this special ministry of the Spirit are Matthew 3:16; 12:18; Acts 4:27,30; 10:38. This divine unction was a necessary preparation for Christ's work. Heavy tasks were ahead. He must go out to seek and save the lost—die for the world's redemption, and so was endowed marvelously and immeasurably with the Spirit.

Christ's anointing with the Spirit was an evidence of His claim. How were the people to know that this obscure man of Nazareth was God's Chosen? The Father's benediction and the Spirit's descent upon Christ indicated that He was indeed the Sent One (Is. 48:16; John 6:27). One of the most instructive writers on Hebrew ritual and worship reminds us that it was the custom for the priest, to whom the service of presenting offerings pertained, to inspect with minutest scrutiny a selected lamb. If free of physical defect, the priest would then seal the lamb with the temple seal, signifying that it was fit for sacrifice and food.

At Jordan, the Lamb of God presented Himself for inspection and under the Father's omniscient scrutiny was found to be without blemish. Well-pleased with His Son, God anointed Him with the Spirit, who in turn became the seal of Christ's separation unto sacrifice and service (Matt. 3:16,17; Mark 1:10,11; Luke 3:21,22; John 1:32,33).

Christ's anointing with the Spirit was for testing. Immediately after the double attestation at Jordan came the conflict in the wilderness. "Then was Jesus led up of the spirit ... to be tempted of the devil" (Matt. 4:1). As the newly anointed Prophet passed into the arena to meet the satanic foe, it was the Holy Spirit who led Him to such a critical conflict, comforting, equipping, and building Him by the way. Angels might minister to His lower, natural life when the conflict was over, but it must be the Spirit's unshared ministry to bring afresh into view those deep things of God by which His higher life might be sustained. The forces of evil, although far from infinite, are mighty in themselves, and appalling in their resources. Christ could only venture to meet them by the Spirit.

What fools we are if, like Peter, we face the tempter in the spirit of pride and self-sufficiency, in a spirit of recklessness and presumption, madly defying the power of the Enemy and lacking the unction of the Spirit. Jordan and the wilderness go together. First the Dove—then the Devil! And God pity us if we meet the Devil without first meeting the Dove. For a victorious wilderness, we must have a Jordan experience.

Further, as the natures of the Dove and the Devil differ, so do their purposes. The One blesses, the other blasts. Some are all Dove and no Devil. Sin, they tell us, has been eradicated and they are now sinless. Others are all Devil. These are hopelessly defeated. Sin reigns within their lives. The true spiritual progressive life, however, is the one in which both the Dove and the Devil are to be found, with the Dove continually keeping the Devil at bay. The question is, do we deliberately help the Spirit in His lusting against the flesh (Gal. 5:17)?

Two thoughts suggest themselves as we think of our Lord's temptation, the first being that the wilderness came before His ministry. The first, direct outcome of the Spirit's anointing was not to cast out demons, but to defeat the Devil himself, both for His sake and ours. He had to experience the full strength of the foe before He could deliver those who were bound.

The second thought is, Christ's testing followed a deep, spiritual experience. After the waters, the wilderness. After heaven's voice, hell's venom. After the benediction, the battle. After the Dove, the Devil. This is ever the order. Pentecost was quickly followed by persecution (Acts 4:1-3). What we fail to realize is that our most critical moments are those immediately following some deep, spiritual experience. After some mountain-top revelation we find ourselves assailed most bitterly by the enemy, so much so that we are tempted to doubt the validity of our Jordan. How essential it is to realize in such hours that Satan is out to reclaim all territory lost to the Spirit: the Devil is endeavoring to displace the Dove.

Christ's anointing was for service. What a divine sequence Christ's relation with the Spirit affords! The Dove . . . the Devil . . . the dynamic. Luke reminds us that "when the devil had ended all the temptation . . . Jesus returned in the power of the Spirit into Galilee" (Luke 4:13,14). Jordan, wilderness, Galilee; these three, and their order is never reversed.

The dovelike form of the Spirit, implying peace, tenderness, holy and gentle fellowship, suggests the nature of the One thus anointed for service. The name *Galilee* means "circle," and Jesus now goes into every circle of need in the Spirit's power to diffuse all that the nature of the Dove portrays.

God's Spirit had no need to come to God's obedient, undefiled Son as scorching fire. The blessed Third Person came with new anointings, discernments, and prerogatives to the humanity of Christ. He came as a fresh vehicle of fresh visions, fresh powers, fresh aptitudes, fresh vocations, and these mighty things were by and by to pass from the risen Head to the members of His body.

Fame went from Christ, and glory returned to Him in various ways as He exercised that dynamic ministry of His.

He had power over demons. All in vain did Satan try to induce Jesus to work in His own strength, in the power of His inherent Godhead, tempting Him to reverse the self-renouncing humility of His incarnation. Christ stoutly affirmed that demons were expelled by the Spirit of God (Matt. 12:28; Acts 10:38).

He had power over disease and death. Another specific result of the anointing with the Spirit was the action of Christ in healing all who were oppressed of the Devil. Having gained a decisive victory over the source of all evil and suffering, Christ was now able to deal with the results of same. As the Spirit of life, the Energizer enabled Jesus to quicken the diseased and pain-stricken bodies and minds of men, and also raise those whom death had claimed.

He had the power to preach and teach. Recognizing Himself as the Sent One of God, the perfect anti-type of all Old Testament types, symbols, and ordinances, Christ definitely declared His divine commission to proclaim a divine message. "The Spirit of the Lord is upon me, because He hath anointed Me to preach . . . to preach . . . to preach" (Luke 4:18,19). As the result of this equipment the people "wondered at the gracious words which proceeded out of His mouth" (v. 22). Surely this is evidence enough that the ministry of Christ was the product of His implicit dependence on the inward Counselor. The Father gave the Word, and by it gave the continuous elucidation of the Spirit who indwelt Christ.

This also must be acknowledged: Christ came to His oral ministry because He was divinely called to it and divinely anointed for it. The usual rabbinical training He lacked. "How knoweth this man letters, having never learned?" (John 7:15). He possessed, however, the greatest of all equipment for His witness, namely an intimate knowledge of Scriptures and the fullness of the Spirit. Lacking these two most vital and essential requisites, all the academical training gathered at cultural centers is but futile and useless.

Christ gladdened by the Spirit

As the hour of Christ's rejection drew near Luke tells us that He "rejoiced in the Holy Spirit" (Luke 10:21 asv). Weymouth translates the passage, " [He] was filled by the Holy Spirit with rapturous joy." Another rendering has it, "He thrilled with joy at that hour in the Holy Spirit." Thus, the Spirit was the source of our Lord's joy, enabling Him to triumph over His circumstances and to glory even in His tribulations. Anointed with the oil of gladness, He possessed an inward peace and joy

THE ATTRIBUTES OF THE SPIRIT

independent of all outward experiences and happenings (Heb. 1:9).

Have you ever noticed the somewhat unmistakable connection between the Spirit and joy? On the day of Pentecost, the waiting disciples were anointed with the Spirit in such a way as to make them God-intoxicated men. "These men are full of new wine." Theirs was a gladness, a hilarity others could not miss. Later on, when persecution came to these same men we read that they were filled with joy and with the Spirit (Acts 13:52). Paul speaks of "joy in the Holy Spirit" (ASV), and of joy as "the fruit of the Spirit" (Rom. 14:17; Gal. 5:22; Col. 1:11; 1 Thess. 1:6).

There is a false rejoicing, a superficial, effervescent ecstatic feeling worked up by those who resort to a purely psychic appeal. Jesus spoke of His own sharing His joy (John 15:11). Such a brand of joy can come only through the Spirit and is a joy independent of all circumstances. This was the joy Paul and Silas experienced when suffering in a prison cell. In spite of much physical pain and discomfort, they could forget sleep and sing praises unto God at a midnight hour.

What do we know of this joy unspeakable and full of glory? Are we sharing Christ's joy? Is ours the right foundation of joy (Luke 10:20)? "There is a river, the streams whereof shall make glad the city of God . . ." (Ps. 46:4). And this gladdening river is the Holy Spirit (John 7:37–39). The city of God is a symbol of the church John saw coming down from heaven as "the holy city" (Rev. 21:2). The Spirit in these days of the church's need and challenge is the source of her abiding, captivating joy.

Christ died by the Spirit

The writer to the Hebrews informs us that it was "through the eternal Spirit" that Jesus offered Himself to God as the sinless Substitute for sinners (Heb. 9:14). The same Spirit who had formed Christ's human body at the Incarnation enabled Him to become strong, wise, and gracious (Luke 2:40). The

Spirit guided and empowered Him, prepared Him for sacrifice and sustained Him as He died. "It was through the eternal Spirit," says one expositor, "that His sacred will conquered its aversion to death and for love to His Father and His people made Him a sacrifice for sin, without blemish as a perfect offering. The Prophet now becomes the Victim, and is shortly to be the Priest."

The Cross is eternally efficacious, not only because Christ as the perfect sinless One was there offered, but because all the members of the Godhead were involved in our redemption. God was in Christ and also the Spirit, reconciling earth to heaven.

The Spirit was present at Calvary as a witness of the act of eternal redemption and is the only witness in the world to the sufferings of Christ. Speaking of the cruel death of the Savior, Peter declared the apostles had been witnesses of such a bitter end, and went on to say, "so is the Holy Spirit" (Acts 5:32 ASV). The first generation of witnesses have been dead for almost nineteen hundred years, but the divine Witness remains (1 Pet. 5:1; Heb. 10:14,15). As the writer quoted above states it,

There were human witnesses of the outward tragedy, but the Spirit who had been the lifelong companion of Christ's deepest and most secret thoughts was the one solitary witness of the infinite and eternal virtue which enforced and informed the sacrifice. . . . Just as an attendant waited upon the steps of the sacrificing priest, who scrutinized the victim to be placed upon the altar, and was a sponsor for its unblemished health, so the Spirit who had watched with unresting jealousy and vigilance over the life of the Son, mediated in His last offering, and as earth and heaven became the sponsor for its spotlessness and soul-cleansing power.

What a sublime truth! Wonderful it is indeed to realize that it is through the faithful influences of this unseen Companion the work of salvation wrought out by Jesus Christ was crowned.

Because of the Spirit's association with the Cross, He ever blesses the preaching of the cross. He can illuminate such a truth and visualize the facts of Christ's death. Therefore, let us exalt and magnify the finished work of Christ in absolute dependence upon the blessed Spirit who witnessed its completion. And coupled with our witness, may there come the full offering of ourselves for whatever service He may appoint, without spot of self-interest or self-glory. With a crucified Savior and a crucified saint what untold wonders the Holy Spirit can accomplish in a world of sin!

Christ raised by the Spirit

With united voice, the New Testament affirms that the Spirit was "the efficient cause" of our Lord's resurrection: "The Spirit of Him that raised up Jesus from the dead" (Rom. 1:4; 8:11); "Put to death in the flesh, but quickened by the Spirit" (1 Pet. 3:18). As the Spirit of life, the Spirit of the conception, He was likewise the Spirit of the Resurrection. The power giving the antenatal life and bringing it to birth was the same who quickened that body in the tomb and helped to bring it forth as "the first begotten of the dead."

The Resurrection, then, was the supreme effort of the Giver of life: "By it He gave life to the dead body of Christ, but reunited the human spirit to its proper dwelling, not as a mere tenement, but as a home, insusceptible of further death."

The question may be asked, "Where was the Holy Spirit while the body of Jesus rested in the tomb?" Surely, it is not fanciful to imagine that the Spirit was in the tomb guarding that sacred tabernacle of flesh He had possessed, led, and strengthened through all its earthly pilgrimage. The Roman authorities had their seal on the outside of the tomb declaring that Jesus would not rise again; God had His seal, the Holy Spirit, inside proclaiming that His Son would rise again. And rise again He did, on the third day, robed with life forevermore! Thus, as in the virgin womb of Mary the Spirit fashioned the physical body of Jesus, so in the virgin tomb of Joseph of Arimathea He prepared the glorified body of Jesus. It was the Spirit, then, who quickened into life that holy body, which, the psalmist prophesied, should not "see corruption" (Ps. 16:10).

The same Spirit within believers is the pledge of our final resurrection (Rom. 8:23; Eph. 1:13,14; 4:30). As the "earnest," the Spirit is the guarantee of our victory over death. Presently, He is able to quicken us spiritually, physically, and mentally. "The Spirit of him that raised up Jesus from the dead . . . shall also quicken your mortal bodies" (Rom. 8:11). An ancient creed refers to the Spirit as "the Lord, the Life-Giver," and as such He can impart to us the resurrection life of the Lord Christ Himself.

Christ gave commandments by the Spirit.

Overcoming the limitations and humiliations of His earthly lot, Christ, even in His resurrection form, was still related to the Spirit: "Through the Holy Spirit He gave commandments unto His disciples" (cf. Acts 1:2). By the inspiration of the Spirit the risen Lord instructed His immediate followers about how His work would continue. The Book of Acts proves how those Spirit-filled men preached the Word received from Christ, with mighty power (Matt. 28:19; Acts 1:8; 2:41; 1 Thess. 4:2).

Looking at ourselves, we realize that our preaching and teaching can only be effective as we communicate to others what we are taught of the Spirit. If Christ in His risen life was Spirit-inspired to instruct His disciples, how deep must our need be of the Spirit's teaching ministry (John 14:16; 15:26).

At Pentecost the ascended Lord sent His Spirit to His previously instructed disciples so that they might bear testimony to His fullness. From that time, their duty, and ours, has been to understand the Savior's work and worth, and in reliance upon the Spirit's unction convey the saving message to Jews and Gentiles alike.

It is worth noting that in the final revelation given to the churches, Christ and the Spirit are still together. The mystic union abides. In Revelation 2 and 3, for example, each letter sent to the churches begins with a glorious title of Christ and invariably ends with, "Hear what the Spirit saith unto the churches." Well might we pray, "Make Thou the blessed motto of my life to be ever thus, in the name of the Lord Jesus and by the Spirit of our God, joining Him and Thee together in one secret of power and peace, O Spirit, glorify Christ to me, that Christ may be glorified, in some measure through me."

One final word of appeal. Our gracious Lord realized and enjoyed the Spirit's indwelling and fullness. His own forceful word was true of His own life and experience: "Out of [Him] . . . shall flow rivers of living water" (John 7:38). Christ submitted to the sway of the Spirit, and now commands all His followers to be filled with the Spirit (Eph. 5:18).

John reminds us that we are to walk even as Jesus walked (1 John 2:6). How did Jesus walk? He walked in the Spirit, and we must go and do likewise (Gal. 5:16).

We are apt to forget that the same resources of the Spirit appropriated by Christ in the days of His flesh are at our disposal, with one notable addition, namely all the virtue and efficacy of a crucified, risen, glorified, interceding Lord. What a vast heritage is ours! No gift of the Spirit bestowed upon Christ is denied to His followers if only we seek what the Spirit has for Christ's glory, and as loyal and uncompromising servants of the divine counsels. As the Spirit was not given by measure unto Christ, so the same unstinted generosity awaits our appropriation. Our merciful heavenly Father ungrudgingly gives the Spirit to those whose needs are deep, pressing, and manifold (Luke 11:13).

May our lives then reveal the permeation of the Spirit! He waits to dominate and control our thoughts, words, feelings, actions, pleasures, and pursuits, making us, even as Christ before us, "fine flour mingled with oil." To know what it is to be Spirit-possessed we must claim the promise of Acts 1:8: Forsake all that is alien to the mind of the Holy Spirit and respond immediately to the least whisper of His voice.

CHAPTER FIVE

The Symbols of the Spirit

The Bible contains the mind and will of God communicated to man in human, everyday language he can readily understand. By means of symbols and metaphors it pleases God to reveal Himself to our hearts. "I have . . . used similitudes, by the ministry of the prophets" (Hos. 12:10), the Lord has said.

Types, parables, and emblems abound to illustrate the work of the Father, Son, and Spirit, as well as the Bible's own nature and ministry. And the metaphor in Scripture is a most fascinating form of Bible study.

Among the most helpful books dealing with the symbolized work of the Spirit, mention can be made of the exhaustive study, *Emblems of the Spirit* by F. E. Marsh. Summarizing these emblems we can tabulate them as symbols from natural life—air, water, fire, salt, oil, wine, seed, seal, earnest, clothing, the number seven, dove—and symbols from human life—doorkeeper, Paraclete, witness, and finger.

Symbols Drawn from Natural Life

How generous of God it is to convey heavenly truth through emblems associated with the world in which we live. He speaks to us in language we can understand. This is the only way infinity can enlighten finiteness.

Wind

"The wind . . . so . . . the Spirit" (John 3:8).

The wind is invisible, inscrutable, not amenable to human control, but is known by its effects. Therefore it is a fitting symbol of the mysterious work of the Spirit in regeneration (Eccl. 11:5). He is not seen in His operations, but definitely felt.

When the prophet recorded the command of the Lord, "Prophesy unto the wind . . . breathe upon these slain, that they may live" (Ezek. 37:9), he had before him the vivifying principle in nature and applied it to the life-giving, resurrecting power of the Spirit.

Luke describes the appearance of the Spirit on the day of Pentecost "as a rushing mighty wind" (Acts 2:2). "Mighty" speaks of power, and the Spirit, who came imparting power, is all-powerful in Himself. "Rushing" suggests the approach, efficacy, filling. Taken together, the language symbolizes the secret of effective testimony in service and speed of accomplishment as witnesses are borne along by the invigorating, energizing power of the Spirit.

Wind is a great power; yet it can be modified. It is varied in its manifestations. Sometimes it comes as a mighty tempest or cyclone and with the relentlessness of a tornado. This was the work of the Spirit the jailer required (Acts 16:28). At other times, the wind is as gentle as a zephyr, the soft breath of evening. As such the Spirit influenced Lydia, whose heart silently opened to the Lord. Let us be careful never to ape another's experience. If you never had a cyclone conversion, do not criticize the man who has.

> Come as the wind! with rushing sound
>   And Pentecostal grace!
> That all of woman born may see
>   The glory of Thy Face.

Water

Water is one of the most common of symbols used to describe the varied ministry of God's Spirit. It can assume many forms, all of which are employed to unfold the blessings of the Spirit.

There is water. "Whosoever drinketh of the water" (John 4:14). From the context we have the idea of the clear, clean, refreshing work of the Spirit who alone can quench the thirst of the human heart. He it is who brings satisfaction for the soul's deep thirst. Cleansing (Ezek. 36:25–27), life, fertility, beauty (47:1–12), joy (Is. 12:3) are all aspects of water's beneficial usefulness.

There are rivers. "Rivers of living water . . . the Spirit" (John 7:37–39). How many mighty rivers there are on the earth, and no two of them alike! Cast in the plural, our Lord's prophecy indicates the many-sidedness of the Spirit's work. He is not confined to one avenue of expression. Diversity characterizes His activities.

There are floods. "Floods upon the dry ground" (Is. 44:3). Even though water comes as an avalanche, it is still water. God flooded the earth with a judgment of water in Noah's day and is just as able to flood it with blessing (Rev. 21:6). Floods, then, can stand for the superabundance of the Spirit's supply.

There is rain. "He shall come down like rain" (Ps. 72:6). Absence of rain means famine, scarcity, ruin. As rain, the Spirit is the fertilizing, life-giving power of God. He can transform the desert, causing it to blossom as the rose (Is. 35:1).

There are springs. "A well of water springing up" (John 4:14). "All my springs are in thee" (Ps. 87:7). Under this figure we have the Spirit as the perennial source of supply. Within, He is the Creator of all spirituality.

There is dew. "I will be as the dew" (Hos. 14:5). Here we have represented the secret, unnoticed, yet effectual work of the Spirit. He is the early dew of morning.

> Come as the dew—and sweetly bless
>   This consecrated hour;
> May barrenness rejoice to own
>   Thy fertilizing power.

Fire

In Scripture, "fire" is used in many ways. It is the consistent symbol of the holy presence and character of God (Deut. 4:24; Heb. 12:29). Various times it is applied to the Spirit (Is. 4:4;

Acts 2:3): "Cloven tongues like as of fire." (See also Luke 12:49; Rev. 4:5).

Used of the Spirit's operations, it is a most expressive figure for fire gives warmth and light. It consumes what is combustible and tests that which is not so. It cleanses that which neither air nor water can cleanse. Its action is life-giving, as is the warmth of the mother bird while she broods upon her nest.

Fire gives light and therefore indicates the knowledge and illumination the Holy Spirit imparts. "The eyes of your understanding being enlightened" (Eph. 1:17,18; Heb. 6:4).

Fire gives heat. It warms cold things and persons and thus symbolizes the Spirit's power to warm cold hearts (Rom. 5:5).

Fire gives power, generates steam, and so represents the energizing influence of the Spirit (Acts 2:3,4; see Lev. 9:24; 10:2; Mal. 3:2; 1 Cor. 3:13,14, for other actions of fire).

Salt

Another reason why the Bible abounds in symbols is the fact that it was written in the East where language is very picturesque; hence our Lord's constant use of common objects. The parables and symbols He used bear the stamp of His years of association with the simple, everyday life of the people. Salt, for example, was taken to express the influence of the saint's spirituality in a corrupt world. "Ye are the salt of the earth" (Matt. 5:13). "Salted with fire" says Mark 9:49,50.

The Holy Spirit alone can preserve our character from deadly insipidness and give it savor and pungency. How tragic it is when, as salt, we lose our power to arrest the evident decay all around us!

To be "salted with fire" implies the twofold influence of the Spirit. First, as "fire" He cleanses the life of the believer, consuming all uncleanness and putrefaction. Then, as "salt" He keeps the believer clean, preserving him day by day from sin's corruption.

Let us guard against losing our saltiness, that is, our Spirit-created spirituality. When this goes, Jesus said, " [We are] good for nothing" (Matt. 5:13; Col. 4:6).

Oil

The use of oil in Bible times makes a profitable study. For example, it played a large part in Old Testament days.

Oil was associated with food: "Fine flour mingled with oil" (Lev. 2:4,5). Here Christ—the "fine flour"—and the Holy Spirit—"oil"—are brought together. As the Spirit-anointed One, Jesus was food for man to feed upon.

Oil supplied illumination. In the service of the tabernacle, "pure olive oil" was provided (cf. Ex. 25:6; Matt. 5:16; 25:4). Today it is the Spirit's indwelling that enables the believer to shine and the church to maintain her testimony in the world. We are the lamps and the Spirit is the oil. Light, therefore, comes from within and is contrary to what is known as "the light of reason." The Spirit alone can give us understanding according to God's Word (Ps. 119:18). One duty of Aaron was to keep the lamps dressed (Ex. 30:7,8). How we need the continual dressing of the lamp of witness!

Oil was supplied for various anointings. Anointing oil is beautifully symbolic of the Spirit's actions. There is, for instance, His healing ministry as He pours oil and wine into our bruised hearts.

Prophets, priests, kings, lepers, diseased, and dead are all alike connected with oil-anointing. Christ came as the Messiah, the anointed One (Acts 4:27; 10:38; Heb. 9:11). And the Christian likewise is an anointed one (2 Cor. 1:21; 1 John 2:20). May ours be the experience of a fresh, daily anointing for the Lord's service!

> Thou the anointing Spirit art
> Who dost Thy sevenfold gifts impart!
> Anoint and cheer our soiled face
> With the abundance of Thy grace.

Wine

This striking symbol represents the refreshing, stimulating, gladdening influence produced by the Spirit in the lives of believers. "Wine maketh merry" (Ps. 104:15; Eccl. 10:19). Are we the Lord's merry men? On the day of Pentecost spiritual exhilaration and joy were mistaken for the effects of wine (Acts 2:13–15). The Spirit-possessed disciples became God-intoxicated men. Christ Himself, Spirit-filled, was taken for a winebibber (Matt. 11:19). Paul would have us avoid all fleshly excitement produced by the excess of wine (Eph. 5:18). We can never drink of God's wine to excess.

Seed

As an emblem, "seed" is applied to Christ (Gal. 3:16), the Scriptures (Luke 8:5), and the Spirit: "His seed remaineth in him" (1 John 3:9). "His seed" is the remaining Spirit (John 14:16). John's declaration perplexes many hearts. They argue, "Well, I am born of God; yet I commit sin." But all difficulty vanishes when we remember that the Holy Spirit is the seed and that the new nature He imparts cannot sin. Are we allowing Him, as the seed, to grow and reach full fruitage?

> Plant and root, and fix in me
> All the mind that was in Thee.

Seal

Like his Master before him, Paul knew how to use what was around him to illustrate divine truth. Ephesus was a maritime city having an extensive timber trade. Great logs and planks would be brought in and then sealed with burnt-in marks, indicating ownership. Thus he reminded the Ephesian believers of their sealing with the Spirit (Eph. 1:13;4:30; cf. 2 Cor. 1:22; 2 Tim. 2:19).

A seal was also used to convey to wax the design of the seal. Such monograms often implied a finished transaction when applied to documents. "Him hath God the Father sealed" (John 6:27). Jesus was the perfect reflection of God, "the express image of his person" (Heb. 1:3). Are we carrying the correct impression? Is the Holy Spirit as the Seal stamping our life with divine holiness? Perhaps the wax of our hearts is not soft enough to receive divine impressions.

THE HOLY SPIRIT OF GOD

Earnest

An "earnest" was a deposit paid by a purchaser to give validity to a contract. In Scottish transactions the term used is "arle." One farmer buying land from another would be handed a bag full of the earth bought, a part of his full purchased possession, an "arle." In this sense Paul uses the symbol of "the earnest" in reference to the Spirit, "Who hath . . . given [us] the earnest of the Spirit in our hearts" (2 Cor. 1:22; 5:5; Eph. 1:13,14).

The gift of the Spirit is a partial deposit of our complete inheritance. What God has already given in part, he will bestow at last in perfection. In the Spirit we have a little piece of heaven to go to heaven with. Presently we have the firstfruits of the Spirit, but the present enjoyment of Him is a pledge of future glory.

> If here it is so blessed
> What will it be up there?

Clothing

"Clothing," as a verb, is frequently used in a figurative sense. In connection with the Spirit's empowerment it can be compared to an act of clothing. "The Spirit of the Lord clothed himself with Gideon" (Judg. 6:34). "Tarry ye . . . until ye be endued" ("clothed with power from on high"—Luke 24:49; cf. Is. 61:10).

Seven

Representing perfection, "seven" is symbolic of the Spirit as the perfection of deity and the perfection of His work. Having "seven eyes" (Zech. 3:9; 4:10; Rev. 5:6), He possesses perfect insight. Having "seven horns" (Rev. 5:6), He possesses perfect power. As "seven Spirits" (1:4), He possesses perfect obedience. As "seven lamps of fire" (4:5), He possesses perfect holiness.

We sing of Him as "the sevenfold Spirit," and so He is, seeing that light, life, holiness, power, joy, love, and hope spring from Him.

As the sevenfold Spirit He is related to the seven churches

(Rev. 1:3,4), suggesting the beautiful truth of a separate aspect of His ministry for each separate church. He is not the same to all, but gives Himself to each as specifically as a mother gives her whole self to each of the seven children she may have borne.

Dove

Charles Wesley taught the church to sing,

> Expand Thy wings, celestial Dove
> Brood o'er our nature's night
> On our disordered spirits move
> And let there now be light.

Such an expressive emblem speaks of the Spirit's nature and office.

"The Holy Ghost descended in a bodily shape like a dove upon him" (Luke 3:22; Gen. 1:2). Such a type speaks of the Spirit's nature, *loving;* of the Savior's mission, *peaceful and sacrificial;* of the saint's character, *innocent and harmless.* It is profitable to note the sixfold characteristics of the Dove as given in the Bible:

It is swift in flight. "Wings like a dove" (Ps. 55:6).

It is beautiful in plumage. "Wings of a dove covered with silver" (Ps. 68:13).

It is constant in love. "The eyes of doves" (Song 5:12).

It is mournful in note. "Mourn sore like doves" (Is. 59:11).

It is gentle in manner. "Harmless as doves" (Matt. 10:16).

It is particular in food. "The dove found no rest for the sole of her foot" (Gen. 8:9).

All these qualities are marks of the Spirit. Would that each of us could aspire to the dovelike life!

Symbols Drawn from our Daily Walk and Work

At least four symbols from human life are used in Scripture to emphasize the Spirit's omnipotent operation in our daily walk and work.

THE HOLY SPIRIT OF GOD

Doorkeeper

The word as used by our Lord in John 10:3, "To him the porter openeth," carries a double meaning (cf. Mark 13:34; John 18:16,17). One is "a doorkeeper," from *porta,* one who waits at a door to receive a message. The psalmist was content to be a doorkeeper (Ps. 84:10). A second is "a burden bearer," from *portare,* "to carry," akin to a station porter.

Christ is before us as the Shepherd, and the Holy Spirit is the Doorkeeper. As such it is His work to open and keep open doors for the Savior. It may be that John the Baptist was in our Lord's mind when He spoke of a doorkeeper. The Holy Spirit, however, is ever the divine forerunner of Jesus.

He it is who opens up the door of the heart, preparing the soul for the entrance and reception of Christ (John 16:8–11; Acts 16:14).

He it is who opens up the door of the world at large. The progress of missionary effort is due to the Spirit's promptings, as the Book of Acts clearly proves. He is found shutting a door into Asia and opening another into Europe (Acts 16:6–11).

Not only does the Spirit open doors, He also guards them so that strangers and hirelings cannot pass through. And we have the blessed privilege of assisting Him as the doorkeeper. But are we opening doors for Jesus?

Paraclete

This appears to be our Lord's favorite designation of the Spirit, for at least four times He is spoken of as the "Comforter." In John 14:16 He is Christlike and abiding. In verse 26, He comes as the gift of the Father. In 15:26, He is represented as the gift of the Son. In 16:7, Christ's ascension is the basis of such a gift.

As the Greek is such a pliable language, a word is capable of many meanings. Thus, we have three words in English for the one used to denote "the Spirit."

Comforter

"Walking . . . in the comfort of the Holy Spirit" (Acts 9:31

ASV). As Augustine expressed it, "He is our sweetest Comforter." As such He is connected with our sufferings.

Advocate

"Spirit [Himself] maketh intercession" (Rom. 8:26,27). The same word is used of Jesus in 1 John 2:1. "We have an advocate." Such a term implies a pleader who comes forward in favor of and as the representative of another. We have two advocates, the Holy Spirit within us that we may not sin, and Jesus with the Father to plead His efficacious blood if we do sin. Here, the Spirit is related to our sins.

Helper

"The Spirit also helpeth our infirmities" (Rom. 8:26). Scofield has it, "One called alongside to help." God has promised help from One who is mighty (Ps. 89:19; Acts 26:22; Heb. 4:16). Do we require help? Then why turn to human sources for succor, when we have such a willing, all-powerful Helper as the Spirit? He is ever the "help of the helpless."

Witness

Doddridge has it,

> Cheered by a Witness so Divine,
>   Unwavering I believe;
> And Abba Father; humbly cry;
>   Nor can the sign deceive.

Paul refers to the Spirit in this telling fashion: "The Spirit Himself beareth witness" (Rom. 8:16 ASV); "My conscience also bearing me witness in the Holy [Spirit]" (9:1).

Who, and what, is a "witness"? The word itself is from *witan,* meaning "to know." A witness is one who sees and knows. A witness in court is brought there because of his knowledge of a case before the court.

As a witness, the Holy Spirit witnesses in and to the believer in three ways. First of all, there is pardon (Rom. 5:1; 8:1). Here we are as sinners in the court of divine justice, guilty of crime.

101

But we plead the atoning work of the Savior, and we are forgiven our crimes. The Spirit enters as the witness of pardon. He gives the assurance that there is now no condemnation.

Then there is adoption (Rom. 8:14–17; Gal. 4:6). Here we are as sons. From a court, we go to a home where we find ourselves brought into a divine family, with the Spirit as the witness of our adoption. His indwelling makes us perfectly at home.

Last of all, there is sanctification (1 John 4:13). The pardoned one in court becomes a son in the Father's house and then enters a holier sphere, the temple. Here we are as saints. As the Sanctifier, the Spirit witnesses to our sanctification. He it is who prompts us to dedicate all we are and have to the Lord, not that we might become His, but because we are His already. And the consciousness of the presence of the ungrieved Spirit within is a witness of our growing likeness to Jesus.

Finger

The early Fathers spoke of the Holy Spirit as "the Finger of the Hand Divine." The oft-repeated phrase "finger of God" like "hand of God" is synonymous with power or omnipotence, sometimes with the additional meaning of the infallible evidence of divine authorship, visible in all God's works.

Combining our Lord's words as recorded by Matthew and Luke we discover that the Spirit is the finger of God. "I cast out devils by the Spirit of God" (Matt. 12:28); "I with the finger of God cast out devils" (Luke 11:20).

References to the Spirit as the "finger of God" describe Him as the indispensable agent accomplishing the purpose of the divine will.

The Law of God

"Two tables . . . written with the finger of God" (Ex. 31:18; Deut. 9:10). The Holy Spirit was associated with the Father in framing and writing the Word of God. Human fingers actually penned the Scriptures, but they were ever under the control of the divine finger (Prov. 22:20,21; 2 Pet. 1:21).

The judgment of God

When the magicians with their enchantments no longer could produce the same plagues with which God smote Egypt they confessed to Pharaoh, "This is the finger of God" (Ex. 8:19). Belshazzar saw those fingers as of a man's hand (Dan. 5:5). The sinner is met on his own level and the divine fingers write in language humanity understands.

The power of God

David considered God's heavens as the work of His Spirit. "Thy heavens, the work of thy fingers" (Ps. 8:3), and the Scriptures offer abundant evidence that the Third Person is the Creator-Spirit. The word "firmament" is a wide extent of space, and such expanse is the production of the executive of the Godhead, the Holy Spirit. He it is who ever strives after a wider expanse in our hearts for the glory of God to be revealed in some new measure through us.

The saint of God

To Orientals, fingers are essential in conversation as they indicate what mouths dare not utter, namely concern or grave insult (Prov. 6:13; Is. 58:9).

Paul uses the figure of the "finger" in describing the Spirit's fashioning of the saint of God. "The epistle of Christ . . . written not with ink, but with the Spirit of the living God" (2 Cor. 3:3; Heb. 8:10; 10:16). Do we permit this blessed Writer to pen something fresh upon our life as day follows day?

> Write Thy new name upon my heart
> Thy new, best name of love.

CHAPTER SIX

The Fruit
of the Spirit

In his Galatian epistle, the apostle Paul depicts the ideal Christian character (Gal. 5:22,23). What Paul calls "fruit" is the sole product of the Spirit-possessed life. It is the fruit of the Spirit; that is, it is His fruit and not that of the believer. All that the Christian can do is to bear the fruit; he cannot originate it. Note the contrast: "Fruit unto himself"; "From Me is thy fruit found" (Hos. 10:1; 14:8).

Fruit is no mere self-development. It is the outcome of the Spirit's unhindered indwelling. It is the Spirit's transplantation of Christ's nature into the character of the Christian. Taken together, the rosary of graces in these verses presents a moral portrait of Christ, into whose likeness the Spirit strives to bring us.

The Holy Spirit Himself is our divinely-bestowed income. His fruit is the divinely expected outcome. Too often the outcome is far below the income! Such fruit is the consummation of the Spirit's indwelling and inworking and also forms the result of our union with Christ.

One or two introductory thoughts must claim our attention before we consider all that is involved in functioning as fruit-bearing branches of the living Vine. For a clear perspective of the spiritual truth before us, three portions of Scripture dealing with fruit bearing must be closely studied.

The source or foundation of fruit in John 15.
The nature and results of the fruit in Galatians 5:22,23.
The progress of a fruit-bearing life in 2 Peter 1:5–9, where the apostle gives us nine stages of spiritual progress.

Fruit as an Organic Whole

In Galatians 5:19–23, Paul indicates the diametrical differences between "the works of the flesh" and "the fruit of the Spirit."

The plural "works" is attributed to the flesh, because they are divided and cause division. Dr. Alexander Maclaren calls these works a "huddled mob." They have no order or regularity. Their interests and purposes are scattered. The works of darkness have no unifying principle. Their only binding element is sin.

Further, the multiplicity is contrasted with the unity of the Spirit's graces. The works of the flesh are independent of each other, and it is seldom that an unregenerate person commits them all. Any Christian, however, can manifest all the graces of the Spirit.

And "works," it would seem, are more numerous than the nine graces represented by the fruit of the Spirit. In fact, there are seventeen manifestations of fleshly works, and more still in the phrase, "and such like." Bishop Lightfoot remarks that the flesh is a rank weed which produces no fruit properly so-called. "Fruit" implies life, growth, spontaneous outcome, but "works" are often forced, strained, artificial, not indigenous.

In the singular "fruit," we have the thought that in spite of the manifold operations and results of the Spirit's ministry, they yet form one harmonious whole. The man who walks in the Spirit truly lives. He has a unity, wholeness, and completeness about life the sinner lacks. The life of a Christian is one undivided whole.

Again, in the "fruit" we have a unified variety. The cluster is one although the grapes are different. The effect of the Spirit's work is viewed as one perfect whole. The strength of those who follow the works of the flesh runs to waste. Such "works" form a prolific crop of weeds. The work of the Spirit is entirely different. United to Christ, the true Vine, we have fruit unto holiness (Rom. 6:22). Scientists tell us that the chemical analysis of the grape reveals nine ingredients, all essential to the perfection of the fruit. If one ingredient is missing, then absolute perfection is not assured. Thus it is with the ninefold fruit of the Spirit.

It is somewhat interesting to take the Ten Commandments and Beatitudes and compare them with the nine graces we are considering, and discover that taken together, they depict, not different characters, but different manifestations of the same character.

Fruit in its double operation

Because the Holy Spirit is not a mere figure of speech or dry dogma, but a living, life-giving person, the results of His work are sweetly positive as well as negative. His gracious indwelling is both an invoking and an outworking. No one can receive and obey the Spirit and remain the same in life and character. As He assumes control, there will be a change—clear, definite, noticeable, and attractive.

The believer is able to offer an eager, curious world, glorious evidence that the fruit of the Spirit is a loftier ideal than the works of the flesh. The Holy Spirit always produces a nobler standard of work than the flesh. And such an outcome does not come through human power but from a holy Presence pervading the life. The fruit of the Spirit is character rather than conduct—being rather than doing. In so many of our highly organized churches people are urged *to do* something. The Lord, however, wants them *to be* something. There is never any difficulty about service once true sanctity operates within the life.

Further, the fruit of the Spirit produces undeniable proof of His vital energy, and of what He is able to do in and through the believer. As already hinted, the fruit is His work, not ours. We do not manufacture the fruit; we only manifest it. The Spirit is the irresistible force within our life, supplying sap for fruit-bearing. And, as we shall see, the apostle gives us nine lovely graces, expressive of the loveliness and charm of a Spirit-filled, Spirit-led life.

Fruit as the climax of union

As the grape is the climax of the vine, the end for which it exists, so the outward fruit described by the apostle Paul is the manifestation of inner life and power. Fruit is the proof of root and sap.

Fruit is the consummation of the tree's origin and possibility. Fruit or flower represents the perfection of development, final cause, ultimate results. Thus, the great purpose of our salvation and sanctification is to bear fruit to the glory of God. Let us not deem such fruit-bearing a remote possibility. There is no reason whatever for a withered, barren, feeble witness. Peter in his word on fruit-bearing tells us how to escape being barren or unfruitful.

Another aspect of fruit is that it does not exist for its own sake or even for the sake of the tree, but for the support, strength, and refreshment of those who care to gather the fruit. Christ, as the Vine, did not live unto Himself. Himself He did not save. If we live for our own sake, we live in vain.

Fruit is also essential, seeing that the reproduction of the fruit tree comes through seed. Winter rains, spring air, and summer sun all combine to produce fruit, and through the fruit make possible still more fruit. The counterpart in the spiritual realm is not hard to see. Living under the sway of God's Holy Spirit, we not only manifest the fruit of personal holiness; by our Spirit-filled life we influence other lives, and they in turn bring others to the feet of the crucified One. Is the Spirit reproducing Christ in you and through you, in the lives of those around you? By character, conduct, and confession are we propagating the gospel?

Coming to the nine virtues representing the fruit of the Spirit, it is necessary to understand that they are not isolated graces. Springing from one root, they constitute an organic whole. "The graces named," says Bishop Moule, "are not isolated things of which you may choose to appropriate one, and I another. The complete Christian character is the fruit of the Spirit."

The Three Triads

The nine graces, it would seem, divide themselves into three groups or triads. We have three sets of triplets, treated in various ways by expositors. For example, the late Evan H. Hopkins, of the English Keswick Convention, used this effective outline of Galatians 5:22,23:

1. *Condition.* Love, joy, peace; disposition of soul.
2. *Conduct.* Long-suffering, gentleness, goodness; external manifestations.
3. *Character.* Faith, meekness, temperance; personal results in life.

Alexander Maclaren, in his matchless *Expositions,* has a slightly different outline:

1. The life of the Spirit in its deepest aspects: love, joy, peace.
2. The life of the Spirit in its manifestations to men: long-suffering, gentleness, goodness.
3. The life of the Spirit in its relation to the difficulties of the world and of ourselves: faith, meekness, temperance.

Griffith Thomas classifies the cluster of fruit as the relation to God, to man, and to self.

A somewhat unique treatment is given by Russell Caley, who reminds us that all perfect fruit has three distinct characteristics. There can be no fruit without this combination of qualities, and upon their respective relationship and development depend its beauty and use.

1. *The color of the fruit.*

2. *The flavor of the fruit.*
3. *The form of the fruit.*

Seeking to be somewhat original, we offer the following divisions of the fruit of the Spirit:

1. *What the Trinity inspires.*
2. *What the world admires.*
3. *What the saint requires.*

Under the guidance of the Spirit Himself, then, let us look at these various aspects of a fruit-bearing life.

What the Trinity inspires: Love, joy, peace

In these first three graces we view the life of the Spirit in its deeper aspects. And the Godward relationship indicated by these virtues comes as the result of union and communion. All three form the product of heavenly inspiration and indwelling, and are attributable to the Trinity in which we have the love of God, the joy of the Spirit, the peace of Christ.

Love

Love heads the list, seeing it is the foundation, the moving principle of the other eight graces. Love is the leader of the band. John Bunyan has it, "Love is the very quintessence of the gospel." Love, then, stands first, not as distinct from, but including all the rest. It is the root of all fruit. Love binds the three triads together. There is no separating all nine virtues, just as there is no separating the root, stem, and fruit of a tree. Of love, joy, peace, Bishop Lightfoot writes, "The fabric is built up, story upon story. Love is the foundation, joy the superstructure, peace the crown of all."

Love is the life sap giving form and substance to the rest of the cluster. And it is evident from the narrative that the Galatians were in sad need of the initial grace of love. In verse 15 of Galatians 5 Paul rebukes them for biting and devouring one another, while in the previous verse he tells them that "the law is fulfilled in one word, even in this; Thou shalt love . . ."

A. B. Simpson, of reverent memory, wrote of Galatians 5:22,23, "It is all one fruit. We have not a great many things to do, but just one, and that one thing is love, for all these manifestations of the fruit are but various forms of love.

> Joy is love exulting
> Peace is love reposing
> Long-suffering is love enduring
> Gentleness is love refined
> Goodness is love in action
> Faith is love confiding
> Meekness is love with bowed head
> Temperance is true self-love

so that the whole sum of Christian living is just loving."

The fruit of the spirit is "love"; then follow the outworking of love, the manifold colors of the prism.

> Love is the brightest of the train
> And strengthens all the rest.

We link love on to God, for God is love. And the fruit of the Spirit is love, seeing He is the Spirit of love (Rom. 15:30). Love is the greatest and grandest of the results of His inworking. He is ever active, shedding abroad the love of God within our hearts. It is the Spirit who creates love for God, for Christ, for the Spirit Himself, for the world, for fellow believers, for the lost around.

Love is the infallible credential of heart union with Christ. "By this shall all men know that ye are my disciples, if ye have love . . ." (John 13:34). Love is the color of the fruit. No matter what else we have, if love is lacking, the fruit is unripe. As a deep, rich color is the glory of the grape, so love is the chief glory of the believer. "Love is the Christian's livery; by it man knows his Master." Archbishop Trench has given us the couplet,

> The wind of love can be obtained of none
> Save Him who trod the winepress all alone.

Love was the bond of Christian brotherhood in earlier days, when it was said, "See how these Christians love one another." Minutius Felis said of the early Christians, "They love before they know each other." To which Lucian sneeringly replied, "Their Master makes them believe that they are brothers."

There is no conception of love in heathenism. Love is a Christian fruit. The works of the flesh combine to destroy love—love for God, for home, for society, for self-respect.

And the kind of love the Spirit produces is fully expounded by Paul in his "Hymn of Love" (cf. 1 Cor. 13).

> Love suffers long and is kind,
> love does not envy; love does not
> parade itself, is not puffed up;
> does not behave rudely, does
> not seek its own, is not provoked,
> thinks no evil;
> does not rejoice in iniquity,
> but rejoices in the truth;
> bears all things, believes all
> things, hopes all things, endures
> all things.
> Love never fails. . . . And now abide
> faith, hope, love, these three;
> but the greatest of these is love. Pursue love. . . .
> (1 Cor. 13:4–8,13; 14:1; NKJB-NT)

In his soul-stirring hymn, "Love Divine, all loves excelling," Charles Wesley has taught us to sing,

> Breathe, O breathe Thy loving Spirit
> Into every troubled breast!

May such a prayer be answered for us all!

Joy

"Love is the first fruit," says Charles A. Fox, "for it is called out in response to God's love, and it includes all; joy is next, and has its place between love and peace, a sheltered place, for it withers if either is wanting."

If love is the color of the fruit, joy is the bloom of the fruit. This second ingredient is of great attractiveness in the believer's life. Joy is the flower of love, the very loveliness of love. A joyless Christian is a contradiction of terms. Faber has reminded us that

> God's will on earth is always joy
> Always tranquility.

But sin and worldliness can rob a saint of joy. Like parasites, they suck out life's pure joy. David felt this and cried, "Restore unto me the joy of thy salvation" (Ps. 51:12).

Christ pledged Himself to impart joy, His own untainted joy. Anointed with the oil of gladness above His fellows, he bestows a joy unspeakable and full of glory. And such a divine joy springs from a realization of forgiveness; it comes as the result of abiding in Christ.

Further, this joy is of the Spirit. It is not something the believer has to work up. We are familiar with the line of Newton's hymn, "Joy is a fruit that will not grow." No, we cannot produce it. "The fruit of the Spirit . . . is joy." It was the Spirit who made possible our Lord's joy, for He was "filled with rapturous joy by the Spirit" (cf. Luke 10:21).

And such imparted joy is not solely cheerfulness, hilarity, or even happiness. There is a distinction between joy and happiness. Happiness, as the word suggests, depends upon what happens; joy is independent of all circumstances. Joy is equanimity, evenness of spirit. It is foreign to the frivolity and foolishness condemned by Paul in his Ephesian letter (5:4).

The fruitage of joy implies glad acquiescence in the promises of God. It is a joy that becomes our strength, leading to vigorous action (Neh. 8:10). As the work of the Spirit, this joy makes the child of God genuinely happy, and how the sad world around needs the glow of such gladness!

A casual reading of Acts proves that the unhindered action

of the Holy Spirit is ever accompanied with a baptism of divine joy (Acts 2:13,46; 5:41; 8:8,39; 13:52). Truly we "joy in the Holy Ghost" (Rom. 14:17). Because this joy is His, it is not fleeting but full; never perturbed but perfect. There may be certain aspects of pleasure associated with the works of the flesh, but it is only as Robert Louis Stevenson writes, "A pleasure with a thousand faces, none of them perfect; with a thousand tongues and all of them broken; with a thousand hands and all of them with scratching nails." The pleasures of the world are hollow, false, momentary. It is only in God's presence that we have fullness of joy, and pleasures forevermore.

> There is a heritage of joy
>   That yet I must not see,
> The Hand that bled to make it mine
>   Is keeping it for me.

As an acrostic, J-O-Y has been used in various ways: J for Jesus; O for others; Y for you. And blessed joy is ever ours as we place Jesus first, others second, and self last. Another way of using the word is to say that abiding joy always comes when Jesus is first, You last, with nothing (O) between.

It is profitable to take the graces of the Spirit and contrast them with the ugly works of the flesh. "Love," for example, throws into sharp relief the hatred, variance, and wrath that Paul mentions. Over against "drunkenness, revellings," producing a false pleasure, we can place "joy." And "peace" is never a companion of "emulations . . . strife." As for "faith," this fruit of the Spirit is dead set against "seditions, heresies."

In his *Bible Students' Companion,* William Nicolson has this profitable comment: "Joy, an agreeable emotion of the soul, arising from the hope or possession of some good . . . is the fruit of the Spirit—because the Spirit produces conviction of sin, leads to a knowledge of Christ—to repentance and faith—to pardon of all sin, freedom from condemnation by the Law—holy fellowship with God and His people—security under the care of Almighty God—and to the hope of a glorious resurrection to eternal life."

113

Peace

Griffith Thomas says that "Peace is the restfulness of our abiding attitude and disposition of the soul in relation to God." Peace, built on love and joy, is not the absence of trouble, but the realization of the presence of God in all circumstances, pleasant or painful.

Peace is a close relative of faith and joy, seeing there is "joy and peace in believing." Peace is "faith's first resting place." If love is the color of the fruit, joy its bloom, then peace is the skin, seeing it is the binding and covering element. Love and joy can only exist and develop upon a groundwork of peace. The "unity of the Spirit" is kept in "the bond of peace" (Eph. 4:3).

Peace is of a threefold nature. There is peace *with* God, which was made by Christ, who became our Peace. There is the peace *of* God, the impartation of His own attribute, a peace passing all understanding (and also all misunderstanding). There is peace *in* God, which is a tranquil attitude of soul, which He alone can make possible.

Peace such as the Spirit produces is not a state of spiritual coma, a condition of mental or spiritual insensibility, but a conscious resting in the will and Word of God. It is a deep, perfect, settled peace of heart and mind amid the turbulent experiences of life. Very often the vast surface of Lake Superior is swept by storm, but the tempest's rage only affects the surface. In the great depths of the lake (and it is some nine hundred feet deep) a wonderful calm reigns. Thus it is with the child of God, who in the world has tribulations, but in Christ enjoys an untroubled peace. Here we learned to sing, "There's a deep, settled peace in my soul."

Peace is associated with Christ, just as love is of God, and joy of the Spirit. Peace is Christ's legacy to His own. And He has no shortage of peace, seeing He is the Prince of Peace. The question, however, for each of us to answer is, "Am I bearing this precious fruit of the Spirit?" If of the earth, earthy, and therefore agitated, disturbed, confused, then such fruit of the Spirit will not adorn the tree of our profession. God knows there are too many of us restless amid the restlessness of the world! As a blind man knows nothing of the glorious colors of earth, sky, and sea, and a deaf man cannot hear the sweet strains of music, so a carnal mind is a stranger to the peace of God. Love, joy, and peace are opposite to the hatred, dissatisfaction, and restlessness characterizing a war-torn world like ours. God grant that the color, bloom, and skin of the fruit of the Spirit may be evident in our lives!

> Like a river, glorious
>   Is God's perfect peace,
> Over all victorious
>   In its bright increase;
> Perfect, yet it floweth
>   Fuller every day,
> Perfect, yet it groweth
>   Deeper all the way.

A perusal of the hymn books of all denominations discovers many beautiful and expressive hymns on *peace*. Hymnology, however, has failed to produce anything to supersede E. H. Bickersteth's masterpiece. To our way of thinking it is one of the finest expositions of *peace* extant. Here is the entire hymn:

> Peace, perfect peace, in this dark world of sin?
>   The blood of Jesus whispers peace within.
> Peace, perfect peace, by thronging duties pressed?
>   To do the will of Jesus, this is rest.
> Peace, perfect peace, with sorrows surging round?
>   On Jesus' bosom naught but calm is found.
> Peace, perfect peace, with loved ones far away?
>   In Jesus' keeping we are safe, and they.
> Peace, perfect peace, our future all unknown?
>   Jesus we know, and He is on the throne.
> Peace, perfect peace, death shadowing us and ours?
>   Jesus has vanquished death and all its powers.
> It is enough: earth's struggles soon shall cease,
>   And Jesus calls us to heaven's perfect peace.

What the world admires:
long-suffering, gentleness, goodness

If it be true that the first triad of love, joy, and peace constitutes what the Lord inspires, then it goes without saying that when He inspires, the world must ultimately admire and desire.

In the first set of triplets we have *character*. Here in this second set we come to *conduct*. "All these three obviously refer to the spiritual life in its manifestations to men." Passing from the color of the fruit, we now come to the flavor of the fruit. Flavor is a virtue fruit possesses, but which must be tasted by others if it is to be realized and praised.

It will be noticed that this second triad is arranged in an ascending scale. Grouped together we have, as Elder Cumming suggests, "The Christlike graces under suffering and provocation."

Long-suffering

The first virtue can be translated "good temper" and implies the ability to avoid quarrels, heal injuries, promote good will, forgive, and forbear. Martin Luther in his valuable commentary on Galatians interprets "long-suffering" as being that grace "whereby a man doth not only bear adversities, injuries, reproaches and such like, but also with patience waiteth for the amendment of those which have done him any wrong." *Long-suffering* is love enduring; love not easily provoked; love able to avenge wrongs but studiously avoiding them. Of such a grace, Bishop Lightfoot writes, "It is a patient endurance under injuries inflicted by others." Long-suffering can mean "long on suffering."

It is a quality marking divine dealings. Long-suffering is an attribute of the Trinity. We have, for example, "the riches of His . . . forbearance" (Rom. 2:4). God also "endured with much long-suffering the vessels of wrath fitted to destruction" (9:22). Long-suffering is shown forth in Christ (1 Tim. 1:16). And divine long-suffering is ever to us-ward (1 Pet. 3:20; 2 Pet. 3:9; Jer. 15:15).

The long-suffering of God is responsible for the delay of the day of final judgment for sinners, affording them time to repent. Because of their blindness of heart and bent to evil, the ungodly certainly need God's long-suffering. And this spirit of forbearance toward others was constantly shown by Christ. Think of how He bore the prejudice, dullness of understanding, pride, and jealousy of those around! "How long shall I suffer you?" Oh, how eternally patient the Lord is!

It is a quality unnatural to man. If long-suffering is grace to resist anger, smother hate, or endure animosity, then the natural heart will never be able to manufacture it. No earthly influence can produce such a fair, attractive virtue. The best of us are apt to be impatient over the faults of others. We are critically-minded, easily offended, eager for reprisal. For the unregenerate man nothing is sweeter than revenge. Alexander Maclaren says, "It takes two to make a quarrel, and no man living under the influence of the Spirit can be one of such a pair." Alas, however, we are short-sufferers! Unspiritual in our thought-life, we are somewhat willing to make up the pair. Flesh meets the flesh, and there is further trouble. Unless Spirit-possessed, as we come forth from the fragrant chambers of love, joy, and peace, we are not prepared to meet "the cold gust of indifference or the icy wind of hate."

It is a quality the Holy Spirit alone can produce. As *long-suffering* means that we are approachable, easy of access; suspending our judgment; not too ready to censure and condemn as we discern the faults and failures of others, then such a grace must be imparted.

If the depth of the reality of love, joy, and peace is tested by adversities and proves to be triumphant, if we are to get beyond repaying hate for hate, paying people back in their own coin, fighting fire with fire, surely we want to know the secret of having the soft answer turning away wrath.

Our only hope is the long-suffering Spirit Himself. It is His grace we need to bear quietly the insults and injuries of others. One whose life exhibited the fruit of the Spirit wrote, "I have tried for thirty years to see the face of Christ in those I differed from." Can we subscribe to this testimony?

"Christianity," it has been said, "is the Academy of Patience," and in such an academy the Holy Spirit is our tutor. He alone can inspire what the world quickly admires. There may be a few souls born with a kind, forgiving, charitable nature. It is somewhat easy for them to manifest Christian graces. With the majority of us, however, it is otherwise. With shame we have to confess that we are easily moved to passion, quick to take offense, impatient. We jump off at the deep end over the least thing. Constantly we struggle against our natural disposition. But what is hard and impossible for ourselves is blessedly easy to the Holy Spirit. He it is who can impart that "good temper" recommending the gospel we profess.

In one way long-suffering is linked on to the grace of peace for "the heart at peace with God has patience with men."

> There is a patience that endures
>   Without a fret or care,
> But joyful sings, "His will be done,
>   My Lord's sweet grace I share."

Gentleness

The grace we have just considered presents us with the passive side of Christlikeness. Gentleness and goodness, which naturally glide into one another, bring us to the active side. *Gentleness* means "benignity, being conciliatory to others." Jerome says, "Goodness, though ready to do good, has not such suavity of manner." *Gentleness* can be translated "kindness" or "kindliness," and is a further evidence of the flavor of the fruit. It suggests "a nature permeated by kindness." Graciousness and friendliness at all times are before us in *gentleness*. Combining two marks of true love, Paul says it is able to "suffer long and is kind." Gentleness, then, is love refined. Matthew Arnold's comment is, "The word which our Bible translates by *gentleness* means more properly 'reasonableness with sweetness' or 'sweet reasonableness.' " Bishop Lightfoot speaks of this virtue as a "kindly disposition toward our neighbors."

Gentleness means that we are inspired by the Spirit to hold all turbulent feelings in check. Submissive to the Spirit, we are enabled to preserve a tranquil demeanor when provoked.

Gentleness is Godlike. The Bible has a lot to say about the gentleness of God. "Kind, kind, and gentle was He." Kind hearts, we say, are more than coronets. Well, God has both the kindness and the coronets. The life of Christ offers a beautiful illustration of the spirit of selflessness found among the fruit of the Spirit.

The proud Corinthians were urged to emulate the gentleness of Christ (2 Cor. 10:1). Martin Luther tells us that "it is written of Peter that he wept so often as he remembered the sweet mildness of Christ which He used in His daily conversation." Is the Spirit producing this "sweet mildness" in your life and mine? Must we not confess that sharpness, bitterness, harshness, too often escape us? And yet, true followers of the "gentle Jesus, meek and mild," must exhibit the excellent quality of gentleness, if others are to be won as they hear us speak about the kindness and love of God, our Savior.

Gentleness is power. How slow we are to learn that greatness depends upon gentleness, and not upon mightiness! Worldly axioms have it that knowledge is power; money is power. The Scriptures say gentleness is power. "Thy gentleness hath made me great" (Ps. 18:35). Henry Martyn found that kindness was the only effective weapon he could use against the pride and prejudice of the Brahmins. "This also I learned," he wrote, "that the power of gentleness is irresistible." Have we found it so? Gentleness, of course, is a scarce commodity among dictators, but it ought not to be scarce among followers of the Lamb.

Gentleness wins hearts for Christ, and often conquers those

119

who are dead set against His will. The grace and sweetness Isaac manifested toward the Gerarites over the wells greatly impressed them as they wrongly insisted on their rights. His attitude also brought Isaac the benediction of heaven (Gen. 26:20–24).

The margin notes of Philippians 4:5 gives us "gentleness" for moderation. How thought provoking! "Let your [gentleness] be known unto all men." Martin Luther contended that the Greek of the quality we are considering conveys the thought of "giving way," and is thus translated in the German Bible as "yieldedness." And, truly, the world needs to know more of the milk of human kindness. Lack of gentleness is responsible for unnecessary tears and heartaches. "Be ye kind one to another" (Eph. 4:32).

Gentleness is the work of the Spirit. Courtesy of manner, sweetness of disposition, the willingness to give way, come hard to the flesh. Naturally we are hard, rough, rude, bitter, coarse. But such is the work of the gentle Spirit that He is able to transform our whole deportment and give us a charm and sweetness of manner commending Christ and His gospel.

> Every virtue we possess
> And every victory won,
> And every thought of holiness—
> Are His alone.

This word found its way into what we understand by noble manhood and womanhood; thus the terms *gentlemen* or *gentlewomen*. Are we among God's nobility? Whether we have social superiority or no, do we possess that chivalry and well-bred manners the Holy Spirit can make possible for all God's children?

Goodness

Here is another grace the Spirit inspires, the world admires, and the saint requires. Goodness is the practical side of love, as Paul proves in the opening verses of 1 Corinthians 13. "Goodness is love in action." Bishop Lightfoot reminds us that "goodness is beneficence as an energetic principle." This trait gives moving influence to the parable of the Good Samaritan (Luke 10:30–37).

Goodness implies a kindly disposition and temper in all things; doing good to others; lightening the loads of sufferers, as Jesus lightened ours. Comparing the former trait and this one, we can say that gentleness is benevolence in well-wishing to those around. It wishes to make others well.

Goodness is beneficence or generosity in welldoing. It is benevolence in action. And, as *good* is something translated "beautiful," the "good works" are also "beautiful works."

Goodness is embodied in the Trinity. Victor Hugo is credited with saying that the only thing he learned to bow the knee to was goodness. Well, "goodness" is active in the Father, Son, and Spirit, thus giving us cause for continual worship. "How great is thy goodness" (Ps. 31:19; Eph. 5:9; 2 Thess. 1:11). Lord Bacon pointed out that goodness is the greatest of all dignities and virtues of the mind, seeing it is a reflection of the character of God. *God* and *good* spring from the same root word.

It was by the Spirit's power that Jesus "went about doing good" (Acts 10:38). He came as the embodiment of the goodness of God. As we think of His good life and good deeds, we find ourselves praying, "Lord, I wish to be good and do good."

To do good we must be good. The manifestation of the active grace of goodness depends upon rightness of heart. "Thou art good, and doest good" (Ps. 119:68). Streams and source must correspond, otherwise goodness will be forced, artificial, hypo-critical. A fountain cannot bring forth sweet water and bitter (James 3:11; cf. Matt. 12:33: "Make the tree good"). To which agrees the wise comment of Evan H. Hopkins, "Character and conduct; creed and deed; word and work should always be united."

Do you remember the prayer of King Arthur for Galahad, "God make thee good as thou art beautiful?" And Sir Walter Scott's dying words are apt at this point, "Be good, my dear.

Whatever else you are, be good." If destitute of gold and gifts, we can yet be good and do good, as Charles Kingsley has reminded us in the well-known words, "Be good, sweet maid, and let who will be clever."

What a different world this would be if only more of us exhibited the attractiveness of goodness! David Livingstone, in the interior of Africa, learned that nothing impressed the hearts of the savages like the possession of "the daily beauty of goodness in his life." Can we say that our lives are resplendent with this daily beauty of goodness?

Goodness is the fruit of the Spirit. "Thy Spirit is good" (Ps. 143:10). It is because of the goodness of the Holy Spirit that He is able to produce such a quality in your life and mine. "The fruit of the Spirit is in all goodness" (Eph. 5:9). As the result of our union with Christ, the Holy Spirit can bring this flavor of the fruit to perfection. As the embodiment of grace, goodness means the burning out of our heart, by the fire of the Spirit, all vanity, selfishness, evil temper, malice, and envy. Such is His negative work, the positive side being the impartation of warmth, tenderness, charity, and generosity. The late Queen Victoria the Good made the noble resolve early in her life, "I will be good." And the British have never forgotten her good and gracious reign. By the Spirit, has a similar resolve become ours? F. Robertson, the renowned preacher of Brighton, wrote of what he called, "The Supremacy of Goodness." Truly, goodness commands respect and wins its way where beauty has no spell and knowledge can exercise no power. God's good and gentle Spirit can make possible for each of us a happy heart, a beautiful character, and a useful life.

What the saint requires: faith, meekness, temperance

We have now reached what we might term the foundational graces, for the three before us have to do with the mastery and subjection of self within and without. Taking us back to the first principles, these basic virtues help to make the rest of the fruit commendable to God and to man. If love, joy, and peace are the lovely color of the fruit; long-suffering, gentleness, and goodness, its inimitable flavor, then faith, meekness, and temperance, in their order, complete the perfect unity of the fruit.

Faith

If we take the King James translation we have "faith" as a gift of God—Christ's faith, seeing He is the author of it (Eph. 2:8). As the Spirit of faith, He makes over to us the fruit of faith. And such faith we love reposing in God and His Word. It is hard for the natural heart to accept the revelation of God. This is why faith comes as a gift. True, the sinner exercises a natural faith in things around. Faith to believe what God has recorded in His Word about His Son, however, can only come as the fruit of the Spirit.

But the word Paul gives us for faith is not to be used in the theological sense of belief in God. It is not a justifying faith or believing dependence upon Him, although such are necessary.

Faith implies fidelity. Here Paul has before him the idea of honesty, truthfulness, and reliance. The American Standard Version has it, "the fruit of the Spirit is ... faithfulness" (another translates it "fidelity"), which is simply the quality of trustworthiness. Multitudes who make no profession whatever of faith in Christ admire the sincerity, unquestionable honesty, and sterling faithfulness of those who are the Lord's. It was the transparency and uprightness of Joseph that kindled a corresponding trust in the heart of Potiphar for "all that he had he put in his hand" (see Gen. 39:6).

Can we say that our lives reflect the honest, openhearted, genuine confidence and integrity which never fail to inspire trust in others? Isaiah speaks of faithfulness as a girdle (Is. 11:5). Does such an attractive virtue encircle all we do and bind us to one another?

The faithfulness of God runs like a golden thread through the Bible. How "great is Thy faithfulness"! Take your concordance and trace out the passages dealing with this aspect of the divine character, and you will be encouraged to discover that there has never been the least flicker in the lamp of divine fidelity. God is ever the same.

It was for want of this grace that the steward hid his lord's money. Christ, on the other hand, highly commended the loyal servant (Matt. 25:21; 1 Cor. 4:2). Such a quality is also commended by men. It inspires the confidence of others (Titus 2:9,10).

Faithfulness springs from faith. To be faithful simply means to be "full of faith." Honesty and integrity in our dealings with others, as opposed to distrust, springs from faith; that is, a trust uniting us to God. Faith brings about a right relationship with God. Faithfulness means that we are right in our dealings with men. It is one of the manifestations of love. Believing all things, it is also eager to believe and do the best.

Human relations outside of Christianity are full of mutual suspicion. Society suffers from a lack of confidence. Strife, enmities, jealousies, and distrust are only too evident. Too much of the shady and crooked characterize business and politics. But the fruit of the Spirit helps to make men honest, upright, and faithful in all their dealings and relationships. Spirit-born and Spirit-filled men are sincere and without offense. Of the faithful man it has been said:

> His words are bonds, his oaths are oracles,
> His love sincere, his thoughts immaculate,
> His tears, pure messengers sent from the heart,
> His heart is far from fraud, as heaven from earth.

How we praise God because He does not leave us to manufacture the faithfulness He commands and commends! It comes to us as the fruit of the Spirit. By allowing Him to dominate every part of our life, we will see Him produce that which is pleasing to Christ, who is "the faithful and true witness."

What we must not forget in connection with the virtue of faithfulness is that it forms the basis of reward in eternity. Not our fame, but fidelity; not our success, but sincerity, will bring to us the Master's benediction at the judgment seat. "Be thou faithful unto death, and I will give thee a crown of life" (Rev. 2:10).

Meekness

John Perowne tells us that meekness is "a grace of soul which consists in habitual submission to the dealings of God, arising from a sense of His goodness and man's own littleness and sin." Without doubt meekness is a heart virtue. A. B. Simpson says of it, "It is love with a bowed head."

Meekness, which although it indicates our attitude toward others, has its roots in our own temper of spirit toward God. It means that we accept the will of God and His dealings without dispute and rebellion. Meekness is not mere resignation sometimes detected in the spirit, "Well, I suppose I must submit; there's nothing I can do about it." Meekness is the willing, positive acquiescence to whatever God may permit. When Chrysostom was being led into exile, he shouted, "Glory to God for all events!"

Meekness is contrary to the spirit of the age. The ancient world counted meekness a vice. Paganism and its philosophers treated such an attitude of life with profound contempt. The world's tyrants, too, have no sympathy with this virtue. The Greek word Paul uses for *meekness* did not come into current use until the Christian era. It is a term belonging exclusively to the Christian, seeing that Jesus introduced it by practice and precept. Human nature is never fully dignified, nor glorified, until it comes under the gracious, hallowing influence of Christ and Christianity.

Meekness is the opposite of self-parade, self-assertion, self-pride, self-will, and the high-mindedness so common today. As a grace, meekness runs counter to the conceit of the natural heart. All that is selfish, resentful, and vengeful indicates the spirit of the world and not the Spirit of Christ. Meekness will travel far in self-sacrifice for the good of others. This meekness is also foreign to that false humility Charles Dickens has personified for us in his character Uriah Heep, who always contrived to be " 'umble." Let us never be proud of our humility. What is true humility? The most satisfying definition is "realized nothingness."

Meekness is not weakness. Sometimes meekness is mistaken for weakness, lack of character, or flabbiness. Such a reputation is alien to the truth, for meekness blends the harmlessness of the dove and the courage of the lion. It is moral power linked to patience and contentment, which ever endow the soul with irresistible might. Meekness can rise to heights of holy indignation over the iniquitous practices of man and yet treat all who offend with characteristic humility. What a picture gallery the Bible presents of those who were meek yet mighty!

Think of Moses. Meekness is mentioned as his prevailing characteristic (Num. 12:3). Yet the old Adam was strong and fierce in Israel's leader, as can be seen in his murder of the Egyptian, and his anger when he broke the tables of stone. Moses possessed a spirit able to forgive those who injured him, and to speak kindly and gently to those who were adverse to him and disregarded his position. The meek inherit the earth, said Jesus, and as Moses lightly esteemed the riches of life, he gained after his death name and fame as the greatest ruler and legislator of all time.

Think of David. In his treatment of Saul and others, this brave warrior knew how to act in a gentlemanly fashion. Grossly insulted by Shimei, he could yet pardon. Reviled, David never retaliated.

Think of Paul. The apostle not only reached meekness; he practiced it. How his eyes would flash with strong opposition and his voice ring with authority, as he said, "To whom we gave place by subjection, no, not for an hour" (Gal. 2:5). Yet in his writings, Paul ever preserved the affinity between firmness and meekness (Eph. 4:2; Col. 3:12).

Think of Christ. The Master comes before us as the most perfect example of this fruit of the Spirit. Meekness reaches its absolute and lovely perfection in Him who was "meek and lowly in heart" (Matt. 11:29). Look at Him as He stands before the Sanhedrin, Pilate, and Herod. How beautifully He combined majesty and meekness! No wonder George Macdonald wrote:

> In all things like Thy brethren made,
>   O teach us how to be,
> With meekness, gentleness arrayed,
>   In all things like to Thee.

The Holy Spirit, as a dove, came upon Jesus, helping to make possible His dovelike character and ministry. The gentle, unruffled Spirit, with His entire absence of self-assertion or revenge, had full control of the strong, brave spirit of Jesus. Hence, His sweet reasonableness, absence of fear, and true humility in His approach to others.

And what of ourselves? Is such a grace ours? How do we regard all the insults and wrongs inflicted by men? As permitted by God as part of His disciple of life? Alexander Maclaren says of meekness that it "points to submissiveness of spirit which does not lift itself up against opposition but bends like a reed before the storm." Henry Wadsworth Longfellow has it:

> O power of meekness,
> Whose very gentleness and weakness
> Are like the yielding, but irresistible air.

Turn where you may, meekness meets you as a qualification for public leadership in Christ's kingdom (Matt. 11:29,30; 1 Cor. 4:21; Gal. 6:1; Eph. 4:2). It is also one of the blessed graces Jesus named in His Sermon on the Mount (Matt. 5:5). The flesh may want to repay insults. But it is always Christlike to forgive and to repress self when it comes to the claims and needs of others (2 Tim. 2:25; Titus 3:2). Such a heart virtue is of the Spirit, who is also a true embodiment of meekness.

> There is a meekness free from pride,
>   That feels no anger arise;
> At slights, or hate, or ridicule,
>   But counts the cross a prize.

Temperance

We must not confine this word to its usage in connection with the problem of alcohol. The old temperance societies stood for the control or abolition of liquor, and such mastery of passion is included in this last grace of the Spirit. What is intended, however, is the mastery or dominion over *all* passions. It is "self-control," as the ASV translates it. One writer expresses it, "Temperance is the right handling of one's soul." It is the superiority of the spiritual over the carnal, of the eternal over the temporal.

Such self-control is set against the lack of control manifest in the drunkenness and immorality named among the works of the flesh. It was the virtue urged upon Felix by Paul (Acts 24:25), and which Peter exhorted his readers to add to knowledge (2 Pet. 1:6).

It is an absolute control. While certain forms of self-indulgence and the grosser sins of the flesh do not appeal to us, we have to be on our guard lest other, equally harmful, manifestations of carnality ensnare us. Self-control must be practiced in all respects (Rom. 15:1,2). Unruly desires, uncurbed feelings and impulses, rash indiscretion, "harmless" excesses of natural passion, a reckless forgetfulness of others, letting ourselves go in a direction in which we know we are weak, must be brought under control. The voice of the Spirit must not be drowned.

It is a joyful control. Temperance is wedded to joy. True control never produces an inward groan, as if the non-allowance of something the flesh hankers after is a grievous privation. It is not merely the tightening of the reins of our passions and desires in order to appear proper and judicious, but the joyful surrender of all we are and have to the Spirit. It is gladly surrendering our bodies to the Lord so that we can run life's race more freely and swiftly.

Paul mentions two aspects of this control: "I keep under my body" and "I strike it in the face." Here he uses the illustration of the most powerful blow a boxer can deal another.

"I . . . bring it into subjection." Here is something stronger. It means that he is willing to be led into servitude and bondage as a slave of Christ (1 Cor. 9:27).

It is a divine control. Peter the Great confessed, "Alas, I have civilized my subjects, I have conquered other nations; yet have I not been able to civilize and conquer myself." But what is not possible with man is blessedly possible with the Spirit. Self-control is poor defense against self-indulgence. Many of us have tried but with shame confess our failure. Now we know that more than self-control is necessary. We must have what A. T. Pierson called "godly self-control." Victory becomes ours not by self controlling self, but as we allow self to be controlled by the Spirit.

Can we say that all our appetites, habits, sensual attractions and passions, are under the firm control of the loving Spirit? To be overcomers we have to come right over to the Spirit. No matter how great the pressure of the world and the flesh, we can do all things—even control the surging tides of passion—through Christ who strengthens us (Phil. 4:13). Let us hurry to say that such a divine control does not mean the abandonment of pure and profitable pleasures. God never robs us of any ennobling, enriching pursuits. When He placed our first parents in the Garden of Eden, He told them they could eat of all the trees but one. Thus, while the flesh with its affections and lusts must be crucified, there is, at the same time, a joyous realization of all the good things of God which He has so richly given us to enjoy.

The Fruit in Our Lives

Paul concludes the catalogue of the Spirit's graces most pointedly: "Against such there is no law." In his masterly exposition of the Mosaic Law, in Galatians and in other epistles, Paul makes it clear that the Law exists for the purpose of restraint. With the fruit of the Spirit, however, there is nothing to restrain.

"Law neither prohibits nor enjoins Christian graces, which belong to a different sphere." The Law inflicts a drastic penalty upon the persons guilty of the works of the flesh. Excess in any of the dark deeds mentioned by Paul in Galatians 5:19–21 will throw any person into prison. The Law was made to punish such offenders (1 Tim. 1:9). With those who are Spirit-filled, things are different. Thus the apostle substantiates the proposition, "If ye be led of the Spirit, ye are not under the law" (Gal. 5:18).

The word "such" ("against such there is no law") is in the masculine, meaning the character and persons of those Paul wrote to, as well as the graces he exhorted them to exhibit. And, praise God, there is no harm in any excess of the virtues the Spirit makes possible in and through our lives. Here, then, are some things we can never have too much of. If any pearl is missing from this necklace of graces, then life for us is not perfect. Such a chorus of virtues will be marred if one note is omitted from our character. May all be ours in greater abundance!

As we conclude our meditation, it may be profitable to summarize a few features. Are we wearing the "rosary" of Christian graces we have considered? Do we realize that each of us can bear the fruit of the Spirit? Presently faulty and fruitless, we can be transformed into the best God has for us. If only we are willing to become Spirit-possessed, He is able to change even our natural disposition, no matter how unChristlike it may be.

Does our life present the color of the fruit?

Is there a love, which tinges and glows within every relationship of life?

Is there a joy, which in its bloom is rich and glorious, deep and divine?

Is there a peace, possessing and protecting us, even the sweet peace, the gift of God's love?

Does our life preserve the flavor of the fruit?

Is there a long-suffering, displaying itself in a quiet resignation under the providences of God and the provocations of men?

Is there a gentleness, both humble and loving, a kindness reflecting the kindness of God?

Is there a goodness, both within the heart and permeating the whole life?

Does our life possess the form of the fruit?

Is there faith in God and faithfulness in life: a charming, all-round trustworthiness and sincerity?

Is there meekness, seen in deep humility and a true realization of nothingness apart from grace?

Is there self-control, a strong, inspiring, and contagious mastery of all our powers? Are we among Christ's happy warriors?

If we are fully yielded to the Spirit, then our lives will bring forth abundant fruit to the praise and glory of God. Let each of us pray, "Lord, may mine be the fruit of the Spirit that those seeing the most of me may see the best of me."

The Spirit in Galatians

For the guidance of students, the following study of the Spirit in the Galatian epistle will be helpful.

The reception of the Spirit

The special mark of Galatians 3 is the first mention of the Spirit in the book. This is as it should be, for the Holy Spirit is the distinctive work of the new covenant Paul stresses in this epistle. An indirect reference to the Spirit may be found in 1:12; 2:2, where Paul claims that the gospel he preached came to him by revelation. Revelation is made possible by the Spirit of revelation. Power is a person, and that person is God the Holy Spirit. "Received . . . the Spirit" (3:2) and "born after the Spirit" (4:29) are more or less equivalent terms. The faith, appropriating Christ as Savior, receives the Spirit as regenerator, indweller, and sanctifier.

The progress of the Spirit

Paul upbraids the Galatians for treating the flesh as the

finishing school for the child of faith. "Having begun in the Spirit" (Gal. 3:3) they can only be perfected by the same means. The commandment, course, and consummation of those saved by faith is all of the Spirit. "Love perfecteth what it begins." We "perfect holiness in the fear of God" (Ps. 138:8; 2 Cor. 7:1). Arrested spiritual progress is one of the themes Paul develops in Galatians (5:7).

The ministry of the Spirit

On the basis of faith, and faith alone, the Holy Spirit is ministered or given unto us by the Lord Jesus Christ (Gal. 3:5). Therefore every believer has the Spirit. Whether He fully possesses every believer is another matter. Once the Spirit is ministered *unto* us, He graciously ministers to us in various ways.

The promise of the Spirit

Doubly promised by God and Christ, the Holy Spirit came on the day of Pentecost as the gift of the Father and the Son. Thus, the double promise was realized to the full, as divine promises always are (Gal. 3:14). Many promises, however, are conditional—"through faith."

The nature of the Spirit

As the Spirit is related to sonship, He is referred to as "the Spirit of His Son" (Gal. 4:6). The Spirit is described as the Spirit of God and the Spirit of Christ. He came from both and represents both. It is the Spirit who, by His indwelling, actualizes the believer's position and present experience as a child of God (3:26).

The patience of the Spirit

Already we are found in the righteousness of God. We do not have to hope for positional righteousness. Such became ours the moment we received Jesus, the Righteous One, as our personal Savior. Here Paul speaks of "the hope of righteousness" (Gal. 5:5). And what is this particular hope? Is it not the

THE FRUIT OF THE SPIRIT

blessed hope? Before long we are to see the Lord, the Righteous Judge. As the Spirit of glory He keeps the Advent-hope bright and burning, and prepares us for "the crown of righteousness" (2 Tim. 4:8).

The antagonism of the Spirit

Galatians is an epistle of antagonism. Opposing currents are everywhere—the flesh against the Spirit, law against grace, Satan against Christ, the world against the saint. But the believer is not to stand undecided between two opposing currents. It is true that "the flesh lusteth (or is eager) against the Spirit, and the Spirit is eager (or incensed) against the flesh, these are contrary the one to the other, that ye may not do the things ye would" (Gal. 5:17 ASV).

The believer's position, however, is clear. He is to side with the Spirit at once. Without hesitation he must throw his entire weight on the Spirit's side. He must allow the divine current to carry him away. The pressure of the Spirit must never be resisted (Rom. 7:22,23).

The guidance of the Spirit

Two positive statements are vitally related, namely "walk in the Spirit" and "be led of the Spirit" (Gal. 5:16,18). Walking in the Spirit guarantees freedom from the flesh; being led of the Spirit guarantees freedom from the law. Charles A. Fox remarks, " 'Walk' is the active side of faith; 'be led' is the passive side, and our failure may arise from one or the other not being observed. 'Walk' means, step out, venture forth, put your foot down in faith; 'be led' means, yield to, follow, submit and surrender to the promptings of the Spirit."

The fruit of the Spirit

As we have seen in our exposition of Galatians 5:22,23, the fruit of the Spirit is in one cluster like the grapes of Eschol. The same Spirit governs the different aspects of fruit, like the diversities of gifts. Fruit is the product of sap, soil, and sun; the Holy Spirit is the sap, Christ Himself the sun and soil.

THE HOLY SPIRIT OF GOD

The dwelling place of the Spirit

Sometimes we are asked the question, "Where do you live?" And then we try to describe the exact location of our home. Do we realize that the Spirit lives in us? He has taken residence and dwells within, but are we "at home" in Him? Are we living in or by the Spirit? Such a life "is not an occasional influence of the Spirit, but an abiding state, wherein we are continually alive, though sometimes sleeping and inactive" (cf. Gal. 5:25). Living thus in the Spirit, Paul enjoins us to "walk in the Spirit," which means that our life in practice must correspond to the ideal inner principle of our spiritual life. The Greek suggests the thought that "walking" implies "by the rule of the Spirit."

The harvest of the Spirit

Our last glimpse of the Holy Spirit is that of One who can produce a bountiful harvest for all those who care to sow for Him. "He who sows for the Spirit will reap life eternal from the Spirit" (cf. Gal. 6:8,9). What sowing for the Spirit really means is explained for us in verses 9 and 10. We are never to "grow tired of doing what is right, . . . do good to all men and in particular to the household of the faith." A. R. Fausset in his *Commentary on Galatians* says of these verses, "We shall not always have the opportunity we have now. Satan is sharpened to the greater zeal of injuring us, by the shortness of his time (Rev. 12:12). Let us be sharpened to the greater zeal of well-doing by the shortness of ours."

CHAPTER SEVEN

The Fullness
of the Spirit

The last century has witnessed a revival of interest in the truth of the Spirit's personality and work. Never has there been such a wealth of printed material dealing with such a theme. At an ever-growing number of Bible conferences, too, this truth is given prominence, causing multitudes of believers to realize that they have by no means exhausted the riches treasured up in Christ.

With many, a sense of defeat has driven them to the New Testament to discover what it says about the victory the Holy Spirit makes possible through the crucified, ascended, and glorified Savior. Truly if all the facts and promises of holiness and holy living through the Spirit are not in the Bible to mock us but are capable of realization, then surely it ought to be our desire to understand and experience such promises of victorious living.

The Truth Outlined

Because of conflicting ideas regarding the Spirit's ministry in the life and work of the believer, we deem it necessary to closely examine New Testament teaching on the subject. Too often this truth is neglected due to error and confusion about the functions of the Spirit. Our prayer therefore, is for divine guidance as we endeavor to rightly understand the word of truth.

"I am amazed at a man like you going to these conferences where you hear a lot about the Holy Spirit," said a critic to a pastor. "What new thing can these conference speakers tell you? It is all in the New Testament." Replied the seeker for truth, "Yes, that is the trouble. We have left this truth in the New Testament, whereas we want to get it out of the New Testament and into our hearts and lives."

His ministry of incorporation

The great work of the Spirit's incorporation operates in a twofold way. It is essential to distinguish between the *fullness* and the *filling* of the Spirit. Such terms describe, as we hope to prove, the different actions of the Spirit as He seeks to incorporate Himself within the lives of those who are obedient to His sway.

The filling

Several persons in the Scriptures are referred to as having received "the filling of the Spirit" (see Luke 1:15,41,67; Acts 2:4; 4:8,31; 9:17; 13:9,52). "Filled" as a participle refers to an occasional experience, a more abundant blessing for the time being than "fullness." This "filling" denotes a special inspiration, a momentary action or impulse of the Holy Spirit for particular purposes.

Those who are habitually full of the Spirit need to be filled to meet a particular need. In times of peculiar difficulty or trial we can count upon the additional supply of the Spirit's grace and wisdom. Extraordinary endowments for special needs and emergencies can be looked for. Thus, the formula condenses the truth. "One baptism of the Spirit—many fillings."

The fullness

"Fullness" is an adjective suggesting a permanent position or a habitual, abiding condition. Barnabas and Stephen are spoken of as being "full of the Holy Spirit" (Acts 7:55; 11:24). Christ also was full of the Spirit (Luke 4:1). He received the Spirit without measure (John 3:34).

What believers should seek and claim as their privilege is the habitual condition: always full of the Spirit. This abiding condition should characterize every believer at all times and under all circumstances. This normal experience can be best illustrated by a vessel filled with water to the brim.

Such a spiritual fullness, however, does not render the believer independent of any further supply of the Spirit's power, nor make him self-satisfied. On the contrary, the fuller we are, the more conscious we become of our own insufficiency, and of the necessity of the Spirit's sustaining and renewing grace moment by moment.

One who is "full" will find that as special difficulties or calls arise, there are always special fillings for witnesses and triumph, and that these fillings come just when God sees they are needed. It is His responsibility to send them, and ours to receive them.

"Fillings" come in the path of service according to need. Therefore, we must not be anxious to receive momentary supplies. The Lord will bestow according to His riches in glory. In this chapter it is rather the "fullness" of the Spirit, the believer's normal life, we desire to emphasize.

His blessed incoming

The fullness of the Spirit rests upon the basis of His presence in the life. We cannot be filled with anything we do not possess. Regeneration brings the Holy Spirit into the believing sinner. "If any man have not the Spirit of Christ, he is none of his" (Rom. 8:9). "None of His." How emphatic! Such a serious statement demands attention. Where the vital bond does not exist between the soul and Christ, the divine Spirit is not to be found. Whatever virtues a person may possess or whatever attractions and qualities may adorn his character, if unsaved, he is destitute of the Spirit. One therefore must make sure of the initial work of the Spirit; otherwise, it is useless to cry for His fullness seeing the infilling is based upon regeneration. The Holy Spirit unites us to Christ, making us "accepted in the beloved." We are joined unto the Lord by one Spirit (1 Cor. 6:17).

So, the first pulsation of divine life is due to the divine Spirit. What the soul is to the body, the Spirit is to the soul of the believer.

> What are our works but sin and death,
> Till Thou the Quickening Spirit breathe.

The Holy Spirit then, is the "spot" of God's children. "Their spot is not the spot of His children" (Deut. 32:5). The presence of the Spirit in the life is the divine mark or "spot," by which the child of God is distinguished from a child of the Devil.

> Then on each He setteth
> His own secret sign,
> They who have My Spirit,
> These, saith He, are mine.

So far as God is concerned, there is no reason why the fullness of the Spirit should not take place at regeneration. There need be no intervening period in the life, no gaps. One can blossom almost immediately into life more abundant. Only three days elapsed between Paul's conversion and the fullness of the Spirit. Alas, with the vast majority of believers, it is otherwise! Ignorance of the truth of the Spirit and the lack of a full, complete surrender at the moment of the new birth robs them of the Spirit's fullness. Thus, as they journey on they come to yield to the Spirit's infilling and experience a blessing as distinct and definite as that of His initial work in regeneration. Such an experience is sometimes referred to as "the second blessing." Really, it is the other half of the first blessing, the fuller realization of the presence and power of the Blesser who entered once and for all.

His permanent indwelling

Many are kept back from the realization of the Spirit's indwelling through mistaking it with the reception of miraculous gifts. The Spirit's indwelling, however, is distinct from His fullness and infilling. We can possess the Spirit, yet not be possessed by Him. It is said that "Egypt always has the Nile, but Egypt waits every year for its overflow." Having the Nile is one thing; rejoicing in the overflow is another. The Nile's overflow is Egypt's salvation. But to overflow, the river must first be full. The overflow from our lives is the world's salvation. But in order to overflow we must first experience the fullness of the blessing of the gospel of Christ.

This indwelling is personal.

There is a sense in which the Spirit is related to every man, seeing He is the co-Creator of the unregenerated as well. Even the unsaved are dependent upon the Spirit. The physical life they enjoy and their intelligence by which they are gifted are due to the unknown Spirit. But His wondrous indwelling is an altogether distinct aspect of the Spirit's gracious ministry. "He shall be in you." He possesses each and every one accepting Christ as Savior. There may be outstanding gifts of the Spirit for a few, but "the gift of the Spirit" is for every believer, no matter how simple and ordinary.

One of Satan's lies is that such a heritage is not for us. The truth is, he knows only too well that the Spirit is the birthright of every believer, his birthright in virtue of the new birth. He also knows what it means to his evil sway when a believer lives in enjoyment of the Spirit's fullness. The question is, are we living this moment in the realization of this birthright, or like Esau are we despising our birthright? Are we possessing our possessions?

The early church was so dynamic in witness simply because all the witnesses were filled with the Holy Spirit (Acts 2:4). There are no special occasions for such a "filling." It is for all, at all times. It is not the luxury of a few. Whether a week or a century old in the faith, we can claim all there is of the Spirit, if His incoming is a realized fact.

This indwelling is permanent.

When the Spirit enters, He enters to remain. His indwelling is permanent. He abides with us forever (John 14:16). As the

139

holy inhabitant, He remains with us until death. He dwells in our hearts, that is, settles down, never to be driven out (Eph. 3:16). His is an abiding presence. Grieve Him we may, and do, but we can never grieve Him out of our lives. Our spirit becomes the permanent nest for God's holy Dove. And it is necessary to maintain this attitude until it becomes a settled habit.

As we open our window each morning to welcome and breathe in the fresh air, so let us address the Spirit as each new day commences, welcoming Him as the inmate of our being, the fountain of peace and joy, the strength of our heart, the director of our life. And as the day proceeds let us count upon Him, who came as the Helper of the redeemed.

His gracious infilling and outworking

The work of the Spirit within the believer's life is progressive. As the well, He longs to rise and fill every part of the inner life and then flow out to influence other lives. So we come to Paul's great word about being filled with the Spirit, a fuller treatment of which is given under "Marks of Infilling."

Saints are referred to as being filled with God (Eph. 3:19). Christ fills all things (4:10). Conybeare and Howson translate Paul's command in Ephesians 5:18, "Be filled with the indwelling of the Spirit." And if our lives are to function aright as "the mysterious cabinet of the Trinity," we must be filled with the Spirit in the sense of a pitcher sunk in a well and filled in the well. We are to be in the Spirit and fully filled with Him. Bishop Moule expresses the truth thus: "Let in the holy atmosphere to your inner self, to your whole will and soul. Let the divine Spirit pervade your being as water fills the sponge."

Paul urged upon the Ephesian believers the Spirit's infilling as a habitual condition. In Acts, this filling was necessary for daily need in service. For witness before kings and rulers, the apostles were filled with the Spirit, exercising the power of reply and defense as occasion arose. The Spirit gave them the mouth of wisdom so that with simplicity and directness they could answer all questions.

At this point, we pause to indicate the threefold aspect of the apostolic call to a life filled full with the Spirit.

It is a call to receive Someone.

The voice used is passive, not active. Thus, the call is not to do but to permit something to be done in and for us. Such an infilling of the Spirit is, of course, dependent upon the consent of the will and a right attitude before God. We must be willing to open the avenues of our inner being for the inrush of the living waters.

It is a call to a distinct duty.

We enjoy many privileges in our Christian life, but the Spirit's infilling is not one of them. It is not a privilege, a distinction, or an honor to be filled with the Spirit; it is our duty. The language Paul uses indicates an imperative necessity; something each of us ought to be and have.

Banks have what are called "unclaimed deposits." Often these were owned by people who lived and died in poverty. Can it be that we have a vast unclaimed deposit in God's treasury? Do we live in spiritual penury, a hand-to-mouth existence, and yet have such wealth at our disposal? May grace be ours to possess all we have through the Spirit!

It is a call to a positive command.

Paul is giving us an inspired, authoritative command. The Spirit's infilling is not optional, something to please ourselves about. If this is not our normal experience, then we live in disobedience. The Spirit, of course, cannot fill the life if it is full of something else. If full of pride, preconceived ideas, prejudice, or the world, we cannot be full of the Spirit.

Willingness must be ours to let Him saturate every part of our life, expelling everything alien to His will. And the Spirit ever fills by displacement.

> Oh, ye that are thirsting for fullness
> Make room by forsaking all sin,
> Surrender to Him your whole nature
> By faith let the Spirit come in.

The Truth Appropriated

Having noted the difference between the fullness and the filling, the abnormal and the normal, we now come to consider the means whereby we can realize all God has for us in His Spirit.

First of all, let us approach the subject from the negative side. This is necessary in order to discover those things checking the rise of the Spirit as the well of water. No matter how sincere our desire for the Spirit's fullness, if we entertain wrong motives and methods, we cannot experience His best.

Wrong motives

While it is certain that the Spirit is every believer's birthright as well as need, and that His infilling is a command to be obeyed, we can be guilty of harboring wrong motives, hindering the Spirit's work within and through our lives.

We must be filled and filled for one supreme reason, namely the glory of God—not for the glory of self. If we are tempted to think that such infilling will advance our own happiness and merely satisfy, or make us more conspicuous in the eyes of the world, such a blessing of the Spirit cannot be expected. The fountain within must be cleared of all the rubbish of self-advancement and self-glory if the living waters are to rise and saturate the life. Death to self is one of the unalterable conditions of the reception of the Spirit's fullness. If our whole body is to be full of light, our life must be simple. Simon the sorcerer desired the power of the Spirit from wrong motives, and earned the condemnation of Peter (Acts 8:9–25).

Wrong methods

As it is possible to seek a right blessing in a wrong way, it is necessary to guard ourselves from mistakes common to many who thirst for the fullness of the Spirit.

This fullness is a fullness of Someone, not something.

We must never lose sight of the fact that the Spirit's infilling consists, not in the reception of a mere influence or emanation from God, but in the possession of our lives by a divine Person. There can be no infilling apart from the personal Filler. Eager for any of His gifts, we must never divorce them from the Giver Himself.

This fullness does not come by the way of fleshly effort.

We tell the sinner that he can only be saved by grace through faith. Thus it is with the saint. The Spirit's fullness does not become ours by some holy frame of mind producing it, or by working it out of, or in our own hearts. Self-efforts, wrestling, fighting, struggling are useless. No matter how earnest we may be we cannot master all that hinders the Spirit by trying to squeeze good qualifications out of the flesh, as oil out of flint. Sanctification becomes ours by submission and faith.

This fullness does not come as the result of stirred-up emotions.

Certainly warm, gushing feelings may come as the result of a liberation of the Spirit's fullness in the life. But if emotion is lacking we must not doubt the validity of our dealings with the Spirit. We shall be bitterly disappointed if we set our hearts on ecstatic experience or extraordinary inspiration. In some circles, there is much that is purely fleshly and psychic; complete surrender to the Spirit may produce some raptures stirring within, but such is not to be sought for.

This fullness must not be sought as a medium of sinless perfection.

Christians full of the Holy Spirit are not perfect. A tub can be overflowing, yet full of holes. And a believer may be Spirit-filled, yet a very leaky vessel. Certainly one can reach a state in which, at the moment, there is not the consciousness of sin, but this is not perfection. The fuller we are, the more conscious we become of the vileness of our old nature. And this realization of proneness to evil accentuates our thirst for the holiness the Holy Spirit makes possible.

> They who fain would serve Thee best,
> Are conscious most of sin within.

The fullness has not to be agonized for.

If regenerated, then in virtue of the new birth such a fullness is our birthright and must be calmly claimed. The Spirit has taken up His abode within us, and is in us, that He might fill us. There is no need to wait and pray for His fullness. True, the disciples tarried in prayer for ten days for the promise of the Father. He came, however, not because the disciples waited, but because He had been promised by the Father and the Son. They had to wait for the Spirit as the ascension gift of the risen Savior.

We live in the post-Pentecostal era and have not to cry out for the Spirit. Some there are who feel they must tarry and agonize before the Spirit's fullness can be experienced. But all God asks of us is to appropriate and enjoy what he has already given. As we open the sluice gates within to the Spirit, the living water quickly rushes in, filling every part of our being.

Right attitudes and methods

We now come to the positive, practical side of our theme. If it has dawned upon our consciousness that such a blessing can be ours, then we will never rest until it is realized in our heart and life.

Obviously, there must be some kind of action on our part before the Holy Spirit can dominate and control our beings. The question distressing many an anxious soul, and one over which painful hours are spent in vain, is how the promised fullness of the Spirit can be translated into experience. Well, here are three keywords we must keep before us if we personally desire His full possession of the life.

Rectification

Vessels must be cleansed before filling (2 Tim. 2:21). Paul urged upon the Corinthian believers deep cleansing from all defilement of flesh and spirit (2 Cor. 7:1). With the saints of the early church, God first cleansed them, and then bestowed them the heaven-sent gift of the Spirit (Acts 15:8,9). We, too, must be willing to be cleansed of all that is alien to the Holy Spirit. We cannot be filled with the Spirit if we are already full of something else. Who would put pure white milk in a dirty jug?

It must be clearly understood that by a clean heart we do not imply a condition of sinlessness or eradication—that sin is taken out by the root. A clean heart is clean, but "the flesh," that is, the old self-life, remains "latent if not patent." Our fleshly nature can only be kept in the place of daily death through the counteracting power of the indwelling, infilling Spirit. As we walk in the light as He is in the light, He continuously cleanses us from conscious sin. Cleansing is a means to an end, namely the fullness of the Spirit. He garnishes us that He might completely possess us. No person cleans house, then goes out and lives in the yard. It is cleaned for habitation. Our trouble is, we want this needy blessing of the Spirit, but we love our sins. Yet we can be delivered not only from sin, but the very love of it.

The question is, are we spiritually prepared for this necessary rectification or adjustment? Until we are ready to part with all that is contrary to the mind of the Spirit we cannot receive His fullness. Are we willing to be made willing for everything to go that may stand in the way? That temper—are we honestly willing to die for it? That tongue—are we desirous of bidding farewell to those sharp, sarcastic, cynical words, so hurtful to others? Those impure thoughts; proud, vain, selfish thoughts; hatred of others; jealousy—are we prepared to let these vanish before the incoming tide of the Spirit?

Consecration

Sanctification represents separation from sin. When we are conscious that we have parted with all we know to be a hindrance to our spiritual progress, and have a desire to be totally yielded to the Spirit of holiness, then we are ready for His fullness.

When nothing is withheld and we are willing to be a filled spirit, soul, and body, then the surging waters overleap all banks and deluge the life. But if we hold the least little part back, then the Spirit's progress is blocked. "If He is not Lord of all, He is not Lord at all."

One day a small child was playing with a very valuable vase when somehow his little hand found its way inside the vase and could not be withdrawn. His anxious father tried in vain to extricate the hand. He thought of breaking the costly ornament, but made a last appeal. "Now, son, make one more try. Open your hand and hold your fingers out straight, as you see me doing, then pull." To his astonishment the little fellow replied, "Oh, no, Daddy, I could not put out my fingers like that! If I did, I would drop my dime." Our tragedy is that we try to hold on to our dime.

Appropriation

Our true attitude in the presence of a command like, "Be ye filled with the Spirit," is not to ask, but accept; not to supplicate, but submit; not to request, but receive.

One may ask, how can the fullness be obtained? The answer is: be cleansed, consecrated, then claim.

There is, of course, a difference between asking and claiming. If you have money in the bank you do not have to plead with the cashier to give you ten dollars on your account. You present your check and claim what is your own. But suppose your account is overdrawn and you need ten dollars to tide you over a difficulty. Then you have to ask the favor of a loan.

In virtue of our regeneration, we have received the Holy Spirit. Therefore we have not to plead, "Give, give, give," but claim all we have in Him. The two key words helping to make appropriation possible are "desire" and "receive."

Desire. "If any man thirst" (John 7:37–39).

Do we really desire to be filled, experiencing a life of victory over besetting sins? Without desire, we can never be delivered from a dry and thirsty land where no water is. All prayer for the Spirit is formal and unreal if desire is lacking. "Blessed are they which do hunger and thirst . . . they shall be filled" (Matt. 5:6).

Can we truly confess that we have been brought to know our parched and barren condition, the utter folly of all worldly compromise, and the necessity of a full and complete surrender to God? If the language of our inner soul is, "As the hart panteth after the water brooks, so panteth my soul after thee," (Ps. 42:1), then we are halfway on the road to blessing.

To be brought to the place of self-despair, shrinking not from the willingness to go all out for God, fearing not the loss of worldly treasures, then the flood tide of the Spirit can be expected. If we desire to be filled, God is determined to fill us.

Receive. "Receive [ye] the Holy Spirit" (Acts 8:15 ASV).

At Samaria, Peter and John prayed that believers there might receive the Spirit. The fullness of the Spirit, therefore, is not a promise to plead, but a command to obey and a blessing to receive. If some are hindered from appropriation through want of desire, others are destitute of the fullness through lack of reception.

It will, of course, be understood that we do not receive more of the Spirit. Yielding ourselves more completely to His sway, He receives more of us. Through believing reception He permeates every part of our life. If we receive someone into our home, yet only give them the possession of one room, even though it is the best room, they still do not occupy the whole house. If, however, we allow them to take one room after another until they have full control of every part of the house, then and only then can it be called their own. What takes place is not more and more of a man coming into the house, but more and more of the house becoming his possession. Thus is it with the reception of the Spirit's fullness. Our entire life is brought more completely under His control and power.

In connection with such a reception there are two phases to distinguish. First of all, we receive by resting. Already we have noted that there is no need to tarry for a special gift as the disciples had to. It is the Spirit who waits to bless.

But soul-rest is necessary in order that we may be ready to receive all the Spirit is willing to bestow. And such an attitude is an essential condition in all spiritual progress. We wait on the Lord rather than for the Lord. By waiting, or resting, we cease from self, from carrying our own cares, anxieties, and burdens. All is submitted unreservedly into the hands of God. We become as clay in the hand of the Potter. Soul-rest produces adjustment of the whole inner being to the divine will.

Second, we receive by faith. It is our privilege to claim the fullness of the blessing by the simple act of faith. "Receive the promise of the Spirit through faith" (Gal. 3:13,14; John 7:37–39). We have not to wait for feeling, for an experience of overflowing joy, but we accept by faith. Faith acts as if we felt. If we are conscious that all hindrances have been yielded to the blood, then we can claim our birthright by faith believing that as we do so, the Spirit takes full possession.

As we keep believing, God keeps us filled with the Holy Spirit, who, as the Spirit of faith, makes our faith possible. It has been said that "we must take God's checks by faith and cash them by obedience." By faith, we must reckon we are filled, then daily act as if we are.

The Truth Experienced

Seeking to classify the vital results of a life adjusted to the will of God and fully yielded to the divine Spirit, we discover that such cover both what we are and what we do. Our lives and labors are affected by the Spirit's gracious infilling.

Our lives

First, we consider what we are, seeing that what we are determines what we do. The Holy Spirit is more concerned about lives than labors. He knows that if we are right, fruitful service will come quite naturally. Here are some of the evidences of a Spirit-possessed life.

Inward dominion over sin

The Spirit's progress within the life means the instant expulsion of all that He reveals as being contrary to His holy nature and desires. Impure thoughts, lustful appetites, fiery temper, hatred, pride, self-seeking, worldliness all fall before Him as Dagon did before the ark of the Lord.

As we walk in the Spirit, increasingly we realize that the body is His temple, and we crave inner holiness. To be Spirit-filled is the only preventative against backsliding and the secret of the overcoming, ever-victorious life.

Constant victory over Satan

The Spirit-filled life is the life constantly attacked by Satan. It was so with the Master, whose filling led to fighting (Luke 4:1,2). We live in a fool's paradise if we imagine that to be Spirit-filled means to be lifted out of all testings, hostility, and antagonisms.

The more intense and marked our spiritual life, the greater the onslaught of Satan. But "endynamited" with divine strength, we become more than conquerors. Mere nominal Christians are of little account to the Devil. He can afford to let them alone, seeing their unspiritual life is not disastrous to his cause.

Spirit-filled, however, we become the target of his constant determined attacks. Consecration results in conflict. Our spiritual adjustment produces satanic antagonism, but we fight victoriously. We overcome the enemy by the blood of the Lamb. By the Word of God, which is the sword of the Spirit, we can cause Satan to retreat even as Christ compelled him to do so in the wilderness. This means that Spirit-filled Christians must be Bible-filled Christians. They prove the infallible Word to be the source of succor, guidance, and victory. And their appetite for the Book is ever a sure index of their spirituality.

Subjugation of self

The Spirit-filled life is likewise the life in which self is molded and controlled by the will of the Spirit. If self-filled then we cannot be Spirit-filled. As the Spirit of humility, He creates humbleness of mind and brings death to all self-pride and self-will. Through His unhindered infilling He makes possible submission one to another in the fear of the Lord (Eph. 5:21). He realizes for each of us the experience of the apostle Paul, "I live; yet not I, but Christ liveth in me" (Gal. 2:20).

A sense of personal unworthiness and insufficiency

Previously we have indicated that this distinct work of the Spirit does not imply a state of sinless perfection. The more complete the control of our life by the Spirit, the deeper our realization of the wickedness of the old nature. With the prophet we cry, "Woe to me! for I am undone" (Is. 6:5). Holiness, we come to learn, is altogether beyond human achievement.

A life lived in obedience of the Spirit is one in which there is the constant revelation of the need of the cleansing blood, delivering us from a holier-than-thou attitude. We come to know that we are not sufficient of ourselves, but that our power is of God (2 Cor. 3:5–7).

A life of joy and praise

Another evidence of being Spirit-filled is that of holy joy finding expression in secret inner song and heart melody, as well as in outer praise (Eph. 5:18,19). As the Spirit of praise, He creates gladness not of the flesh.

It will be found that any deep work of the Spirit is accompanied by an outburst of song. Martin Luther found the church songless, and through the mighty work of the Spirit in his life he composed spiritual songs carrying the evangelical faith to places where the reformer's voice was not heard.

The revival under John and Charles Wesley also found expression in sacred songs. Every Lord's Day the world over, Charles Wesley's hymns inspire the worship of multitudes.

The great Welsh revival likewise witnessed a revival of singing, becoming known as "a singing revival."

A dead church cannot sing, unless it be by proxy. There may be elaborate performance of music, but spiritual praise is missing. True praise comes only from the Spirit, and thus His infilling is as necessary for organists, choirleaders, and singers as it is for preachers.

Such Spirit-inspired praise can make us triumphant over all adverse circumstances. Paul and Silas could sing praises at midnight, suffering in a prison cell. Under the Spirit, our very trials come to us as chosen of God and are accepted in the Spirit of rejoicing. Spirit-filled, we can sing songs in the night.

Exercise of a prayer-ministry

As the inspirer of all effective prayer, the Spirit creates desire within the heart for intercession (Rom. 8:26; Eph. 6:18). A prayerless believer is one in whom the Spirit is not functioning as the Spirit of intercession.

A quickened prayer life is a proof of His infilling. Of Martin Luther it was said, "There goes a man who can get anything from God." Is such a description true of us?

A consciousness of Christ's reality

As we live in the Spirit, He makes Christ a real, indwelling, all-sufficient Savior to our consciousness. He it is who leads us to be occupied with Christ and produces a complete identification with Him, and our reality of oneness in Him (John 14:26).

To the Spirit-filled, Christ becomes so precious to the heart that we love to hear and speak about Him. It is the Spirit's delight to draw attention to and glorify Christ. "The dispensation of the Spirit is the revelation of Christ." We come to see Jesus as the kind, loving, forgiving, compassionate Savior.

151

Our labors

As the Spirit of power He energizes all activity of life. As service is what we do, so life is what we are, and the Spirit relates the one to the other, and both to the world at large. Three aspects can be noted.

Fellowship of the body

Spirit-filled, we live for each other's edification (Eph. 5:19). We speak one to another, not against one another. Where there are carnal-minded religious people who fight against the deeper things of the Spirit, one usually finds the fellowship of the body marred and broken by gossip, backbiting, and bitter criticism. Our only deliverance from the uncontrolled, unsanctified tongue is by way of the Spirit.

Once God the Spirit totally controls the life, all friction, crosscurrents, and antagonisms vanish as chaff beyond the wind. Peace and harmony prevail when His lordship is recognized.

Inspired witness

A vital testimony is dependent upon the Spirit's entire possession of our life (Acts 1:8). Our obligation is not to save the world, but testify to it "whether [it] will hear, or whether [it] will forbear" (Ezek. 2:5). If filled with the Spirit, we will speak somehow and somewhere of the Savior's grace. The spring will overflow (Acts 2:4). Lack of courage in confession is an evidence of the lack of the Spirit's fullness. If filled, there will be no fear (Acts 4:31).

Boldness will be ours, whether we publicly preach the Word or personally witness to relatives, friends, and those who daily cross our pathway. Of course, one can testify who is not Spirit-filled, but such a testimony is powerless and destitute of the fruit of the Spirit.

Partnership in suffering

This may appear an unwelcome aspect of the theme before

152

us. To be Spirit-filled does not always mean wonderful, visible results. If we judge the movements of God by the activities and requirements of men we are doomed to disappointment. The Spirit-filled life rarely wins the homage of worldly men or the sympathy of half-hearted religious people.

Somehow, the Spirit and suffering go together. Paul in his dungeon, cloakless and cold, could yet pen deeply spiritual letters. John the beloved was banished to Patmos. The aged seer, however, remained victorious until the end of his Spirit-filled life. Stephen, full of the Spirit, had only a short career as an office bearer. The most eloquent expositor of the faith in the early church, he died a brutal death. At the end of three short, mighty years of ministry exercised in the power of the Spirit, Jesus died upon a cross. Opposition, shame, and the desertion of His own crowned His days.

Yet, life in the Spirit is worth all the hatred and animosity such a life creates. The question is, are we prepared to pay the price of a Spirit-possessed life? If we are willing to be cleansed of all that hinders the Spirit's infilling, then we are ready for His endowment, an endowment causing us to glory even in tribulation.

Once all hindrances are removed and by faith we appropriate the Spirit's fullness, we are not long in discovering that such a fullness is to be regulated by the services asked of us and measured out to us according to our faith. We become not reservoirs but aqueducts; we possess in proportion to our need and our faithfulness. The filling becomes ours in an even deeper measure as we go on step by step, from faith to faith.

As we become more humble, more surrendered to the Spirit, more saturated with His presence, we come to experience a life of fruitfulness. We dare not shun this fullness if we desire the Master's smile and approval at the judgment seat.

CHAPTER EIGHT

The Marks of the Spirit

Paul, in affirming that he bore in his body the marks of the Lord Jesus, had in mind the scars covering his body, his insignia of sufferings for Christ's sake. He was as proud of these scars as a soldier is of his medals and decorations.

There are also distinguishing marks of the Spirit, evidences of His possession of us, and of our full surrender to His sway. Life in the Holy Spirit means a cross; not a vicarious Cross like the Savior's, but one that is sore and sharp to the natural mind. The flesh, our old darling sins, our pride, our self-life have no welcome for the Spirit, for He is out to pierce and slay them all until we bear branded on every part of our life the very stigmata of Jesus.

While the word *spiritual* occurs only once in the Old Testament, it is found thirty times in the New and is vitally connected with the Spirit in the life of the believer.

The Spiritual Man—What He Is and Has

Mankind as a whole has been described by Paul in a threefold way.

First of all, there is the natural man. "The natural man receiveth not the things of the spirit of God" (1 Cor. 2:14).

Such a man is under the influence of human nature—learned, eloquent, cultured, and even religious, but unrenewed by the Spirit and therefore incapable of understanding the spiritual content of Scripture. He may be educated with all man's wisdom, having "the wisdom of this world," but being unregenerated, counts spiritual things as foolishness.

Secondly, there is the carnal man. "Carnal, even as unto babes in Christ" (1 Cor. 3:1).

This second man is an improvement on the first, seeing he has the Spirit. In one sense he is spiritual, having spiritual gifts it may be, but not spiritual graces. He walks in the flesh, not in the Spirit, walks as a man guided by principles belonging to men and not of the Spirit. Owing to his carnality he cannot take strong meat—the deep things of the Word. Babes need to be fed with simple food; they cannot feed themselves.

Thirdly, there is the spiritual man. "As unto spiritual" (1 Cor. 3:1).

The spiritual man is the man of the Spirit, the renewed man—Spirit-filled and in full communion with God. Such a distinguished name is his on account of what is most prominent in life and character. Spirit-controlled, he is able to comprehend the sublime revelation of God.

The seven marks of carnality and the seven of spirituality have been classified thus:

The Carnal Man

Carnally minded (Rom. 8:5,7)
Carnally limited (1 Cor. 3:1)
Carnally weak (1 Cor. 3:2)
Carnally bound, enslaved (Rom. 7:14)
Carnally opposed (Rom. 8:7)
Carnally doomed (Gal. 6:8)
Carnally despised (1 Cor. 3:3,4)

The Spiritual Man

Spiritually born (John 3:6)
Spiritually led (1 Cor. 2:11,12)
Spiritually minded (Rom. 8:5,6)
Spiritually renewed (Eph. 4:2,3)
Spiritually sealed (Eph. 1:13)
Spiritually filled (Eph. 5:18)
Spiritually freed (Rom. 8:2)

155

Two great spiritual changes are possible within these three classes forming the human race. First, there is the change from the "natural" to the "carnal." This is divinely accomplished by the Spirit, when by faith Christ is received as the personal Savior. Secondly, the change from the "carnal" to the "spiritual," which is produced when there is complete adjustment to the Spirit in life and service. The spiritual man is the divine ideal.

Examining the spiritual man more closely we find him to be:

A man of the Spirit. He is altogether distinct from the unrenewed, natural man, who is a man of the flesh and of the world. He has the Spirit, whereas the natural man is destitute of the Spirit (Jude 19).

He belongs to the Spirit. He is in subjection to and under the rule of the Spirit. The repeated phrase "in the Spirit" implies perfect agreement with Him in all His wishes and work.

Endowed with the Spirit's attributes. As spiritual, he is infused with all the graces of the Spirit. And the manifestation of these graces is measured by obedience and yieldedness to the Spirit.

If the question is asked, how does one become spiritual, the answer would be:

Believe it to be possible.

Realize it is necessary.

Be willing to be given up to the Spirit.

Yield unreservedly to His claims.

Expressing it more fully, the spiritual man is:

One who has been baptized by the Spirit into the body of Christ.

One who has received the gift of the Spirit, once and forever.

One who has been sealed as God's possession through Christ.

One who has received the earnest of the Spirit as God's pledge of complete redemption.

One who has the indwelling of the Spirit as the evidence of salvation and sonship.

One who has the anointing of the Spirit for service.

One who realizes the constant infilling of the Spirit.

As one writer expresses it, "In the New Testament and in general use, 'spiritual' indicates man regenerated, indwelt, enlightened, endued, empowered, guided by the Holy Spirit; informed to the will of God having the mind of the Spirit, living in and led by the Spirit."

Tracing the usage of the word we find that he:

Feeds upon spiritual food

"Eat . . . spiritual meat . . . drink . . . spiritual drink" (1 Cor. 10:3,4). In the narrative Paul refers to nourishment miraculously supplied in the wilderness, namely manna and water out of the rock, typical of the spiritual food we require for our sustenance. We are what we eat. Man grows by what he feeds on. And as actual meat and drink form the body, spiritual food produces spiritual physique.

The four ingredients of our spiritual diet are:

The Christ of God—John 6:48–58—bread.

The will of God—John 4:32–34—obedience.

The truth of God—Heb. 5:12–14; Matt. 4:4—meat.

The things of God—1 Cor. 3:1,2—milk.

If the prodigal is a type of the wayward son of God, then his disgust over hog's food and his confession that there was bread enough and to spare in his father's house, carry a pointed message for many. Why feed on husks—selfish, sinful indulgences and trashy novels and literature—when the Father has an unlimited supply of heavenly bread?

Exercises spiritual gifts

"Impart . . . some spiritual gift, so that you may be . . . established" (Rom. 1:11 NKJB-NT).

"Concerning spiritual gifts . . . I would not have you ignorant" (1 Cor. 12:1).

"Desire spiritual gifts" (1 Cor. 14:1).

"Zealous of spiritual gifts" (1 Cor. 14:12).

Passages like these indicate that the Holy Spirit bestows various gifts upon believers, equipping them to serve the Lord. To each believer, no matter how humble, is given some spiritual enablement or capacity for specific service. No child of God is destitute of a gift. Having received the Spirit as the gift of God, a gift was received from the Spirit to exercise to the limit. "To every man severally as he will" (1 Cor. 12:11; cf. Eph. 4:7,8; 1 Pet. 4:10,11).

Our obligation, then, is to discover our particular gift and, empowered by the Spirit, employ our talent to gain other talents. As Paul reminds us, each personal gift is necessary for the edification of believers as a whole (Eph. 4:12,13).

Sows spiritual things

"The Gentiles have been made partakers of their spiritual things" (Rom. 15:27).

"If we have sown unto you spiritual things" (1 Cor. 9:11). By these "spiritual things," we are to understand those possessions proceeding from the Spirit which pertain to man's spiritual life, worship, and ministry. Paul, it would seem, is discoursing upon these benefits accompanying our salvation such as faith, hope, love, justification, sanctification, and peace—in fact, all the fruits and blessings and aids of the regenerated life.

As believers, we do not sow merely carnal things for the body, such as food, clothing, and money. Philanthropic work is good and necessary, but the greatest benefits we can bestow upon a needy world are spiritual things. Sowing to the Spirit, we reap life everlasting (Gal. 6:8).

Enjoys spiritual blessings

"Blessed . . . with all spiritual blessings" (Eph. 1:3). Such a phrase can be translated "blessings of the Spirit," which evangelical blessings are enumerated for us in verses 1 to 14 of this chapter. Of course, the phrase can represent any blessing ministered to us in the realm of the Spirit. His greatest blessing is His introduction of us into the heavenlies.

How necessary it is to guard ourselves from being taken up with blessings to the exclusion of the Blesser! Satan is subtle enough to know that even a gift can obscure the Giver.

> Once it was the blessing
> Now it is the Lord.

Sings spiritual songs

"Speaking to yourselves in . . . spiritual songs" (Eph. 5:19). "Admonishing one another in . . . spiritual songs" (Col. 3:16). To remember that we are spiritual and must sing spiritual songs excludes a good deal of worldly trash from our repertoire. These particular songs are those inspired by the Spirit and employed in the joyful and devotional expression of our spiritual life. Some there are, especially in Scotland, who declare that the Psalms are alone inspired and to be used as songs. But Paul's reference to "psalms, and hymns and spiritual songs" excludes such a narrow definition.

Many of our modern hymns and choruses are not worth the paper they are printed on. Purely doggerel, there is nothing divine about them whatever. Hymns from Charles Wesley and Ira D. Sankey have sung more people into grace and heaven than many others (note the songs of Revelation 5:9; 14:3; 15:3).

Part of a spiritual house

"Ye also, as lively stones, are built up a spiritual house" (1 Pet. 2:5). This "spiritual house" is not only the church as a whole, but any body of believers constituting a local church, where the Spirit and power of God are manifested—any company of saints where His glory dwells. For various applications of the term see Matthew 21:13; John 14:1,2; Hebrews 2:3; Ephesians 2:19-22; 1 Corinthians 3:16; 6:19.

159

Offers up spiritual sacrifices

"To offer up spiritual sacrifices, acceptable to God" (1 Pet. 2:5). Peter is here using a figure taken from the tabernacle sacrifices of old when a lamb was killed and placed upon the altar, signifying the complete and acceptable offering of a self-dedicated spirit. As believers are spiritual, so all associated with them bear the same nature, even their sacrifices. By a spiritual sacrifice we can understand any self-dedicatory act of the inner man yielded to God. And the Word leaves us in no doubt as to the nature of these sacrifices.

In them there is Christian benevolence (Phil. 4:18; Heb. 13:16). These sacrifices are inward (Hos. 6:6). They include a broken spirit (Ps. 51:17). They cover our praises (Heb. 13:15,16). And they represent the surrender of all we are and have (Rom. 12:1,2).

Fights spiritual foes

"We wrestle . . . against spiritual hosts" (Eph. 6:12 ASV). Our actual foes are not clothed in flesh and blood. They are invisible, wicked spirits in heavenly places. Too often we are taken up with flesh and blood if antagonism comes from such a quarter. Paul, however, takes us behind the curtain and shows us the invisible inspiring the visible.

> Principalities and powers,
>   Mustering their unseen array,
> Wait for thy unguarded hours,
>   Watch and pray.

Awaits a spiritual resurrection

"It is raised a spiritual body" (1 Cor. 15:44; cf. 46). Here and now, our natural body requires food and clothing and is subject to weakness, pain, and sickness. But our new body will be a wonderful organism similar to Christ's glorified body. All believers await this redemption of the body (Rom. 8:23; Eph. 4:30). Presently our spiritual life is hampered by a natural body, but the promise is "we shall all be changed" (1 Cor.

15:51). The inner is to correspond to the outer. Spiritual life is to have a spiritual body. Love is to perfect what it has begun. The Holy Spirit is to complete His spiritual work and make us wholly spiritual. What a glorious consummation!

The Spiritual Man—How He Is Known

Examining another set of passages where the term "spiritual" is found, we see at least six distinguishing marks by which we can know the spiritual man. During the Tribulation era none will be able to buy or sell except those who carry the mark of the Beast (Rev. 13:16,17). In the spiritual realm, unless we have the mark of the Spirit we cannot traffic in holy things. Let us look at some of these marks.

Misunderstanding

"The prophet is a fool, the spiritual man is mad" (Hos. 9:7). The only reference to "spiritual" in the Old Testament can be translated, "Crazed is the prophet, mad the inspired one." Here a prophet is described who has been driven mad, distracted by the persecution to which he was subjected. But is not the spiritual man today looked upon as a fool by Mr. Worldly Wise? "He himself is [discerned] (or understood) [by] no man" (1 Cor. 2:15). Often he does things that appear to be against reason.

The cleaner, more spiritual, and more marked our separation unto God, the greater the misunderstanding we create. But if there are no mad actions on our part, causing folks to think us crazy, then we are not responsible for what they call us. To many, Christ was a winebibber. God will take care of those who because of their distorted vision of the nature of the spiritual life misjudge us.

What we have to guard against, if we claim to be spiritual, is self-created misunderstanding. Acting without the Spirit's aid and guidance may occasion the just ridicule of the world. If we walk in the Spirit we will receive enough contempt without

161

adding to it unnecessarily. While it is true that we are to be fools for Christ's sake, we must not make ourselves foolish.

Development

"I . . . could not speak unto you as unto spiritual" (1 Cor. 3:1). "He that is spiritual" (1 Cor. 2:15). This should be the normal designation of every believer. Paul reminded the Corinthian believers that there was a higher state than that of spiritual babyhood. A beautiful baby is a most wonderful sight to behold, but a baby remaining a baby all its days is a monstrosity.

Are we spiritual? Are we daily growing in grace? The renewed are like a mirror, and the all-important matter is, which way is the mirror turned? If downward it will reflect only earthly things, the mire, the filth, and dirt of earth. This turning down of the mirror produces carnality. And if we are in the flesh, we cannot please God. If the mirror is turned upward then it will reflect the heavens with all their glory of sun, moon, and stars. Spirituality is simply the spiritual mind reflecting the things of God.

Fundamental

"If any man think himself to be . . . spiritual, let him acknowledge that the things I write unto you are the commandments of the Lord" (1 Cor. 14:37).

All who are born and taught of the Spirit are ever true to the divine revelation. It is impossible to find a spiritual man doubting the infallibility of the Scriptures. Not only so; a man's spirituality can be judged by the way he handles God's inspired Word. Why do some men criticize the Bible, reject its great fundamental truths, and appear ignorant of spiritual things although they appear to be learned in the wisdom of the world. There is only one answer—they are not spiritual; that is, they have not the Spirit, are not truly born again. Reason, and not revelation, is their starting point.

There is a world of difference between mere cleverness and spiritual discernment. One is worldly acumen; the other is heavenly wisdom. A Spirit-taught mind is the first requisite rather than a certain quality of intellect modernists dote upon. It is the spiritual mood and not a learned mind which gives the soul its initial posture for discovering the deep things of God.

Discernment

"He that is spiritual [discerneth] all things" (1 Cor. 2:15; 3:2). This mark of the spiritual man is really a development of the one we have just considered. If we live in the Spirit, then there is no limitation to our understanding of divine truth. We find ourselves in the attitude to freely receive and glory in holy truths that the natural man cannot comprehend. The natural man counts spiritual things dull and stupid, and is therefore one in whom truth does not produce its proper effect. To him truth is insipid, tasteless, distasteful. He cannot discern its proper nature, that it is beautiful, and good. And his difficulty is not so much in the will as in the inward state, for truth can only be spiritually discerned, by and through the Spirit. All truth is revelation, but one who is spiritually blind has not the inward condition necessary to the reception of a divine revelation. Spirituality, as we shall now see, covers the entire range of a spiritual man's faculties, namely, his heart, mind, and will.

The mind. The curse of today is the divorce of the intellectual from the spiritual—wisdom of words versus words which the Holy Spirit teaches (1 Cor. 1:17). The spiritual, however, is never divorced from the intellectual, for a spiritual man's intellect is touched and inspired by the divine Spirit. Some of the greatest saints have been the deepest thinkers.

Almost the first result of the adjustment of a regenerated life to the Holy Spirit is the adjustment of human reason to divine reason. Now the believer no longer argues about a divine revelation. He accepts it by faith and is enabled to think God's thoughts after Him and to clearly discern His purposes. "Filled with the knowledge of his will in all wisdom and spiritual understanding" (Col. 1:9), he revels in spiritual sublimities.

The heart. The spiritual man does not receive truth in a cold, formal way. With a heart pulsating with warm love, he is enabled to lovingly receive all the Spirit reveals to his intellect. He has love for the truth of God, seeing he has first of all love for the God of truth.

Spirituality, then, in the realm of the affections is that state of soul in which the heart with all its holiest love is centered upon God as revealed in Christ. And this is the specific work of the Spirit, for He it is who sheds love abroad within the soul (Rom. 5:5).

Can we say that all our emotions are under the regulating sway of God's Spirit? Such Spirit-love has a keen insight and is blind to all else save the will of God.

The will. George Matheson has taught us to sing, "My will is not my own, Till Thou has made it Thine." Unless our will is harmonized with the will of God we cannot enjoy His favor. To be spiritually-minded is to have the mind of the Spirit and a willing assent to all He desires of us. We cannot be vessels unto honor unless we constantly act under the guidance and dominion of the Spirit.

Thus, "When intellect, heart and will focus their energies reverently and affectionately upon Him, love—a passionate, ever-present, ever-dominant love—is the result. This is the true sphere of the Holy Spirit's indwelling and activity, and the character of such a God-centered and Spirit-filled life is described by the exalted word 'spirituality.' "

To be spiritual, then, means to:

Discern the deep things of God with our minds,
Love these deep things with our hearts,
Submit to them with our wills.

Compassion

"You who are spiritual, restore . . ." (Gal. 6:1 NKJB-NT). The spiritual man is also one who, in all humanity, endeavors to win back to the Lord a fallen brother. But the question arises, are we spiritual enough for the Lord to use us?

Only the spiritual are fitted to undertake this work of restoration. Being in touch with the Spirit, they receive spiritual insight as to the needs of the lapsed one and the message to apply.

Further, we must be spiritual if we are to lift others above their own level. All restoration is undertaken considering ourselves. We have nothing to brag about, even if we are without fault, seeing it is the grace of the Spirit that keeps us where we are.

Victory

"To be spiritually minded is life and peace" (Rom. 8:6). The margin note has it, "To have the mind of the Spirit," as a study in contrast, for Paul speaks of others who have "the mind of the flesh" (ASV).

If not spiritually minded, our joys, exercises, objects, and motives are "not subject to the law of God . . . cannot please God . . . enmity against God" (Rom. 8:6–9).

"Life" is one outcome of the spiritual mind. Death belongs to the carnal mind. Have we this life indeed? Do we by the Spirit bring to the place of death the deeds of the body and thereby live the full, abundant life?

"Peace" is another result of having "the mind of the Spirit" (ASV). This is not the initial peace, peace from God; but peace in God. It is a deep settled peace, passing all understanding, and misunderstanding also. We are no longer at "enmity against God," but at peace with Him. No matter how adverse our circumstances may be, being spiritual we carry a sweet, undisturbed peace.

Manifesting the Love of the Spirit

The love of the Spirit is a forgotten, neglected truth in the thoughts of believers. There is a tendency to dwell on the love of the Father and of the Son to the exclusion of the love of the Spirit. Have you ever heard a sermon on such a theme? If the Spirit is and does love, is it not shameful not to know it and delight in it?

THE HOLY SPIRIT OF GOD

Believing as we do in the equality existing among the persons of the Godhead, then we must be equally loved by the Spirit and the Father and the Son. God loves us and is not satisfied until we rejoice and rest in His love. Christ loves us and poured out His lifeblood for us at Calvary, and lives again to plead our cause above. The Spirit loves us and is content to abide in us until we are as pure as Christ is pure.

R. A. Torrey states the truth in this forcible way:

> We kneel down in the presence of God the Father and look up into His face and say, "I thank Thee, Father, for Thy great love that led Thee to give Thine only begotten Son to die upon the Cross of Calvary for me."
>
> Each day of our lives we also look up into the face of our Lord and Savior, Jesus Christ, and say, "Oh, Thou glorious Lord and Savior, Jesus Thou Son of God. I thank Thee for Thy great love that led Thee not to count it a thing to be grasped to be on equality with God, but to empty Thyself and forsaking all the glory of heaven, come down to earth with all its shame and to take my sins upon thyself and die in my place upon the Cross."
>
> But how often do we kneel and say to the Holy Spirit, "Oh, Thou eternal and infinite Spirit of God, I thank Thee for Thy great love that led Thee to come into this world of sin and darkness and to seek me out and see my utter ruin and need of a Savior and to reveal to me my Lord and Savior, Jesus Christ, as just the Savior whom I need?" Yet we owe our salvation just as truly to the love of the Spirit, as we do to the love of the Father and the love of the Son.

Well, now, let us give ourselves to the study of the love of the Spirit, a heart-warming theme taught directly and indirectly in the Scriptures.

Direct evidences in Scripture

Several passages make it clear that the Spirit is love, just as God is love. Let the following citations suffice.

"Grieve not the Holy Spirit of God" (Eph. 4:30).

Grief is a deeper word than *sorrow*. Herod was sorry over the request of Salome for the head of John the Baptist, and the king's sorrow came because of his respect for John. Grief, however, springs from a relationship of love. Grief is an element of the heart. Where there is no love, there is no grief, and the deeper the love, the more poignant and distressing the grief.

Because, then, the Spirit can be grieved, we know what a loving heart He possesses. And Paul leaves us in no doubt as to those sins stabbing the heart of the Spirit. Oh, to live with an ungrieved Spirit!

"The fruit of the Spirit is love" (Gal. 5:22).

Weymouth translates the phrase, "The Spirit . . . brings a harvest of love." Fruit is ever the same nature as the tree. An apple tree, for example, cannot bear grapes. Therefore, if the Spirit produces love, He Himself must be love. The fruit must correspond to the root.

And such love is the fountainhead of all other virtues, for the eight succeeding graces are a development of the first.

> Joy is love exulting.
> Peace is love reposing.
> Long-suffering is love enduring.
> Gentleness is love in refinement.
> Meekness is love with bowed head.
> Goodness is love in action.
> Temperance is love obeying.
> Faith is love confiding.

"The love of the Spirit" (Rom. 15:30).

Such a Pauline phrase declares not only the love the Holy Spirit produces or inspires, but also His personal love. He cannot lift us above His own level. Having love in Himself He is able to beget the same in our hearts. And "the love that the Spirit inspires," as another translates the above phrase, is a love pure in content.

167

"By kindness, by the Holy [Spirit], by love unfeigned" (2 Cor. 6:6).

Here we have a trinity in unity, and we are only attested as witnesses when our lives manifest these three graces (2 Cor. 6:4). When the Spirit has the central place in life, kindness and love flow out in all directions. Union with the loving Spirit reveals itself in our loving attitude toward others. "Seeing ye have purified your souls in obeying the truth through the Spirit unto unfeigned love of the brethren, see that ye love one another with a pure heart fervently" (1 Pet. 1:22).

"Who [hath] declared unto us your love in the Spirit" (Col. 1:8).

In an epistle preeminently given over to the theme of the fullness and glory of Christ, this is the only reference to the third person. Weymouth translates the phrase, "Your love, which is inspired by the Spirit." We often say that we become like those we live with. Well, if we live in full harmony with the will of the Spirit, we are bound to reflect His character. His love flowing into us will flow through and then out, to bless and cheer a loveless world.

> Holy Spirit, Love Divine
> O'er life's path Thy radiance shine!
> Purify my every thought
> Help me love Thee as I ought.

Indirect evidences in Scripture

Considering various aspects of the Spirit's nature and ministry, we cannot escape the conclusion that He is the Spirit of love. Here are five indirect evidences of His undying love.

He is likened to a dove (Matt. 3:16).

The dove is the lovebird, the bird without gall, and therefore a fitting symbol of the peaceful, loving nature of the Spirit. Solomon speaks of the Beloved as having "the eyes of doves by the rivers of waters," and divine eyes are ever filled with tears of compassion.

> Heavenly—all alluring Dove
> Shed Thy overshadowing love
> Love, the sealing grace impart
> Dwell within a single heart.

He was promised as a Comforter (John 14:16).

The early church walked in the comfort of the Holy Spirit (Acts 9:31). Comfort is a heart-feeling, an outlet of love. God promised to comfort His own as a mother comforts her children (Is. 66:13). As a mother comforts her child, because she loves the child, so the Spirit consoles us because of the love He bears for us. Jesus loved His own (John 13:1), and the Spirit is another like Jesus—Jesus' other self.

> Our blest Redeemer ere He breathed
> His tender, last farewell,
> A Guide, a Comforter bequeathed
> With us to dwell.

He dispenses God's love (Rom. 5:5).

Natural love is an instinct and passion, and is behind every romance. The love with which the Spirit floods our hearts, however, is the imparted fruit of the supernatural life. Furthermore, natural love is based upon attractive qualities in its object. This is why we find it hard to love the unlovable and the unlovely. But the love the Spirit dispenses is not human but divine, and consequently is not exclusive. It has no favorites; it can love the most unattractive. It was while we were yet sinners that God commended His love toward us and Christ died for us.

It is the Spirit, then, who perfumes the life with love. Through us He seeks to love sinners out of their sin. And the more He has of us, the more we are able to exhibit of the love of heaven for all men.

THE HOLY SPIRIT OF GOD

He bestows love as a gift.

Taking 1 Corinthians 12 and 13 together—and they should never be disassociated—we find that the gifts of the Spirit are only effectual as they are ministered in love. We are to covet earnestly the best gifts, and the greatest, says Paul, is love. Particular gifts there may be for certain saints to exercise, but love is the Spirit's gift for all. And His most effective gift, let it be said, is not that of tongues, but of a loving heart. How the church needs a baptism of the Spirit's love!

Bickersteth, in his "Bridal of the Lamb" prays:

> Spirit of love,
> Hear me, who humbly supplicate Thine aid;
> That which is gross in me, etherealize
> That which in me is carnal, spiritualize;
> That which is earthly, elevate to heaven;
> The weak enable, and the dark illume,
> Till love, which is of God, abide in me
> And I abide in God, for God is Love.

He is pictured as a jealous Lover.

Jealousy is a part of the divine nature, "I the Lord thy God am a jealous God" (Deut. 5:9). James reminds us that the Holy Spirit indwelling us "yearns jealously" over us (4:5 RSV).

There are, of course, two brands of jealousy:

Divine jealousy. "I am jealous over you with godly jealousy" (2 Cor. 11:2). This is the jealousy of a true lover who will not brook a rival. And the Spirit is a possessive Lover. He wants us all for God and is jealous to maintain His rights.

Devilish jealousy. "Jealousy is the rage of a man" (Prov. 6:34). It is also as "cruel as the grave." Alas, there is too much of this wrong kind of jealousy among Christians! How grievous to the loving Spirit it must be when one believer is so conspicuously jealous of another! True jealousy guards what is its own. *Envy* covets what is not its own.

The divine association

We now approach a strong, irresistible proof of the Spirit's love. What the Father and Son possess, the Spirit likewise shares. Equality characterizes the attributes of the persons forming the Godhead. The whole doctrine of faith is a most fascinating one. At this point we might be permitted to digress and indicate a comforting fact given by a saintly scholar of a past generation.

The three persons in the Trinity are never brought together in the Bible without a result of blessing. We have instances in which each person standing by Himself, is in an aspect of fear. The Father we have seen clothed with the thunders of Sinai; the Son, as "the falling stone that grinds to powder"; and "The sin against the Holy Ghost shall never be forgiven." But there is not an instance upon record in which the three Persons stand together without an intention of grace. And it is a magnificent thought, that the completeness of deity, in all essence and all operation reveals that all three Persons stand together in "love." The third person is "the Spirit of God" and as "God is love" (Matt. 3:16; 1 John 4:8,16), therefore the Spirit is love. He is also called "the Spirit of Christ" and Christ is love (Rom. 8:9; Gal. 2:20). The Spirit, then, shares Christ's nature. In fact, each loved the other. A study in the New Testament reveals a blessed partnership between the Holy Son and the Holy Spirit. Jesus was full of the Spirit, and the Spirit is ever full of Jesus. Jesus sends us to the Spirit, and the Spirit points us to Jesus.

The association bathed in love is of a twofold nature.

The divine benediction

Any passage of the Bible suggesting the Trinity proves that the Holy Spirit is indeed "the sacred Being who is the love knot in the Trinity."

The great benediction of the church universal proves the love of the Trinity. "The grace of the Lord Jesus Christ, and the love of God, and the communion of the Holy Spirit" (2 Cor.

13:14 ASV). *Communion* here can be translated "fellowship," and there cannot be true fellowship unless there are true fellows. Such an association springs from the same love characterizing God, and the grace Christ brought and personified.

The divine sacrifice

Because of His connection with the redemptive work of Calvary, the third person must have a heart of love. "Christ, who through the eternal Spirit offered himself without spot to God" (Heb. 9:14). This great Trinity passage clearly teaches the Spirit's share in the Cross. He enabled Jesus to die and was a witness of His sufferings (Acts 5:32). And now the Spirit is the heavenly Eleazer seeking a bride for the heavenly Isaac. One day He will bring the beautiful Rebekah home and witness the blissful union (Rev. 22:17).

The Spirit's present love-ministry is to lift up Christ, extol His love and sacrifice, quicken the sinner's conscience, lead to Christ, impart faith, and grant the assurance of salvation.

Too often we forget the Holy Spirit's own sacrifice. The sacrifice of the Father and of the Son was indeed great; yet think of the length of the Spirit's sacrifice. Willingly, Jesus tarried in the world with all its corruption for just over thirty-three years. He dwelt among men, untainted as a sunbeam. But the Holy Spirit has been in the world for over nineteen hundred years. What a voluntary sacrifice!

He not only dwells among men but within them. Mary Slessor of Calabar tells of the horror she felt when she was forced to live in the vile atmosphere of a harem. How must the Spirit abiding in our hearts feel, for alas, we are so unlike Him, so disappointing, disobedient, and sinful! Such sacrifice has been fittingly expressed in these words:

> What a tenement He has condescended to enter, and what a glorious work He is pleased to be bearing forward there! He found it dark as night, and foul as the very grave. From a den so filthy, from a cage so full of unclean birds, He might well have turned

away. But the Spirit of grace, He unbarred the gate, and entered in. And what a change He has wrought! Where darkness long brooded, light now shines; where Satan held sway, Jesus now sits enthroned; where enmity long burned, love now glows; where death—the worst of deaths, the death of sin—long prevailed, life now reigns, life with its beauty and the bliss of holiness.

This Holy Spirit will not leave the bosom He enters. Grieved He may be ten thousand times; yet despite unnumbered provocations to depart, He remains—to finish the work He began, till at length He presents us faultless before the throne of God and of the Lamb. Truly, such pursuing love is without compare!

The practical import of this blessed meditation can be found in the apostle's exhortation, "I beseech you . . . by the love of the Spirit" (1 Cor. 1:10 ASV). What an incentive this presents to holy loving and living! If men are to know that we are filled with the Spirit, we must be filled with love (John 13:35). We must reflect His loving nature. As Andrew Murray put it, "Oh, do let us learn the lesson and pray God fervently to teach it to His people, that a church or a Christian professing to have the Holy Spirit must prove it by the exhibition of Christlike love."

But what unlovely traits are ours, and how unlovable we are! Unconquered temper, prevailing selfishness, harsh judgments, unkind words, unlovely ways, impatience all alike proclaim the absence of the Spirit's love. Well might we pray with Horatius Bonar,

> Love of the living God,
>   Of Father and of Son;
> Love of the Holy Ghost
>   Fill Thou each needy one.

Experiencing the Plenitude of the Spirit

By the Spirit's plenitude we imply that fullness and completeness characterizing all His works and ways. Four times

173

over we read of Him as "the seven Spirits of God" (Rev. 1:4; 3:1; 4:5; 5:6), a phrase describing the perfection of the Spirit. There are not seven Spirits, only One, who has a sevenfold manifestation.

The number seven

The Hebrew significance of *seven* suggests "to become satisfied, satiated, or filled." Thus, the primary idea is that of abundance and is descriptive of nature's perfection with its seven-colored light and seven notes of music.

The divine significance of *seven* carries the similar thought of perfection, whether of good or evil. There were seven days of Creation. We are to forgive seventy times seven. There were the seven sayings of the Cross. Seven other spirits speak of the completion of satanic possession. Seven also played a prominent part in Levitical requirements.

Spiritually, *seven* speaks of the plenitude of the Holy Spirit's power and of His diversified activity. As the "seven devils," or "seven other [evil] spirits" (Luke 8:2; 11:26), indicate perfection of evil, so the Spirit, as "the seven Spirits of God," refers to the abundance and the perfection of all that is good. "Seven was the expression of the highest power, the greatest conceivable fullness of force and, therefore, was early pressed into service of religion," and it is thus we come to apply it to the Spirit's ministry. Such a fullness is evident in a fourfold way.

In the Spirit

John in his Revelation applies *seven* to the Spirit thus:

"Seven Spirits of God" (Rev. 1:4; 3:1; 4:5; 5:6). All His fullness and perfection are derived from God.

"Seven lamps of fire burning before the throne" (Rev. 4:5). To the Spirit is granted the perfection of governmental action.

"Seven horns" (Rev. 5:6). As the "horn" is the symbol of power, we here have the Spirit's fullness of power to execute judgment.

"Seven eyes" (Rev. 5:6). As the "eye" is the symbol of understanding, we understand by "seven eyes," perfect vision or intelligence. As eyes, the Spirit penetrates; as lamps, He reveals and exposes; as horns, He destroys and overcomes.

Amid all the Spirit's diversity, however, there is an inescapable unity. Varied though His work was and is, He is yet "one Spirit."

In the Old Testament we have His manifold operation as a physical and material power.

In the Gospels, all His grace and energy were concentrated upon one person, the Lord Jesus Christ. Into Him the Spirit poured His abundance (John 3:34).

In the Acts, we witness the plenitude of His power in the establishment and extension of the church.

In the Epistles, He is brought before us as the source of all spiritual gifts among the members of Christ's body, the church.

In Revelation, the Spirit is seen acting governmentally from heaven on earth.

It will also be noted that in the economy of God, one member of the Godhead is present on the earth at one time. For example, during the Old Testament dispensation, the tabernacle and then the temple localized the presence of God. His "Shekinah Glory" was real to men. The Gospels present us with God tabernacling among men in the person of His Son. There He was not in a cloud but in a man. Now, in this church age, the Spirit tabernacles within saved men and women.

In Christ

Under "Messianic activities" we have already traced the Spirit's abundance in the life and labors of our Lord. He was fully possessed and energized by the blessed Third Person.

Christ was anointed by the sevenfold Spirit in a sevenfold way, namely as:

The Spirit of the Lord
The Spirit of wisdom
The Spirit of understanding
The Spirit of counsel

The Spirit of might
The Spirit of knowledge
The Spirit of the fear of the Lord (Is. 11:2).

As a prism can reflect the seven different colors forming light, so our Lord manifested all the diverse yet unified operating of the Spirit.

Christ received, by the Spirit, His sevenfold name as:

Child
Son
Governor
Wonderful Counsellor
Mighty Lord
Father of Eternity
Prince of Peace (Is. 9:6 ASV).

Christ was energized by the sevenfold Spirit to perform the sevenfold ministry prophesied of old:

To preach good tidings unto the meek
To bind up the brokenhearted
To proclaim liberty to the captive
To open the prison to them that are bound
To proclaim the acceptable year of the Lord
To declare the day of vengeance of our God
To comfort all that mourn (Is. 61:1,2).

Luke mentions only six aspects of Christ's ministry and omits the sixth from the list, "the day of vengeance," synchronizing with "the day of the Lord," a period covering Revelation 4 through 22. This is man's day, and "six" is man's number. But God's Day is coming, and when it is here it will be one of judgment.

In the church

When Paul outlines the gifts of the Spirit (1 Cor. 12:4–11), he proves that in spite of the diversity of His gifts a unity binds them together. He refers, does he not, to "the unity of the Spirit" (Eph. 4:3-6). And seven unities are to be kept, seven strands in the cable of Christian unity.

One body—the true, invisible church, the mystical body of Christ.

One Spirit—the One forming, indwelling, sustaining the body.

One Hope—the completion and translation of the church.

One Lord—the Christ, the head of the body.

One Faith—the full revelation of God in the gospel.

One Baptism—the work of the Spirit, whereby we are incorporated within the body.

One God and Father—the Fountainhead of all supply.

He is Father of all—possession; He is above all—pre-eminence; He is through all—providence, and He is in you all—presence.

In the believer

Seven terms associate the Spirit with the believer. Confusion, bondage, and darkness abound if the differences existing in the Spirit's seven operations are not distinguished. Some of these operations are initial and final; others are initial and continuous.

Initial and final operations

Under this heading we place the baptism, the gift, the sealing, and the earnest of the Spirit. Let us briefly summarize these aspects. For a fuller treatment of all the seven words used to set forth the mission and ministry of the Spirit in relation to the believer, one is referred to W. Graham Scroggie's excellent tract "The Fullness of the Holy Spirit," published by Moody Press. As Scroggie points out, we must not regard the seven words as synonymous, but as flashes from the diamond of truth, indicating some of its many facets.

THE HOLY SPIRIT OF GOD

Baptism with the Spirit

The Bible nowhere speaks of "the baptism of the Holy Spirit." It is always "with," or "in," the Spirit, for He is not the baptizer but the element in which we are immersed. There are seven passages in all mentioning this particular baptism, five pointing to Pentecost and two going back to Pentecost. Originally and fundamentally, therefore, the baptism with the Spirit is that coming of the Spirit whereby the church was instituted, and is equivalent in our experience to regeneration, when we are baptized into or incorporated within the mystic fabric of the church. " [Through] one Spirit we [have been] baptized into one body" (1 Cor. 12:13).

I am aware that *the baptism* and *the filling* are treated as interchangeable terms, but I am persuaded that these two aspects of the Spirit's mission are to be distinguished. We are not urged to be baptized of the Spirit. The Scripture does command us to be filled with the Spirit.

Some teachers, like the late R. A. Torrey, affirm that the Spirit's baptism is a definite experience to be sought by every believer. This renowned scholar taught that the baptism and filling cover the same experience. "One may have the regenerating work of the Holy Ghost and yet not have the baptism with the Holy Spirit." I believe, however, the baptism with the Spirit is the initial work accomplished in the moment of regeneration, and not another blessing to be sought. Whether we speak of the baptism or the filling, doubtless we are all after the same spiritual experience. Yet, surely, it is more God-honoring to seek a biblical blessing, using biblical language.

The gift of the Spirit

Once bestowed, the Spirit, as the gift of the ascended Lord to His believing people, is never withdrawn. Peter makes it clear that this gift is received when one is regenerated. "Repent, and let every one of you be baptized in the name of Jesus Christ for the remission of sins, and you will receive the gift of the Holy Spirit" (Acts 2:38 NKJB–NT).

178

This coming of the Spirit into a life is both initial and final. It is therefore an insult to ask God to give us what He has already bestowed. Of course, the realization of such a gift as the Spirit may be akin to the joy of receiving the gift, but the fact remains that He came as the gift of the Father and of the Son at Pentecost, and that He is the possession and possessor of all believers (Rom. 8:9,15).

The sealing with the Spirit

Under "The Symbols of the Spirit" we have considered the Spirit as the seal. The sealing of the believer with the Spirit of God is another initial and final work, accomplished as the soul accepts Christ as Savior, when he is sealed as God's (2 Tim. 2:19). The possession of, and by, the Spirit indicates that we have been purchased and are now owned by one Purchaser.

Such a seal can never be destroyed nor withdrawn. The Spirit within is the pledge of our full and final redemption. As dirt and rubbish may obscure a signature sealed upon wax, so sin and disobedience in a life can prevent the manifestation of the Spirit's presence and power in and through such a life.

The earnest of the Spirit

The third person of the Trinity is a foretaste of all the Lord has stored up for His own. As Scroggie reminds us, "The grapes brought into the wilderness from Canaan showed the quality of the fruit which the Israelites might enjoy to the full in the land; so the Spirit is the foretaste of heavenly fullness." As the earnest, the Spirit was another initial and final blessing from God (2 Cor. 1:22).

Initial and continuous operations

Because of a deficient understanding of the continuous work of the Spirit, the lives of so many Christians are devoid of fragrance and fruitfulness. Truly, there is One among and in them whom they know not!

What a different testimony many of us would have if only we realized that there are blessings of the Spirit which are the complete and permanent portion of all believers. But there are other operations—progressive and various in their nature, extent, and efficiency—according to individual faith, obedience, and spiritual understanding.

The progressive operations of the Spirit in the very soul vary. Through His continuous inworking the believer is led into fuller knowledge of the truth, into closer fellowship with the Father, and into richer and deeper experiences of the sustaining, satisfying, and sanctifying graces of Christ.

The indwelling of the Spirit

Nothing a believer can do affects this indwelling. The Spirit, once He enters, as Augustine put it, becomes "our perpetual Comforter and our eternal Inhabitant." Weymouth translates John 14:17, "He remains by your side and is in you." Dwelling within (1 Cor. 3:16), He fashions the body of the believer into His temple.

The anointing with the Spirit

Such an anointing, necessary in view of service, is not a blessing, gift, or grace. It is the blessed Spirit Himself in all His fullness, resting upon us. Jesus, as He faced His ministry, received this anointing (Acts 10:38). How tragic it is if we are not equipped and endued for service in the same way. Let us not forget that this anointing must be claimed, not only for special ministry, but for every fresh act of service (Ps. 92:10; 1 John 2:27).

The filling of the Spirit

The apostles, although baptized with the Spirit at Pentecost, were filled again and again. Thus as C. I. Scofield expresses it, "One baptism, many fillings," or infillings. By the baptism, we are put into the divine element. By the filling, the divine element fully possesses us.

Two words are used to describe this aspect of the Spirit's work, and recognition of the distinction between the two will save us from confusion. The words are *filled* and *full*.

Filled with the Spirit. Here the verb suggests an intermittent experience—an aspect of the Spirit's ministry commensurate with need, *e.g.*, Bezaleel, Mary, the apostles.

Full of the Spirit. Here the adjective implies a normal, habitual experience. Christ, Stephen, and Barnabas are spoken of as being "full of the Spirit."

We are commanded to be "filled with the Spirit" (Eph. 5:18). At least two thoughts emerge as we think of the study of this express command. First, it is a definite act, for the present tense is used. At this moment, one must humbly yield to the Spirit, allowing Him to rise as the well and permeate the life. Second, it is a continuous attitude. Crisis leads to process; act becomes an attitude.

Fellowship in the Suffering of the Spirit

Having proved the personality and deity of the Spirit, it is clearly evident that He is capable of being wrongfully treated. Because of who and what He is, any kind of sin committed against Him is grievous and condemnatory. The dignity of a person aggravates any crime perpetrated against him. Insulting a prince brings more punishment than the mistreatment of a nameless pauper.

Equality among the persons of the Godhead means that there is equality of suffering. What One feels, the Others feel. Let us, therefore, classify the various sufferings personally endured by the Spirit. They can be self-imposed, caused by sinners, caused by sinners and saints, and caused by saints.

Sufferings self-imposed

Like the Savior, the Spirit also had sufferings self-imposed. Groanings are His (Rom. 8:26). He also is "touched with the feelings of our infirmities." As the eternal Spirit, He suffered in Christ's sufferings (Heb. 9:14). Have you ever thought of it like this? Jesus lived on earth for just over thirty-three years, but while He endured so much anguish, particularly during the last three years of His life, His sufferings ended with His resurrection and ascension. The Holy Spirit came to earth, as the gift of heaven, on the day of Pentecost over nineteen hundred years ago and has been enduring all kinds of insults since then. Willingly, He remains among men, and from the multitudes, in succeeding generations since His advent, has suffered much at the hands of both saints and sinners.

Sufferings caused by sinners

As this is "the dispensation of the Spirit of grace," and He is definitely related to all who are out of Christ, at least three aspects of unworthy treatment are meted out to the Spirit by such sinners. For example—

He is blasphemed. "The blasphemy against the [Holy] Spirit" (Matt. 12:31 ASV). This declaration of the Master proves the great importance of the Spirit's ministry in this age of grace. The Holy Spirit is God's ultimatum, His last witness to men. Therefore if they treat Him as they treated the Savior, then their doom is sealed. This "blasphemy" has become known as "the unpardonable sin" and consists of the willful, conscious, final rejection of the Spirit's revelation of Christ.

He is spurned. The Holy Spirit says, "Today, if you will hear His voice [Spirit's voice—Rev. 2:7], harden not your hearts" (Heb. 3:7 ASV). As the direct agent between the Savior and sinners, it is His work to convince and convict the lost of their need (John 16:8). But there are multitudes who are continually convicted of their sinful condition, but who constantly say "no!" to the Spirit. He warns that refusal follows refusal, links are added to the chain, binding the soul forever.

He is insulted. "Hath done despite unto the Spirit of grace" (Heb. 10:29). The New American Standard Bible translates this verse: ". . . has insulted the Spirit of grace." The word *despite* actually means "to shamefully treat." It was thus that Simon Magus treated the Spirit (Acts 8:20).

Any sinner insults the Spirit when he refuses to obey His voice. When as He says "Today," to reply, "No, not today, there is plenty of time," is to despise His entreaty.

Further, as the Spirit testifies to the deity of Christ and the necessity of the Cross, to deny these fundamental truths is to insult the Spirit.

Sufferings caused by sinners and saints

Certain passages having to do with the Spirit are capable of a double application, and some are here set forth.

He can be angered. "They disobeyed and made angry the Spirit of God" (cf. Ps. 78:40). The Spirit's sudden descent upon Saul roused his anger and action. "The Spirit of God came upon Saul . . . and his anger was kindled greatly" (1 Sam. 11:6). The Jews made angry the Holy Spirit (Is. 63:10). It is indeed terrible to have the Spirit as an enemy.

Thus, there is "the wrath of the Spirit," as well as "the wrath of the Lamb." Divine anger, however, is different from human anger. Divine anger, speaking of wounded heart, cries out for atonement; human anger, expressive of wounded pride, cries out for revenge.

The sinners of Noah's day were guilty of arousing the wrath of the Spirit, so that he ceased to strive with them (Gen. 6:3). Saints, although redeemed, can rebel (Is. 63:10). When the Spirit reveals unexpected ugliness within, the proud heart acts in a way displeasing to the Spirit.

He can be resisted. Stephen condemns the nation, of which he formed a part, for resisting the Holy Spirit. "Ye do always resist the Holy Spirit: as your fathers did" (Acts 7:51 ASV).

Sinners resist Him when they fail to respond to His promptings. His pleading voice is heard but the heart is kept fast closed. Walls of excuses are built and bulwarks of indifference are thrown up, resulting in active resistance to His gentle persuasion.

Saints resist the Spirit when they doubt the Word and power of God. Prejudice, the result of sectarianism, sometimes leads one to resist the Spirit as He prompts us to obey specific commands.

He can be lied against. In the tragedy overtaking Ananias and Sapphira, Peter ascribes deity to the Holy Spirit. "Lie to the Holy Spirit . . . Lied unto . . . God" (Acts 5:3,4 ASV). The implication here is that the Spirit is God. This tragic pair were guilty of acting a lie. They represented themselves to be what they were not. How we have to guard ourselves against secret falsehoods of the heart and deceptive appearances!

Sinners lie against the Spirit when they pretend to be converted, or when they make a superficial profession for some ulterior motive.

Saints lie against the Spirit when they profess to have all on the altar but keep back part of the price. What wholesale death there would be in our churches today if the Spirit dealt with us as He did with Ananias and Sapphira! God save us from pretending to be wholly devoted to Him, while guilty of indulgence in things He hates.

He can be tempted. Peter refers to Ananias and Sapphira as agreeing "to tempt the Spirit of the Lord" (Acts 5:9). Dean Alford's comment on this passage is, "To test the omniscience of the Spirit, then visibly dwelling in the apostles and the church, which was in the highest sense to tempt the Spirit of God." Weymouth has it, "How was it . . . that you two agreed to try and experiment upon the Spirit of the Lord?"

We speak of "tempting Providence," and this is what these two disciples were guilty of doing. They thought the Spirit was either ignorant of their deed or that He would wink at their duplicity. They forgot that He is full of eyes.

Have you never read of arrogant sinners who, denying the reality of God, have blatantly said, "If there is a God, let Him strike me dead"? Mercifully, He does not manifest His power toward those who try to deny His existence. Asking for signs is a form of tempting God.

Sufferings caused by saints

One way by which we can discover the treatment saints give to the Spirit is to patiently study what the Bible says of the Spirit. It is more profitable to read what the Scriptures say about His activities than a multitude of good books on the subject. Satan knows only too well, that, so long as truth

184

regarding treatment of the Spirit is forgotten or neglected, saints make slow progress in spiritual matters.

He is ignored. "Did you receive the Holy Spirit when you believed?" (Acts 19:2 NKJB–NT). Rebuked by Paul for the lack of spiritual power in their lives, the Ephesian disciples confessed, "We have not so much as heard whether there be any Holy Ghost." A great many are still ignorant of His personality! "There standeth one among you, whom ye know not" (John 1:26). Ignorance of His person and presence contributes to spiritual barrenness.

The New Testament ideal for the Christian life is the constant recognition of the Spirit's reality and His daily enthronement over every part of the life.

Ignorance, then, is the sin of the saved. It affects the progress of spiritual experience and proves a lack of knowledge.

He is grieved. "Grieve not the Holy Spirit" (Eph. 4:30). *Grieve* is a Gethsemane word. It means "to afflict with sorrow." Of Jesus we read that, "He began to be sorrowful" (Matt. 26:37). The implication is that we can give the Spirit His Gethsemane.

This grieving is the sin of sealed ones, but can never affect the sealing which is "unto the day of redemption," that is, the day of the redemption of the body.

Things pleasing or painful to the Spirit are outlined in the narrative. Grieving the Spirit is the sin of the saved as saints, and is related to holiness of life—inward, outward, upward. The reader is referred to a fuller treatment of this aspect under "The Grief of the Spirit."

He is quenched. "Quench not the Spirit" (1 Thess. 5:19). The word "quench" means to "put out the fire" and carries a double significance. We can quench the fire in other hearts. By criticism, jealousy, unkindness, lack of understanding, or prejudice against a message of the truth, we can dampen the faith of those we thus treat.

We can quench the fire in our own heart. By sin, disobedience or worldly desires we extinguish His flame. Quenching is the sin of the saved as servants and is connected with service, either personal or general. See fuller treatment under "Quenching the Spirit."

Praying in the Spirit

I fear that the majority of Christians fail to realize how dependent they are upon the varied ministry of God's Spirit. The Scriptures, for example, teach that He is the Spirit of supplications (Zech. 12:10) and, therefore, the one who becomes at once the sphere and atmosphere of all true prayer.

When the Spirit takes possession of a soul, He becomes essentially the Spirit of intercession. Yearning for heart-communion with God, yet unable to express ourselves aright, we have the Spirit at hand to help us in such an infirmity. He is our aid in prayers and inspires every outgoing of the mind toward God whether in the nature of supplication, confession, thanksgiving, or intercession.

Without the Holy Spirit our prayers are as lifeless as a body without a soul, as ineffective as an arrow without a bow. In his most illuminating and helpful book, *His in a Life of Prayer,* Norman B. Harrison writes, "As the telephone is dead and impotent without the electric current, so is prayer apart from the Spirit. He supplies the sending power; He secures the access; He forms the contact; He molds the pray-er into the mind and will of God. The Spirit is at once the Guide of prayer and the Guarantor of its success."

Martin Luther once confessed, "If I fail to spend two hours in prayer each morning the devil gets victory through the day." Luther's motto was "He that has prayed well, has studied well." From which we learn it is only by the Spirit that we can pray and live effectually.

As we approach the outstanding features of the mystic truth of prayer in the Spirit, it may be found helpful to group together the different passages associated with such a theme.

"Likewise the Spirit also helpeth our infirmities: for we know not what we should pray for as we ought: but the Spirit itself maketh intercession for us with groanings which cannot be uttered. And he that searcheth the hearts knoweth what is the mind of the Spirit, because he maketh intercession for the saints according to the will of God" (Rom. 8:26,27).

"And because ye are sons, God hath sent forth the Spirit of His Son into your hearts, crying, Abba, Father" (Gal. 4:6).

"For through him we both have access by one Spirit unto the Father" (Eph. 2:18).

"Praying always with all prayer and supplication in the Spirit, and watching thereunto with all perseverance and supplication for all saints" (Eph. 6:18).

"For we are the circumcision, which worship God in the spirit . . . and have no confidence in the flesh" (Phil. 3:3).

"But ye, beloved, building up yourselves on your most holy faith, praying in the Holy Ghost" (Jude 20).

The Spirit is the Inspirer of all true prayer.

Responsive prayer is impossible except as we are enabled to pray, and this ability is conferred upon us by the divine Spirit. First of all, He brings the soul into right relationship with God. Being born of God, we have the privilege of sons and as sons we can pray (Gal. 4:6). Spiritual sonship, then, is the true starting point of all access to God. Fear, with its enslaving influence, is driven out and spiritual adoption takes its place. Contact with God rests upon the basis of regeneration. Prayers are not accepted and are not acceptable unless the praying one is truly saved. The Holy Spirit is not able to pray in and through a life He does not possess, and which has not been adopted into the family of God. It is the Holy Spirit who becomes the filial Spirit, whereby we cry, "Abba, Father."

Three elements are associated with all mighty praying.

Prayer is impossible without an act of memory. There must be the recall of all we desire to present to God. Whether it be God's mercies, our sins or needs, or the needs of others, the Spirit must bring to our remembrance all we desire to pray about.

Prayer is impossible without an act of mind. As the Spirit of wisdom, He can cause us to use the acceptable words as we express our adoration, supplication, and petitions. Only by His power can we be delivered from distractions and develop that necessary concentration prayer demands.

Prayer is impossible without an act of love. As the Spirit of love, shedding abroad in our hearts the love of God, He is able to lead us to present sympathetically the needs of others. Intercession, whether divine or human, rises on the wings of love.

It is the Spirit, then, who quickens the mind and the emotions and imparts the ability to continue in prayer. This mighty, heavenly intercessor prepares and possesses and prompts our minds. We easily tire, for true prayer is exacting. We ought always to pray and not to faint. However, we are better at the fainting than the praying. To pray without ceasing comes hard to the flesh (Luke 18:1; 1 Thess. 5:17). But the Spirit helps such an infirmity. We can only pray always with all prayer and supplications *in the Spirit* (Eph. 6:18). To quote Norman Harrison again:

> Were we left to ourselves and our own effort in prayer, we could not be heard. We would be as impotent as a radio set or a telephone without electric current. As electricity gives carrying power to the human voice, projecting it for thousands of miles, so the Holy Spirit performs a like service in winging our worship, petitions and aspirations "unto the Father." We may be well assured that, "praying . . . in the Spirit," they do not fall short of His throne of heavenly Grace . . . That which enables us to "reach" the Father, giving us "access" to Him, is the Spirit-quality.

The Spirit arouses within the soul a sense of need.

Prayer can never attain true perfection unless it is transacted "in the Spirit." Only through His illuminating grace and personal promptings can we come to know the hidden consciousness of our own needs.

The Holy Spirit opens to our spiritual vision a new world of purity and power by revealing the contrast between the old world of the natural life and the glorious world of victory and spirituality. Until we are right with Him on the matter of personal and practical sanctification, we cannot expect His help in prayer. Allowing the Spirit to awaken desires to which we have been strangers and then adjust us to those spiritual desires, we fit ourselves to pray with all prayer and supplication in the Spirit.

Further, the Spirit knows what we do not know, and thus works in the heart of the believer, begetting earnest longings and groanings after those things He knows to be good and according to the will of God for us. As A. R. Fausset expresses it, "God as the Searcher of hearts watches the surging emotions of them in prayer and knows perfectly what the Spirit means by the groanings which He draws forth within us, because that blessed Intercessor pleads by them only for what God Himself designs to bestow."

But Paul's thought of the Spirit's intercessory ministry goes down to the depths, and includes more than those ordinary and coherent expressions before God. Within man there is an unfathomed depth in which there are feelings so vast and mysterious, that the human mind cannot give definite form to nor articulate in fitting words.

Deep down within human personality, from which our yearnings come, the Spirit moves with perfect familiarity. Sympathizing with these mysterious longings for which we have no language but a sigh and a cry, He lays hold of the inarticulate groanings and gives them fitting and definite meaning before God. "He that searcheth the hearts knoweth what is the mind of the Spirit." As we are constantly beset with imperfection, weakness and ignorance, this peculiar office of the Spirit will be necessary and complimentary until we need to pray no more. It would seem as if the depth and ripeness of our spiritual experience produce a deeper sense of our requirements of the Spirit's aid as Interpreter and Intercessor.

The Spirit intercedes for us.

As God's free Spirit, he mingles with our spirit and makes our prayers His own, or rather creates the prayers we should pray. As the Spirit of intercession, He exercises His function within us even as Christ exercises His intercessory work in heaven for us. "Who is he that condemneth? It is Christ that died, yea rather, that is risen again, who is even at the right hand of God, who also maketh intercession for us" (Rom. 8:34). "But this man, because He continueth ever, hath an unchangeable priesthood" (Heb. 7:24). The Holy Spirit prays in, as well as with and for us. He is our Paraclete on earth as Christ is in heaven.

The object of the Spirit's petitions is the laying bare before God all the deep and hidden needs of saints. The glorified Christ intercedes in heaven for us, obtaining the full fruits of His sacrifice for all the needs revealed and voiced by the Spirit.

Two features of this unheard and mysterious groaning can be observed. Such unutterable groanings are known and understood by the Father. And they are also presented in accordance with the will of God. Human needs and divine requirements are thus harmoniously blended.

Another thought emerging from a full realization of our need of dependence upon the Spirit's ministry in prayer is deliverance from all bondage in praying. Instead of saying prayers, we *pray*. We follow inward guidance and promptings rather than outward, mechanical forms. And with such a mighty Intercessor there is no reason for prayerlessness.

Pray, always pray, the Holy Spirit pleads;
Within thee all thy daily, hourly needs.

The Spirit bestows full assurance of faith.

Because we are exhorted to draw near to God with a true heart and full assurance of faith (Heb. 10:22), it is necessary to have such an atmosphere created for us. The Spirit alone enables us to pray believingly. He creates faith in the promises

190

and ability of God, thus making our prayers, prayers of faith.

This Spirit-begotten assurance produces a clear recognition of God as the divine Source of all supply (James 1:17). It also unfolds to faith His power and willingness to bestow all that is necessary through Jesus Christ (Eph. 2:18). Whether it be within the realm of nature or of grace, He is able to answer all true spiritual prayer prompted by the Spirit.

> There is an eye that never sleeps
>   Beneath the wing of night;
> There is an ear that never shuts
>   When sink the beams of light.
>
> There is an arm that never tires
>   When human strength gives way;
> There is a love that never fails
>   When earthly loves decay.
>
> That eye is fixed on seraph throngs;
>   That arm upholds the sky;
> That ear is filled with angel songs,
>   That love is throned on high.
>
> But thee's a power man can wield,
>   When mortal aid is vain;
> That eye, that arm, that love to reach,
>   That listening ear to gain.
>
> That power is prayer, which soars on high,
>   Through Jesus, to the throne;
> And moves the hand which moves the world,
>   To bring salvation down.

CHAPTER NINE

The Anointing of the Spirit

The apostle John reminds us that "as [Christ] is, so are we in this world" (1 John 4:17). To the patient student of the New Testament it is evident that our Lord is our example in all things, especially in His relationship with the Holy Spirit.

Possibly, it has been noted that there are three general passages describing Christ's anointing, just as there are three other verses taken up with the anointing of the believer.

The anointed Savior

"The Spirit of the Lord is upon me, because he anointed me to preach good tidings" (Luke 4:18 ASV).

"Thy holy Servant Jesus, whom thou didst anoint" (Acts 4:27 ASV).

"God anointed Him with the Holy Spirit" (Acts 10:38 ASV).

The anointed saint

"Now He that stablisheth us with you in Christ, and anointed us, is God" (2 Cor. 1:21 ASV).

"Ye have an anointing from the Holy One, and ye know all things" (1 John 2:20 ASV).

"The anointing which ye received of Him abideth in you" (1 John 2:27 ASV).

The Occasion of the Anointing

Seeing we live in days of unscriptural teaching regarding the exact ministry of the Spirit, in and through the life of the believer, it is imperative for us to understand the plain teaching of Scripture. Some views commonly held are:

Received at regeneration

Some teachers affirm that the anointing of the Spirit is equivalent to His indwelling, and that such an aspect of His work synchronizes with His regenerating power in the hour of one's acceptance of Christ as Savior.

Certainly the tenses employed confirm the thought of "a completed act of anointing"—"hath" (2 Cor. 1:21), "ye have" (1 John 2:20,27). Combining the passages dealing with our anointing we have four immediate results of this work of the Spirit.

The baptism with the Spirit places the believer in Christ; we are thereby "established" in Him (cf. 1 Cor. 12:13; Gal. 3:27).

With the impartation of the Spirit, God anoints us.

God, through the Spirit, has sealed us, the Spirit Himself being the seal (Eph. 4:30).

The Spirit is given as an "earnest." Since an earnest is a part of the purchase money or property given in advance as security for the remainder, the Spirit is seen to be the earnest of the whole heavenly inheritance which belongs to every believer through infinite grace (2 Cor. 5:5; Eph. 1:14; 1 Pet. 1:4).

The tragedy, however, is the fact that many of us are so powerless, although we have received this initial anointing. "Weak, though anointed" (2 Sam. 3:39).

Received at fuller surrender

Others hold that the Spirit's anointing is an experience distinct from His incoming at regeneration. They say that as our Lord possessed the Holy Spirit from His birth, but a special unction became His at the age of thirty at Jordan, so the child of God requires a specific anointing of the Spirit before he can witness in power and fruitfulness.

For our part we prefer to combine both of the above views. Namely, there is a once-and-for-all incoming or anointing of the Spirit, and there is also an infilling or anointing of the Spirit, conditional upon the adjustment and resulting in spiritual blessing all around.

With the psalmist we have every right to pray, after wrong

things have been righted, "I shall be anointed with fresh oil" (Ps. 92:10). And then have the assurance that our head has been anointed with oil (23:5; Eccl. 9:8).

Even Hopkins, one of the first theologians of the English Keswick Movement, expressed it thus:

> The holy oil has been poured upon the head of our mystical Aaron, and by virtue of our union and fellowship with Him we are under the same divine anointing. But only those who are walking in fellowship with Christ know what this means as a continuous blessing. For we must observe, the words do not put before us one complete act, something experienced on some one occasion, or at a particular time in the past, but rather the words point to that which is a present and continuous privilege. It is not "ye were anointed," but "ye have an anointing" (ASV). The question to settle then ere we proceed further is this—"Have we received, or are we receiving our share of this anointing? Is ours a claimed, or unclaimed share?"

Might it not be better to say that the act must become an attitude—the crisis has developed into a process? There is the initial anointing constituting a crisis, but there is also the continuous anointing for service.

The Subjects and Objects of Anointing

Under the old law, the ceremony of anointing was related to all the important offices and ministries of those called of Jehovah.

Persons were anointed.

Five classes of persons are specified as being anointed with oil. It is most profitable to study the significance of their setting apart in this way, and also the spiritual applications of such.

The prophet

Special prophets, like Elisha, were anointed not only as one

194

claimed wholly for God, but as one set apart to be the oracle of God to the people. Such an anointing was the outward, visible sign of the impartation to the prophets of those gifts and graces qualifying them to function as ministers of the Lord, and as the teachers, guides, and intercessors of the people (1 Kin. 19:16). It was thus that Christ, as the prophet, received His Spirit-anointing (Is. 61:1; Luke 4:18).

The priest

Priests were anointed in order to be sanctified, or set apart, for divine service. No priest would attempt to touch the holy things of the sanctuary without having been sprinkled with holy anointing oil. God was so jealous of the sanctity of those who had been anointed for service that the penalty of failing to wash their hands and feet as they drew near to minister unto the Lord was death (Ex. 30:19–21). It was presumption to attempt priestly work without priestly preparation. Would that as priests unto God we could ever remember this!

As Aaron and his sons typify Christ and His own in their anointing, we have the counterpart of their setting apart in the Spirit's relationship both in the life of our Lord and also in our life and labors (Ex. 40:15; Lev. 8:12; Acts 1:8; Heb. 9:14).

The king

"Arise, anoint him . . . Then Samuel . . . anointed him" (1 Sam. 16:12,13). Israel's kings were anointed with oil as God's representatives. Saul, for example, was anointed by Samuel to rule and lead the people on God's behalf. And, as with earthly kings, so with "the King Eternal" of whom it is said, "God, hath anointed thee" (Ps. 45:7).

The guest

The anointing of a guest, as he entered the home of a friend, was the signal of honor as well as a means of refreshment (Ps. 23:5). It was thus that Mary signally honored her Lord. "Anointing a person was a mark of respect to a guest so common," says Fausset, "that to omit it implied defective

hospitality" (cf. Luke 7:46; John 11:2; 12:3). The original of
Psalm 23:5 reads, "Thou hast made me fat," or "unctous."

The sick

In some unexplained way, healing was imparted to the sick
and diseased by means of anointing oil. Doubtless, the oil in
question carried healing properties (Lev. 14:14–17; Mark 6:13;
Luke 10:34; James 5:14). The dead were also anointed (Mark
14:8).

As born-again ones, anointed with the Holy Spirit, heaven's
most precious anointing oil, who are we but:
Prophets, sent forth into the world to preach the gospel with
power (Acts 1:8).
Priests, to offer up spiritual sacrifices and to minister unto
God in holy things (Rom. 8:26; 12:1).
Kings, empowered to reign in life.
Guests, living in God's house, feeding at God's table upon
God's bounty.
Sick ones, healed of the plague of sin and kept healed
through the constant anointing.

Things were anointed.

As with persons, so with things; contact with the anointing
oil sanctified them (Ex. 40:9–15; Lev. 8:10). And the Spirit
sanctifies both the believer and his associations (Rom. 15:16; 1
Cor. 6:11; 2 Thess. 2:13; 1 Pet. 1:2). Every tabernacle article
had to be set apart for God, suggesting the complete dedication
of all that we are and have (Rom. 12:1,2).

We herewith enumerate the sanctuary possessions anointed
in this way:

The tabernacle (Ex. 40:9)

The anointing of this holy structure as a whole is typical of
Christ's complete dedication as He tabernacled among men.
This truth is also applicable to the child of God, who is likened
to a tabernacle or temple. We are comprised of the outer court

of the body, the holy place of the soul, and the holy of holies of the Spirit (1 Cor. 6:19,20).

The ark of testimony (Ex. 40:3)

This beautiful chest, with its mixture of wood and gold, is typical of the combination of deity and humanity found in Christ—a combination the Holy Spirit made possible within the womb of Mary. The body of the God-man can be represented by the wood, speaking of His peerless humanity, and then overlaid with gold, symbolic of His glorious deity. Through the constant anointing with the Spirit, our Lord's two natures were kept harmoniously blended, as His miracles clearly prove.

The table (Ex. 40:4)

This part of the tabernacle furniture, along with its bread, prefigured fellowship between God and man through Christ, who, as the Bread, is the satisfying food for both God and man. Such fellowship, typified by the anointed table, can only be maintained through the constant infilling of the Spirit. He it is who presents Christ to our hungry souls as the only Source of sustenance and satisfaction.

The lampstand (Ex. 40:4)

Within the tabernacle there were so many "figures of the True." The lampstand is one of the most conspicuous figures, seeing it speaks of Him who came as the light of the world. The testimony He bore was made possible by the power of the Spirit of truth.

Oil for the lamps is specified (Ex. 25:6) and contains an application for our hearts as those within whom the Spirit dwells. It has been suggested that the Spirit is the oil; the wick, the believer as the channel; the light, the outshining of Christ. The wick must rest in the oil, so the believer must walk in Christ (Gal. 5:16). The wick must be free from obstruction, so the believer must not resist the Spirit (1 Thess. 5:19). The wick must be snuffed, so the believer must be cleansed by the confession of sin (1 John 1:9).

The incense altar (Ex. 40:5)

This particular, precious altar speaks of the excellence of Christ as our great high priest as He exercises His intercessory ministry at the right hand of God. As the Holy Spirit is the great interceding force, He ever seeks to empower us to pray, even as did our Lord while in the flesh (Rom. 8:26; Eph. 6:18; Jude 20; Heb. 5:7; 7:25).

The burnt-offering altar (Ex. 40:6)

Upon this altar, found at the entrance of the outer court, were laid the various, commanded offerings, all of which are wonderfully typical of our blessed Lord.

In the burnt offering, we see Jesus wholly devoted to His Father.

In the meal offering, we have Him in the purity of His nature.

In the peace offering, He is the medium of restored and continuous fellowship with God.

In the sin offering, Christ endures the wrath of God for us.

In the trespass offering, He is presented as the releaser from sin's guilt and government.

In the drink offering, Jesus is represented in the joy of His heart as He followed God.

As our all-sufficient sacrifice, He offered Himself without spot to God through the Spirit's energies (Heb. 9:14).

The laver (Ex. 40:7)

This anointed article symbolizes the Word of God in its cleansing power. But both Christ and the Scriptures are called "the Word of God" (John 1:1; Heb. 4:12; Rev. 19:13). Both the living Word and the written Word are powerful means of cleansing, as the Spirit brings us under their sway.

The Oil of the Anointing

Great care had to be exercised in the compounding of the holy anointing oil. Nothing was left to human invention. All Moses had to do was simply carry out the distinct and specific instructions given him by God (Ex. 30:22–28).

Four specified spices in certain proportions were mingled with a particular oil in the composition of the anointing oil (Ex. 30:22–36). These four sweet spices represent the four peculiar virtues found in Christ as indicated by Paul (1 Cor. 1:30). In turn, these four spices are taken by the Spirit and made over to the believer.

Along with minute instructions regarding the manufacture of the oil were also given three rigid prohibitions regarding its sacred use (Ex. 30:30–33).

It must not touch flesh.

"Upon man's flesh shall it not be poured." Our flesh, because of the Fall and also the practice of sin, has become the seat and source of evil and can never, therefore, be used of God. In the believer, the old nature is to be reckoned as dead through the death of Christ.

When the natural man is exalted and the necessity of the Spirit's regenerating work rejected, then it could be said that his flesh is anointed—anointed only by man's pride. How guilty man is of yielding to the voice of carnal, natural reason, rejecting altogether the illumination of the Spirit! And how guilty believers are of trying to accomplish God's work in the strength of human energy! But God cannot sanction that which is fleshly or carnal, even in His own. No activity or zeal, without the Spirit's anointing, can ever accomplish God's purpose.

It must not touch the stranger.

"Whosoever putteth any of it upon a stranger, shall even be cut off. . . ." To Israel a stranger was one outside the pale of Israel's blessings and privileges. The Gentiles were treated as strangers (Eph. 2:12). Typically, the stranger is the unsaved person, who is indeed a stranger to God and to grace. Upon such the blood must first be placed, meaning, of course, that the reception of the crucified Savior precedes the gracious work of the Spirit in and through the life.

Within the church, too many strangers are anointed. Persons find their way into the service and ministry of the church who have never experienced the Spirit's regenerating work. They labor *for* the faith but are not *in* the faith (2 Cor. 13:5). Outside the family of God and the household of faith, they are as much strangers as the most irreligious.

It must not be imitated.

"Neither shall ye make any other like it." May God enable us to pause and ponder over this prohibition! Any artificial imitation of the Spirit's ministration is disastrous.

God abhors substitutes and imitations. He cannot accept anything but the manifestation of life in Christ, a manifestation produced wholly by the Spirit and impossible of imitation by man (Phil. 1:21).

Acting in the energy of the flesh or seeking to serve God apart from a regenerated heart means the absence of spiritual power. Because this is so, man is tempted to produce effects or work up a semblance of power.

False spirituality can show itself in the matter of guidance as well. Is there not a danger, even among Christians, of assuming to be Spirit-guided when all the time we are indulging our own self-will or self-deceit? Our safety lies only in abiding in Christ, in humble dependence upon Him. Nestling close to Him, ever conscious of our proneness to go astray, restfully confident that He can keep us from falling, is the only way by which we can manifest the anointing that is of God.

The spiritual application, then, of the holy anointing oil is not far to seek. It supplies us with a fitting type of the Third Person, even the Spirit who is declared to be the oil. He it is who comes upon us as the anointing oil. And such an anointing is not a blessing or a gift, such as grace, peace, or power. It is a person, the indwelling of a person with all His influence, even the Spirit Himself. He is not the agent in imparting the New Testament anointing, but is Himself the anointing.

As the Spirit is the anointing, so the risen, ascended Lord is the anointer. He who was anointed with the Holy Spirit anoints the believer. Asks a writer, "What is the source of this anointing?" It is "from the Holy One" (1 John 2:20; Acts 2:27; 3:14; Mark 1:24; Luke 4:34). The Lord Jesus is the "Righteous One" (cf. 1 John 2:1,2) and He is the "Holy One." Our first need has reference to our guilt and sin; thus our first view of Christ is as the "Righteous One." We have not been called, however, to a life of perpetual falling, so we have the anointing of the Holy One as well as the atonement of the Righteous One. How often we take the one and neglect the other!

The Outcome of the Anointing

Elder Cumming tells us that "whatever else this anointing, this 'Chrism' of the Holy Spirit, is and does, here are five things attributed to it:

"It is abiding.

"It makes us independent of the teaching of man.

"It teaches us of 'all things.'

"It is absolutely true.

"Even according as it teacheth us so is our abiding in Christ."

Among the chief benefits received as the result of the anointing with the Spirit, mention can be made of the most conspicuous.

Identification

Greek words for *anoint* are *chrisa* and *chrisma* from which *Christos* or *Christ* come. Thus, *Christ* means "the anointed One." And the honorable name *Christian* signifies an anointed one belonging to Christ, the anointed. The first direct outcome of the anointing at its initial impartation then is the placing of the believing sinner in the same position as Christ. His distinctive name in the Old Testament is "the Messiah," that is, "the anointed One," a name used not only of our Lord, but also to designate others chosen of God. It is applied to Samuel (1 Sam. 2:10), Saul (1 Sam. 24:6), saints (Ps. 105:15), and Zedekiah (Lam. 4:20).

In the New Testament, our Lord's corresponding title is "Christ" implying the same as "Messiah." The Hebrew *Messiah* is the Greek for *Christ*. It is, therefore, remarkable that when Paul and John desire to set forth the position and privileges of the saint they both use the same word for Christians and for Christ. We are also "the anointed ones" of God. "You have an anointing" (NJKB–NT), the same as the Lord had. And we bear it in our name, as He did. He was called *Christ,* and we are *Christians*, the anointed ones of the anointed One—Messiahs of the new dispensation! Christs of God!

Bearing His name we must likewise bear His character (2 Tim. 2:19). A man brought into the presence of Alexander the Great and charged with an offense was asked his name. "Alexander," replied the man. "Well, either change your name or your character," said the unconquered sovereign as he dismissed the offender.

Protection

What a great portion of Holy Scripture is Psalm 105! Listen to these words as they depict the impregnable position of those upon whom the holy anointing oil rests: "When they went from one nation to another, from one kingdom to another people; He suffered no man to do them wrong: yea, He reproved kings for their sakes; saying, Touch not mine anointed, and do my prophets no harm" (vv. 13–15).

The psalmist's many allusions to the "anointed" proves the divine protection afforded them. And the certainty of such a protection is a source of comfort in the hour of trial. David himself had a great dread, before he was fully recognized as God's anointed king, that he might harm Saul, whom he constantly spoke of as "the Lord's anointed" (1 Sam. 24:6).

Surely, there is no truth more plain than this: God makes it

His business to defend those He sets apart for Himself. "Who is he that will harm you, if ye be followers of that which is good?" (1 Pet. 3:13; Ex. 14:19,20). During the Wembley Exhibition many years ago, a section displayed pearls and gems of rare value. An ingenious electrical system protected these priceless treasures so that anyone seeking to snatch them would be rendered powerless in the attempt. One day a clever jewel thief tried to steal the treasures, but found himself almost electrocuted, and speedily caught.

God's anointed ones are His "jewels" and of these He says, "He that toucheth you toucheth the apple of [Mine] eye" (Zech. 2:8). He knows how to preserve His own, so that no weapon formed against us can prosper. And the holy anointing oil is God's electricity preserving His jewels.

> Enemies may seek to injure:
>   Satan all his arts employ:
> God will turn what seems to harm me,
>   Into everlasting joy.

Separation

We have already observed that everyone and everything anointed with the anointing oil was given up to the Lord and belonged only to Him. Oil was the last operation in the Levitical code, completing consecration or separation unto God. Is it not so with we believers? Receiving the Holy Spirit at regeneration, we allow Him to appropriate continuously the regenerated life in order that our entire domain of spirit, soul, and body may be wholly dedicated unto God.

The possession of the Spirit commits the believer irrevocably to separation from sin. "What is holiness," asks A. J. Gordon, "but an emanation of the Spirit of holiness who dwells within us?" The great office of the Spirit in the present economy is to communicate Christ to His church which is His body. And what is so truly essential of Christ as holiness? "In him is no sin. Whosoever abideth in him sinneth not . . ." (1 John 3:5, 6; 5:18). The body can only be sinless by uninterrupted communion with the Head: the Head will not maintain communion with the body except it be holy.

Our sad confession is that communion is so often interrupted; hence our lack of entire separation unto the Lord. Would that we would submit to a complete anointing, resulting in a complete separation from all known sin, and a more complete separation unto the Lord who died for us, and by His redemptive work owns every part of us!

Illumination

John uses two phrases in connection with the anointing: "Ye know all things" and "His anointing teacheth you concerning all things" (1 John 2:20,27 ASV). What is this, but spiritual illumination?

By illumination we mean spiritual insight into divine things, even into the "all things," by which we understand all that it is essential to know as given in Scripture. In his comment on Acts 2, A. T. Pierson observes,

> This chapter contains the first great exhibition and illustration of the power of the Holy Spirit. It is, specifically, power in connection with witnessing. We fall into loose ways of using Scripture terms. "Unction," or "anointing" seems to be used quite uniformly by the apostle John in the sense of spiritual knowledge, insight, or the power of spiritual discernment. . . . There are three grand departments of Christian experience—salvation, sanctification, service; and unction as Pentecostal power appears to be specially connected with the last of the three, giving spiritual discernment of truth, and so, also, effectiveness in the utterance of the truth.

Two characteristic features of the divine illumination reach us because of the bestowal of the Spirit.

It is perfect.

This aspect is indicated by the words "you know all things." The anointing results in the immediate illumination and instruction of the Spirit. Things hidden from the "wise and prudent" are revealed unto the most ordinary believer who lives in harmony with the Spirit's will.

This anointing delivers the recipient from doubt, hesitancy, and uncertainty, for the Spirit conveys nothing but that which is authentic. "You know all things."

One of the four possessions of Christ referred to by Paul is "wisdom" (1 Cor. 1:30). This spice mingled with oil indicates the action of the Spirit as He makes us partakers of our Lord's knowledge as well as His holiness. Moreover, we cannot understand Christ and the things of Christ apart from the perfect illumination of Him who is the Spirit of wisdom (cf. 1 Cor. 2:11 ASV).

Without doubt there are many things, even about the Bible, one can know apart from the revelation of the Spirit, but for deep insight into the secrets of God we are entirely dependent upon the divine Revealer. As it has been expressed, "The horse and his rider may see the same magnificent piece of statuary in the park; the one may be delighted with it as a work of human genius, but upon the dull eye of the other it makes no impression, and for the reason that it takes a human mind to appreciate the work of the human mind. Likewise only the Spirit of God can know and make known the thoughts and teachings and revelations of God."

Such an "unction," with its accompanying illumination, is what the Lord promised to give at His departure (John 16:13). Thus, all the spiritual truth we have, comes from the Spirit of truth. We have no wisdom of our own. As the holy place of the tabernacle had no light except from the golden candlestick, which was ever burning, so our knowledge of God is from the divine Light, even the Spirit Himself.

It is direct.

Do we not have to confess that we have failed to realize the full import of John's assertion, "Ye need not that any one teach you . . . His anointing teacheth you"?

Does this mean that we are not to follow human teachers, read helpful books, or listen to Bible expositions? Of course not. It implies that in proportion as we have this anointing, we have direct access to the Teacher of teachers, and direct wisdom from Him. He speaks to our hearts and minds and leads us into all truth as we rely upon Him. The more pronounced the anointing, the more unmistakably do we detect the voice of the Spirit and follow Him.

It is encouraging to know that no matter how limited our secular knowledge and mental capacity to comprehend avenues of earthly wisdom, we can yet grapple with profound spiritual truths. If we are dependent upon the Spirit, He will make old things new, stir us with the freshness of old Scriptures, cause the eye of sense to discover the hidden nuggets of gold in the mine of the Word. And Spirit-taught souls come to lean less upon the thoughts and theories of men, suggestive though they may be.

It is the prerogative of the Spirit to impart divine knowledge. Without His illumination, the inner glory of truth remains hidden from understanding. Indirect, human sources of wisdom can never help us understand God's Word from God's standpoint. Conscious then, that truth is revelation and that we must have the Spirit of revelation Himself to unfold to us the treasures of Scripture, what else can we do but echo the prayer of George Matheson in his "Voices of the Spirit."

Thou divine Spirit, illuminate to me the words of the Lord. Show me the wealth of glory that lies beneath the old familiar stories. Teach me the depth of meaning hid in the songs of Zion. Raise me to the height of aspiration that is compassed by the wings of the prophet. Lift me up to the summit of faith that is trod by the feet of the apostle. . . . I shall find treasures in my earthen vessels when Thou hast made known the words of the Lord.

Fragrance

The conspicuous, practical manifestations of the anointed life are many. We are told that the holy anointing oil used by the priests was "a perfume compounded after the art of the perfumer" (Ex. 30:25 asv). How sweetly the priestly garments must have smelled after they had been sprinkled with such fragrant oil!

Can we say that ours is the fragrant life? It is said of our blessed King that all His garments smelled of myrrh, aloes, and cassia (Ps. 45:8). Have we that unmistakable and immediately perceived fragrance of holiness the Spirit makes possible?

> As some rare perfume in a vase of clay,
>   Pervades it with a sweetness not its own;
> So when Thou dwellest in a mortal soul,
>   All Heaven's own sweetness seems around it thrown.

May each of us know what it is to carry in our garments the fragrance of the sanctuary above, of the sweet spices of the garden of Christ, of the flowers of grace, the Rose of Sharon and the Lily of the Valley. As His name is as ointment poured forth, may we as we pass through the vitiated atmosphere of the world diffuse abroad the easily detected perfume of our Master's presence.

Mary's box of precious spikenard had to be broken before its fragrance filled the house. And it is only as we are broken and contrite that Spirit-imparted aroma can escape and permeate lives around with its pleasing odor.

Love

The fruit of the Spirit, says Paul, is love (Gal. 5:22). And an effusion of the love of Christ ever results from a fresh, full anointing with the Spirit (Rom. 5:5). Reading the description given of the principal spices forming the anointing oil, it is easy to see that all the ingredients are suggestive of lovableness and sweetness (Ex. 30:23,24).

If anointed with the Spirit, we shall know what it is to be delivered from all the sourness and bitterness of an unsanctified nature. Under the influence of the divine anointing

THE HOLY SPIRIT OF GOD

we are able to administer rebuke with kindness, to disarm prejudice, and lend attraction to the truth. Sternness is also taken out of those of us who are strong, bitterness out of others among us who are quickly indignant. The same anointing enables us to be firm yet loving, and to make a "no" sound kinder than many a "yes."

Joy

On the day of Pentecost the waiting disciples, anointed with the Spirit, became God-intoxicated men, so much so that those around said, "These men are full of new wine" (Acts 2:13). Joy, the fruit of the Spirit, became theirs. In fact, one of the chief secrets of the victory of the early Christians was their joyousness, and the secret of such joy was the Pentecostal anointing (Acts 5:41; 13:52).

Of our Lord it is said, "Thou hast loved righteousness, and hated iniquity; therefore, God, even thy God, hath anointed thee with the oil of gladness above thy fellows" (Heb. 1:9). The word "therefore" implies that righteousness and holiness made possible the anointing. Unrighteousness and iniquity prohibit the possession of joy.

No believer can have a life radiant with the joy of the Spirit if He is not allowed to impart a passionate love of holiness and an equally passionate hatred and disgust for sin.

Service

Another direct and practical outcome of this anointing with the Spirit is a life of usefulness. Thus it was with Him who is our Exemplar in all things (see Acts 10:38; Luke 4:18). Fame, conspicuousness, or wonderful, ecstatic feelings are not to be expected, but serious glorifying of the Lord.

How full of meaning this sentence is: "God anointed Jesus of Nazareth with the Holy Ghost and with power: who went about doing good" (Acts 10:38). Anointed—to do good! Surely this is a very practical outcome of a truly sanctified life. *Goodness* is one aspect of the Spirit's fruit. And the only way to do good, and to be good, is to abide under the shadow of the anointing.

On one occasion a friend went to see a professing Christian and found her miserable, sitting by a fire. She asked the friend to sit down. "No," he said, "argument is unnecessary to know what is the matter. Get up, put your hat on, and go out and try to do some good." She did as she was told, and was soon a different woman. Meeting her spiritual advisor some time later, she said, "Oh, you could not have done me a greater favor than to tell me to go and do something good. Good has come to me in doing good to others."

What must be made clear is that with the anointing, we do not receive a stock of grace, wisdom, and power in advance to be drawn upon as need arises. As we endeavor to serve the Lord, all that is necessary will be supplied at the opportune moment. The anointing with the Spirit does not constitute us reservoirs—it makes us channels. We do not become stored up batteries of electricity, but telegraph wires along which the lightning can flash at any time.

Frances Ridley Havergal had some wise words on this point. Advising one who thought she could write poetry, she said, "God has not given me a chest of poetic gold to order. He keeps the gold, and gives it to me piece by piece just when He will, and as much as He will and no more." Continuing in the same strain the spiritual poetess said, "I am like a little child, who, when writing a letter, looks up and says, 'What shall I write next?'"

The idea before us, then, is a moment-by-moment dependence upon the Holy Spirit. Facing succeeding acts of worship and work we remind our hearts that without Him we are, and can do, nothing. Only then can we rightly discharge our debtorship, Godward and manward. Saintly Samuel Rutherford wrote of the saints as being "drowned debtors to God's grace."

It is therefore essential that we act under the divine anointing, if we would relieve those who are oppressed of the Devil and contribute our quota to the spiritual awakening a sin-cursed, blood-soaked earth so sadly needs. "To him that knoweth to do good, and doeth it not, to him it is sin" (James 4:17). Let us determine not to be among the saints who are sinners in this respect.

CHAPTER TEN

The Grieving and Quenching of the Spirit

In any study of the Holy Spirit it is important to mark the radical change wrought by Pentecost upon the early church. It would seem as if the descent of the Spirit left a more significant influence upon the tone and temper and faith of the apostles than the resurrection and ascension of Christ.

Indeed, the coming of the Spirit was an integral part of the ascension of Christ. In one sense the Spirit's advent is the extension of the resurrection and ascension into spiritual experience. Paul's letter to the Ephesians, for example, illustrates the wonderful change the Spirit's descent produced. Under the teaching of Paul, the believers at Ephesus went forward by leaps and bounds in all the finer, deeper perceptions and sympathies of the regenerated nature. The spirituality of the church is everywhere evident. It is this fact which lends interest to the separate aspect of the Holy Spirit in each chapter of Ephesians. For example, we have Him as:

1. The Spirit of promise (1:13).
2. The Spirit of wisdom (1:17).
3. The Spirit of access (2:18).
4. The Spirit of indwelling (2:22).
5. The Spirit of revelation (3:5).
6. The Spirit of power (3:16).
7. The Spirit of unity (4:3).
8. The Spirit of feeling and sealing (4:30).
9. The Spirit of fruitfulness (5:9).
10. The Spirit of fullness (5:18).

11. The Spirit of conquest (6:17).
12. The Spirit of intercession (6:18).

When Paul speaks of grieving the Spirit, he implies that those capable of such treatment are those who have received the Holy Spirit as the seal of adoption. It is the sealed ones who are saved, safe, and kept, who have it in their power to cause the Spirit such deep sorrow. "And grieve not the holy Spirit of God, whereby ye are sealed unto the day of redemption" (Eph. 4:30).

By grieving Him we do not lose the seal nor drive the Holy Spirit out of our hearts, which, of course, is impossible. When we grieve the Spirit we lose the joy, power, and assurance of the saved state. As sinners we grieve Christ; as saved sinners, we grieve the Spirit. And what is grievous to Him is likewise grievous to the Father and the Son. Unhappily we can hurt the Spirit; thus Paul reminds all saints to be sensitive regarding His feelings, seeing that we owe so much to Him.

Grief Affirms the Spirit's Personality

The word *grieve* implies both the personality and deity of the Spirit, as we have said. Those who deny the Spirit's reality must have a hard time explaining the above Pauline passage, with its sensitive sympathy and sealing of the Spirit.

A mere influence cannot be grieved.

When we speak of grief, we speak of personality. Grief is connected with feelings and feelings with personality. Influence cannot be sorry, no matter what may happen to it. The invisible wind, for example, is an influence but being destitute of personality, it cannot be pained. Paul, however, attributes the personal emotion of sorrow with its correlation of possible joy, to the Holy Spirit. As a person, He can be grieved.

The thought of the Spirit's personality imparts a tender motive, a dissuasive from sin, a persuasive to holiness. Conscious of His tender feelings, we are inspired to walk softly before Him. Many a young man has been kept from doing things and visiting haunts of vice by recalling the sad, pale face of a noble mother at home. And to think ever of the Spirit, who is holy, is sufficient to keep us from the evil forces warring against the soul. To realize that our conflict will either please or pain the Spirit produces a forcible motive for sanctification.

Grieving the Spirit, we grieve a loving friend.

The heart is the seat of love, the source of affection. Therefore, as grief is a feeling of the heart, we must be loved by the Spirit. Tender affections and tender sensibilities go together. The deeper the love, the keener the grief. Thus, the grief of the Spirit can be very deep, seeing His love is divine. In the dove we have a fitting metaphor of the Spirit who, because of His tenderness, can easily be grieved. As the heavenly dove, the Holy Spirit mourns over our sins.

Our thoughtlessness and ungrateful conduct have caused us to lament with the gentle George Herbert,

> Then weep, mine eyes, the God of love doth grieve;
>   Weep, foolish heart,
>   And weeping live:
> Almighty God doth grieve, He puts on sense;
>   I sinned not to my grief alone,
> But to my God's too; He doth groan.

What we must never forget is that in troubling the Spirit we also trouble ourselves. "He was sad . . . and went away grieved" (Mark 10:22). If we make the loving Spirit sad, the reflex of such sadness will be felt in our own feelings. Truly saved, we become sorry for having made the indwelling Spirit sorry. Contrariwise, in pleasing Him we ourselves are filled with pleasure.

How We Grieve the Spirit

In an Old Testament portrait of Christ, we are told that He

THE HOLY SPIRIT OF GOD

was acquainted with grief, grief caused by those who treated Him unkindly (Is. 53:3). That the Holy Spirit endured similar grief, even in Old Testament days, when the truth of His indwelling had not been fully revealed, is evident from a study of several passages. For example, the people "grieved him in the desert" (Ps. 78:40; 95:10), and they "vexed his Holy Spirit" (Is. 63:10); and "the Spirit of the Lord was straitened" by them (Mic. 2:7).

Seeing, then, that the Spirit is a person who is capable of feelings and can be hurt and pained, it is incumbent upon us to find out those things causing Him such grief.

Ignorance of His presence

What Jesus said of Himself is also true of the Spirit. "There standeth one among you, whom ye know not" (John 1:26). Such ignorance of God's presence is the sin of old and young believers alike. At our conversion we receive a twofold gift—Christ is God's gift to us, and the Holy Spirit is Christ's gift. We must fully recognize and appreciate both gifts. As a human father feels a pang if his child takes for granted a precious gift he purchased for him, so the heart of Jesus is wounded if we disregard His blood-bought gift.

Partial possession

We are commanded not only to possess the Spirit, but to be infilled by Him (Eph. 5:18). How grieved He is when we deny Him the full, absolute control of every part of our redeemed being! Moment by moment, we must completely surrender to His holy claims if we would have His approval. Liberty in every sphere can only be ours as His lordship is recognized (2 Cor. 3:17).

Disobedience to His commands and promptings

Christ, we are told, was grieved by the hardness of heart on the part of those who heard Him (Mark 3:5). In like manner, the Spirit is pained when we doubt the possibility of His mystic power. When we disobey His inner voice we lose the sense of

His presence. To obey Him is to please Him. If we have any doubt about certain habits being displeasing to the Spirit, we can look upon doubt as His voice. It is ever safe to give Him the benefit of the doubt. A wise principle to follow is "When in doubt—don't!"

Allowing things He hates

Grieving the Spirit is of a twofold nature. Negatively, we grieve Him when we forget His presence and neglect His power; positively, we grieve Him when we willingly pollute His temple. Because He is the Holy Spirit, the smallest thing in our life can hurt His feelings.

The acid test whether any pleasure, habit, or companionship is pleasing to the Spirit is whether we can ask His blessing upon it. Alexander Maclaren has forcibly expressed it: "Sin, the wrenching of myself away from the influences, not attending to the whispers and suggestions, being blind to the teaching of the Spirit through the Word and through Providence; these are the things that grieve the Holy Spirit of God." May we become more sensitive regarding those things wounding His love, deadening His voice, and disastrous to our own spiritual growth! The great lines of W. M. Bunting come to mind—

> Worldly cares at worship time,
> Groveling aims in work sublime,
> Pride, when God is passing by,
> Sloth, when souls in darkness lie;
> Chilled devotions, changed desires,
> Quenched corruption's earlier fires—
> Sins like these my heart deceive,
> Thee, who only know'st them grieve!

Our treatment of others

It is somewhat illuminating to compare what goes before and after Ephesians 4:30, where Paul mentions the grief of the Spirit. From the context we learn that in the mystical body of Christ, one member affects another. In grieving a fellow believer, we grieve the Spirit who indwells that one. If anyone should slander or ill-treat your best friend, they would be hurting or grieving you. There seem to be two aspects of this particular grief we can cause the tender Spirit.

First of all, He is strung with a keen, inward jealousy when He sees us choosing the little, illusive gratifications of evil-doing and evil-speaking rather than the peace, joy, and confidence afforded by His presence.

What a catalogue of sins Paul enumerates in his loving exhortation about grieving the Spirit! Falsehood, anger, dishonesty, corrupt speech, and all forms of graceless and unedifying conversation are mentioned as disturbing to the holy feelings of the Spirit. How rebuked we are, as we note the feature of each sin!

Bitterness, wrath, anger

We group this triad together seeing they belong to the same evil brood. Quarrels, feuds, and estrangements should be things of the past in those who are Christ's. Because the Spirit is so loving and kind, all unworthy passions alien to His gracious feelings should have no place whatever in the life He indwells.

Clamor

By such a mark of the flesh Paul means all violent assertions of right or wrong. Strife and controversy do not please the Spirit. As loud voices ringing in the forest will frighten the birds, so insistent voices, clamoring for their own way, startle and disturb the gentle Dove.

Evil speaking

The Greek word here is *blasphemia* and can cover all kinds of slander. Sins of the lips certainly pain the Spirit. Uncharitable judgments, hasty and unkind conclusions are besetting sins the best of Christians have to watch. On May 31, 1738, John Wesley wrote in his *Journal*, "Yet on Wednesday did I grieve the Spirit of God, not only by not watching unto prayer, but likewise by speaking with sharpness instead of tender love to one that was not sound in the faith. Immediately God hid His face, and I was troubled." May the same tender conscience be ours!

Malice

Here we have a term denoting an unkind, unjust habit of mind. It is actually "spite" and is mentioned last, seeing it is a deeper, more subtle sin and the root cause of all the others. Our attitude toward all these phases of evil must be that of total rejection. By a decisive, definite act they must be "put away." If we are to be the dwelling of an ungrieved Spirit, an eternal Inhabitant whose love is never wounded, then everything displeasing to Him must be expelled.

In the second place, the Spirit is grieved by whatever discredits His testimony concerning the Father and the Son to the world at large. After the believer is sealed, the Spirit strives to produce in him an ever-growing likeness to the divine character. All the sins Paul mentions, obscure the seal just as dirt hides the image on silver coin for which the woman sought (Luke 15:8).

How Not to Grieve the Spirit

Let us now come to the ways by which we can please the Holy Spirit of God!

Mutual kindness

"Kind" conveys the thought of being useful and helpful, a character reflecting the loving-kindness of the Spirit Himself. It is surprising how unkind we can be to each other, thereby grieving the Spirit.

Tenderhearted

Occurring nowhere else in the New Testament, this virtue suggests being full of pity or kindhearted. When we come pleading God's forgiveness, He offers it freely and willingly.

217

He never demands an apology for our cruel treatment of Him. Because of His tenderheartedness He seeks to inspire the same quality within those of us who belong to Christ.

Forgiveness

All who are Spirit-born and Spirit-filled must exhibit an entire, unreserved, and heartfelt spirit of forgiveness toward those whose actions have grieved them. Divine pardon is at once the supreme example and sacred motive of such a grace. We are to forgive others "even as" God for Christ's sake has forgiven us.

Our actions toward each other determine the joy or sorrow, pain or pleasure of the Holy Spirit. Because love has an infinite capacity of sorrow, as well as of joy, which are we giving the loving Spirit? Do we recognize and regard His sensitive feelings? A. B. Simpson reminds us:

> The Spirit has set His heart upon accomplishing in us, and for us, the highest possibilities of love and blessing; when we will not yield to His wise and holy will, when we will not let Him educate us, mold us, separate us from the things that weaken and destroy us, and fit us for the weight of glory that He is preparing for us, His heart is vexed—His love is wounded—His purpose is baffled; and if the Comforter could weep, we would see the tears of loving sorrow upon His gentle face.

May we endeavor to leave all evil things undone, and all evil words unsaid, and thus add to the joy of the Spirit. God grant us grace to do the things pleasing to the Spirit! Knowing His mind and will, may we be obedient to the faintest whisper of His voice.

The New Testament cites three sins against the Holy Spirit and, taken together, they offer further evidence of the truth of His personality. In order, He can be resisted, grieved, and quenched. We are warned not to:

Resist the Spirit (Acts 7:51). Man as a sinner can resist the Spirit. This was the particular sin of Israel. And such a treatment of the Spirit implies a fight against God, conscience, and light.

Grieve the Spirit (Eph. 4:30). As we have discussed, man as a saint can grieve the Spirit. This is often the sin of those who are sealed. Although regenerated and indwelt by the Spirit, we entertain habits displeasing to His holy mind.

Quench the Spirit (1 Thess. 5:19). Man as a servant can quench the Spirit. Such an attitude indicates that the saved person works against the one great source of power in service. Moffat translates the phrase, "Never quench the fire of the Spirit." Campbell Morgan's illuminating comment on these three aspects is worthy of notice. "To resist presupposes the Holy Spirit coming to storm the citadel of the soul. To grieve presupposes the residence of the Spirit as comforter. To quench presupposes the presence of the Spirit as a fire." These three sins, then, suggest the Spirit as force, friend, and fire.

Bringing together six passages in which the word *quench* appears, we discover that there are three fires we can never extinguish, and three others we can.

Three Fires We Cannot Quench

The fire of true love is unquenchable. Many waters of sorrow and adversity cannot put out such a fire (Song 8:7). Truly, nothing can extinguish the love of our Bridegroom (Is. 49:15).

The fire of tenderness is another defying the efforts of men to damp out. The "smoking flax shall not he quench" (Matt. 12:20). Dictators live by the law of the survival of the fittest. The weak must die, only the strong can live. But Christ restores the fallen and proves Himself to be the defender of the less fortunate.

The fire of hell is likewise unquenchable. There are those who try to extinguish the flames of the lake of fire, but on they burn (Mark 9:44,45). In no uncertain terms we are told that this fire burns on forever and ever (Rev. 20:10).

219

Three Fires We Can Quench

The fire of temptation need not raise fears in the mind of the steadfast believer when we act in the power of God. Again and again the New Testament writers exhort us to resist temptation: "Flee also youthful lusts . . ." (2 Tim. 2:22); "resist the devil, and he will flee from you" (James 4:7); (cf. 1 Cor. 10:13).

The fire of persecution likewise holds no terror for the faithful saint. Confidence in God can quench the violence of fires, as the three Hebrew youths and the early church saints experienced (Dan. 3:25; Heb. 11:34).

The fire of the Holy Spirit is another fire man can quench. Is it not a solemnizing thought, that while man is able to extinguish the fires of temptation and persecution, he can also stifle the Spirit's voice? It was necessary for David to stay at home while the battle raged. If the king were destroyed, then the fire of Israel's hope would be quenched. "Thou shalt go no more out with us to battle, that thou quench not the light of Israel" (2 Sam. 21:17). Would that we were as careful over retaining the constant light of the Spirit!

A study of the Pauline passage in 1 Thessalonians 5:19–22 reveals that the quenching of the Spirit acts in a twofold way. Such an action against the Spirit is both personal and general.

We can put out the fire of the Spirit in another's heart.

The exhortation "Quench not the Spirit" is linked to the injunction, "Despise not prophesyings." One of the gifts of the Spirit is that of prophesying, or preaching, as the word can mean. Some there are who can preach better than others. But good preachers must not dishearten others less gifted and eloquent. We have too many dampers in the ministry.

Whatever we do, let us see to it that we never quench the ardor of a young Christian, even though his testimony is faulty. The fire may smoke a little at the beginning, but give it time and it will burn itself bright. Let us never throw cold water over the efforts of another by unsympathetic criticism and cold looks and words. Let us encourage the fervor, enthusiasm, and passion of those whose zeal may not be altogether according to knowledge.

Do we realize that the tongue of criticism can quench the tongue of fire? To criticize harshly and ridicule the attempts of another often hinders the Spirit within that one. Further, because influence is never neutral, an inconsistent witness can keep others back from a full surrender to the Spirit. Whatever there is in our lives acting as a stumblingblock in the pathway of another, serves at the same time as a check to the Spirit's activities.

We can quench the fire of the Spirit in our own heart.

That "fire" is a metaphor of the Spirit is seen in the description we have of Him as "seven lamps of fire" (Rev. 4:5). Of course, it must be clearly understood that the quenching of the Spirit has nothing to do with casting Him out of our life. Such an action is impossible, since upon His entrance he becomes our eternal Inhabitant. The quenching is simply related to the manifestation of the Spirit's presence and power. Taking the illustration of a fire in the grate or boiler, let us extract a few spiritual lessons and reinforce the apostolic warning regarding the quenching of the Spirit.

Insufficient materials

Scarcity of paper and wood can hinder the progress of a fire. Lack of air or insufficient coal are also responsible for a slow-burning fire.

Very often the fire of faith is kindled, but it soon dies, leaving nothing but ashes. Surrender to Christ was not complete. Materials were insufficient. There was not enough knowledge, repentance, or submission. Has your first love gone? Have you a cold heart? Can it be that you have ashes where there ought to be a blaze?

Neglect

Fires have to be tended. Busy here and there, even with things legitimate, we are apt to forget the fire at home and out it goes. How descriptive of ourselves! Busy here and there, we forget to feed the fires of our inner life. Endeavoring to keep the vineyards of others, we neglect our own. We forget to heap on the fuel. We fail to pray without ceasing. When communion with God, the study of the Scripture, and full obedience to the Spirit are not daily practiced, the fire dies down.

Dross and dirt

Too much dross and coal dust can ruin a fire. Too much rubbish can spoil a fire in the grate. For a glowing fire, one must feed it with proper fuel. In the spiritual realm, proper fuel can only be applied as we trust the Holy Spirit to sanctify us wholly (1 Thess. 5:23). Evidently Paul misses certain traits in the lives of the Thessalonian saints; hence his list of exhortations within the context.

> Spirit of God, descend upon my heart;
>   Wean it from self, through all its pulses move;
> Stoop to my weakness, mighty as Thou art
> And let me love Thee as the angels love.

Dampening the Fire of the Spirit

Do we desire to have a fierce, continual blaze, a fire which, like that on the ancient altar, never went out? Well, let us guard ourselves by thinking of some things calculated to dampen the fire of the Spirit!

Disobedience to the Spirit's promptings

Often His voice urges us to go here or there. We feel led to witness to some soul or obey some command. Without doubt, the Spirit is speaking, but we refuse to answer and, continuing to refuse, we quench the fire.

Self-glorification

The love of self-praise and of self-born aims and wishes can cause the spiritual fire to burn very low upon the altar of the heart. James Denny reminds us that "there always have been men in the world so clever that God could make no use of them; they could never do His work, because they were so lost in the admiration of their own." If we do well, the Devil is the first to tell us so! If we fail, then he is the first to discourage us and whisper, "What's the use of you trying to speak?"

Confidence in the flesh

A self-directed life ever lacks the glow of the Spirit. No flesh can glory in His presence. Uzziah learned this in a harsh way (2 Chr. 26:15,16). The Holy Spirit is always frustrated in His work when we rely upon our gifts, abilities, organizations, and schemes. Fleshly energy will never be able to substitute the might of the Spirit.

The fear of man

Because of cowardice, Peter's fire of devotion burned very low. The fire-flame at Pentecost restored his boldness. Are you timid, afraid, fearful? Do you need to be fired with passion to declare the truth of God without fear or favor? Well, give the Spirit His way in your life!

The mingling of strange fire upon the altar of God

Nadab and Abihu were guilty of this sin (Lev. 10:1). Strange fire will still quench the Spirit. What do you think these strange fires are? Among them we can name unsanctified companionships, the employment of worldly means and methods in God's work, giving way to fleshly passions and lusts, and engaging in pleasures and pursuits not of the Spirit.

May grace be ours ever to feed the flames of the Spirit. As the fire, may He burn fiercely and consume everything alien to His holy will.

> Burn, burn, O fire within my heart,
>   Burn fiercely night and day,
> Till all the dross of earthly loves
>   Is burned and burned away.

CHAPTER ELEVEN

The Evidences of a Spirit-Filled Life

We have now come to an aspect of the Spirit's ministry of deep, practical import. Essential as it is to have correct views on the doctrine of the Spirit, of what good is that if we continue to live unorthodox lives? During a conference of Christian workers convened by D. L. Moody, various addresses were given on how Christians could live a holier, more useful life. At the conclusion of the two-hour session, Mr. Moody, who was acting as chairman, rose and said, "I can tell you in five words how Christians can become more holy, useful, and fruitful—be filled with the Spirit!"

In this concluding chapter, then, let us endeavor to discover the great reservoir of power the Lord places at the disposal of even the humblest child of grace. It is to be doubted whether any believer has fully realized all that God is able to accomplish through a life utterly yielded to the indwelling Spirit.

Marks of Progress

Jerusalem was unlike many great cities of its time, in that it was situated by the banks of a sweeping river. It was this fact, coupled with a constant scarcity of rain, that made the land so dry and barren. What water it did receive ran down to the Dead Sea. In later years, the land around Jerusalem has enjoyed more rain, which is a natural phenomenon full of prophetic significance.

The prophet Ezekiel prophesied of better days. Boundless material prosperity is to be experienced; and the city is to abound in fruitfulness because of perennial rains. Such a prophecy is vividly dramatized in the life-giving river flowing from the sanctuary (Ezek. 47:1–12). In the first six verses, where we have the measured waters, a parabolic narrative full of profitable applications is before us. Taking the section as a whole, we have suggested the twin truths of our inner life and outer service. In verses 1 to 6 we have "The Progress of the Spirit," while verses 7 to 12 provide us with "The Fruitfulness of the Spirit-filled Life."

The arresting theme Ezekiel gives us, of the rapid augmentation of a petty stream into a mighty river as the result of a self-supply from the sacred, miraculous source in the temple, can be used in many ways.

First, the progress of revelation can be viewed as an ever-deepening and widening river. From the dim shadows we come to the full blaze. And with our spiritual perception there is a similar progress. Some truths are easy to understand—water to our ankles. Other aspects of truth are more difficult to comprehend and require deeper search—water to our loins. Then there are yet other phases of the Word almost beyond our reach—water to swim in. All that we can do is to adore their depth (Rom. 11:33).

The river of the human race is another one hardly perceptible at the beginning. From the first human family countless millions have sprung.

Commencing with Abraham, the first Hebrew, God has seen to it that the Jews have become as numerous as the sand on the seashore.

The advance of the gospel affords us another illustration of increasing influence. The growth of Christianity is a miracle! The history of the church reads like a romance. Pentecost marked the planting of a small seed which has become a mighty oak.

From the record of revivals we gather the same principle. One or two earnest souls start to pray, and before long there is an avalanche of blessing.

Coming to ourselves, we can see in Ezekiel's river a type of an ever-deepening spiritual experience. The law of the Spirit of life in Christ Jesus is a law of progress. In the Spirit, life is like a river glorious, deeper and fuller all the way.

Within the context are three words full of spiritual import to underline, namely: waters, sanctuary, altar (Ezek. 47:1).

The waters

If we bend our ear we hear the murmur of the river all the way through the Scriptures, ending as it does, clear and crystal, in Revelation (22:1). From our Lord's own teaching we have authority for using "water" as a type of the Spirit's life-giving ministry (John 7:37–39). It will be noted that "waters" and "rivers," being in the plural, can represent the varied gifts and operations of the Holy Spirit (1 Cor. 12). God's river is for every dry place in our lives.

It is also recorded that the waters "ran," meaning, of course, that they were fresh and fertile. When water fails to run, it becomes stagnant. The waters of the Spirit are flowing waters. "Shall flow . . . This spake he of the Spirit" (John 7:38,39). The resources of the Spirit do not form a Dead Sea, they represent ceaseless progress.

The sanctuary

By the "house" we are to understand the sanctuary or God's immediate dwelling place. In Old Testament days God localized His presence in the temple at Jerusalem and the people had to resort there to worship God (John 4:20,21).

The waters coming from the house indicate that God is the rise or source of the life-giving waters. The Holy Spirit is the Spirit of *God*. And it is said of these "waters" that they "came down." It is ever so. All that is best has its rise in the deep heart of God and comes down to our needy hearts. That which is to bless and refresh the world must necessarily take its rise above the world. We are fond of "getting up" things, such as revivals. It is better for us to allow all spiritual blessings to come down.

A further thought to be gleaned from the "house" is that it represented a place separated from all sinful, common uses.

The tabernacle, and afterwards the temple, were centers wholly dedicated to God for worship and service. Does not Paul use the "temple" as a metaphor of the spirit-possessed believer? (1 Cor. 6:19,20). The Scripture says, "Out of [your body] shall flow rivers of living water." But the body must be holy and entirely occupied by the Holy Spirit.

Again, the waters ran on "the right side." They always do. We cannot expect the divine torrent if we are wrong in any direction. By "the right side" we are to understand the position of power and authority. As Spirit-filled ones, we can exercise all the authority of sonship.

Another interesting detail is the fact that these "waters" came from the East and went out toward the East (Ezek. 47:8). From an earlier chapter we discover that the "East" was the place of His glory (43:1,2). How evocative! The Spirit Himself came when Jesus was glorified, and all He does, in and through your life and mine, is for the glory of God.

The altar

"Afterward." After what? After being at the place where the sacrifice was boiled, Ezekiel noticed that the water came out of the south side of the altar. Sacrifice, then, is the truth emphasized. And is not Christ our altar? (Heb. 10:10). No altar, no water, no Cross, no Pentecost. It is ever thus with ourselves. Have we come to our altar? The position of the altar contains a further truth. The waters came out of the south side. They did not issue out of the north side, the judgment side. The south is the balmy side, the resurrection quarter. And, as the Spirit Himself was not given until Jesus was glorified, a life of fertility and fruitfulness cannot be ours unless we have experienced the death and resurrection Paul expounds in passages like Romans 6 and Philippians 3:10.

Coming to the increasing volume of the living waters which Ezekiel describes, it is spiritually profitable to discern there the progressive life of the believer. A life truly Spirit-filled can never remain static. There must come an ever-deepening experience of His grace and power.

227

The trickle

The margin notes of the American Standard Version gives us "trickled forth" for "ran forth" (Ezek. 47:2). The waters, with their gathering volume, were hardly perceptible as they commenced to flow out of the crevice of the temple. Oozing forth from the temple they would be difficult to distinguish. Thus is it with ourselves. Although at the beginning of our spiritual life evidences of the new life are meager, there they are, proving that we are on the right side.

Faith may be only as a grain of mustard seed, but the tiny seed will grow. The day of small things must not be despised. Through continual yieldedness to the Spirit, the soul is not sluggish growing in grace and knowledge. The keynote of Hebrews is "Let us go on"; *plus ultra*—"onward still!" must ever be our ideal. The trickle must become a torrent. "Though thy beginning was small, yet thy latter end should greatly increase" (Job 8:7).

The tragedy is that so many of the saved never get beyond the trickle. They have just enough grace to keep them alive and get them into heaven. Life they have, but not life more abundant.

The ankles

As the man with the measuring rod led Ezekiel on, the prophet experienced the rising tide of the sanctuary waters. Half a mile from the source, the waters were to his ankles, or "soles of his feet," as the original has it (Ezek. 47:3). And, the further on we travel from self, the deeper the water.

Are we ankle-deep in the waters? Are we walking in the Spirit? Are we able to leap and walk for God? The beggar at the gate of the temple which is called Beautiful was cured of his lameness. "Immediately his feet and ankle bones received strength. And he leaping up stood, and walked . . . walking, and leaping, and praising God" (Acts 3:7,8). Have we weak ankles? Do our feet carry us to questionable places? Are we unwilling to stand firm for the truth? Is it difficult to walk out into the world for the lost? Water to the ankles can save us from straying and unsteadiness.

But water only to the ankles does not mean all the progress we should make. We have far too many paddling Christians. Have you ever paddled on the ocean? Some swim out and meet the tide, but with shoes and socks off, we paddle along the shore and stir up the mud. May God save us from having our feet in grace for safety and the rest of our being in the world for satisfaction! Paddling or carnal Christians can stir up a good deal of trouble in a church. Christians, but not spiritual, they produce a lot of muddy water.

The knees

As Ezekiel followed his guide, he saw less of himself. The tide gradually covered him. The waters are now at his knees (Ezek. 47:4). What do we know of the rising tide? Two thoughts are associated with the knees, namely prayer and worship.

First of all, we have the intercessory life the Spirit makes possible. As Paul prayed for others he wrote, "I bow my knees" (Eph. 3:14). Have we prayer-bathed knees? Do we know what it is to "pray in the Holy Spirit"? If we walk in the Spirit, the waters will rise and ours will be the joy of praying with all prayer and supplication in the Spirit! Our knees, it has been said, are heaven's knockers. Only by the Spirit's energy can we continue knocking until the hinges of the golden door open.

Bending the knee can also represent worship, humility, self-abasement. Have we learned to kneel our way through life? Kneeling thus, we are not inclined to stand up for our rights. Neither have we the desire to bow to the idolatrous things of the world.

The loins

With the next measurement the prophet found the waters up to his loins (Ezek. 47:4). Like a river glorious, deeper all the way, is the Spirit's ministry. But what is meant by "the loins"? From the Bible it is evident that they represent the center of procreative power. "Kings shall come out of thy loins" (Gen. 35:11). Job has a similar idea, "Lo now, his strength is in his loins, and his power is in the navel of his belly" (Job 40:16). Disease in the loins makes one unfit in service or warfare. Are the waters of the Spirit up to our loins? Is He the source of our productive ability and of power in service? The loins are also the seat of the nerves and converging appetites, the waist or stomach being the center of our body. If something is wrong here, the rest of our physical make-up is out of order. Are all our affections nailed to the Cross? Does the Spirit fully control all our appetites? Water to the loins means that we are spiritually healthy and strong.

Waters to swim in

About one mile from its source, Ezekiel found that the river could not be forded. The trickle had become a torrent! "The waters were risen, waters to swim in, a river that could not be passed over" (Ezek. 47:5). How many miles from the initial, regenerating work of the Spirit have you traveled? Is yours the static or submerged life? Is the Man Christ Jesus with His measuring line satisfied with your spiritual progress? As less and less of Ezekiel was seen, so is self submerged with us. The spiritually-progressive life has been forcibly set forth by Theodore Monod in the lines:

> Oh, the bitter shame and sorrow,
>   That a time could ever be,
> When I let the Savior's pity
>   Plead in vain, and proudly answered—
> "All of self, and none of Thee."
>
> Yet He found me; I beheld Him
>   Bleeding on the cursed Tree;
> Heard Him pray, "Forgive them, Father,"
>   And my wistful heart said faintly—
> "Some of self, and some of Thee."
>
> Day by day His tender mercy
>   Healing, helping, full and free

Sweet and strong, and ah! so patient,
  Brought me lower, while I whispered,
"Less of self, and more of Thee."

Higher than the highest heavens
  Deeper than the deepest sea,
Lord, Thy love at last hath conquered,
  Grant me now my soul's petition,
"None of self, and all of thee."

The waters were risen. Risen! Is the risen life ours? Are we out from the shore and plunging into the depths? What have we, a mere trickle, a stagnant pool? Or is ours the submerged fullness the Spirit makes possible for all those who abandon themselves to His tides? "Be ye infilled with the Spirit" (cf. Eph. 5:18). "Ye living waters, rise within me evermore." Is the water above our ankles, loins, heart, shoulders, neck, and head? Have we come to the river that cannot be passed through? Is such a flood-tide experience ours? Are we trusting ourselves to the Spirit as He endeavors to bear us along on His surging tide? Where does our present spiritual experience find us? Like swimmers, are we out in the deep, allowing the waters to bear us along?

The man with the measuring line asked Ezekiel a pertinent question, "Son of man, hast thou seen this?" (Ezek. 47:6). The word *seen* means "experienced," "apprehended." As we take God's measuring line and stretch it alongside our life, can we say that we are apprehending all He has for us? Or can it be that we are far too superficial?

Are we ankle-deep Christians? Content to play along the shore of God's mercy, do we yet allow our feet to stray to questionable places? The old Book tells us that God is able to keep the feet of His saints.

Are we knee-deep Christians? Does the measured distance from our conversion find us mighty in prayer? The Spirit, as "water," can loosen stiff knees and keep them supple and ever bowed before the Lord.

Are we loin-deep Christians? Is self buried deep in the

waters? Are we fully covered? Is the Spirit producing a complete self-effacement? Are we not merely ankle-deep, knee-deep, loin-deep, but self-deep Christians? May grace be ours to bathe in the life-giving waters! Oh to know what it is to be carried along irresistibly and joyfully by the tide of the Spirit! Let us leave the shore lines and claim the immersion in the Spirit the Lord has for His own.

Returning to the opening verse we read that the waters "issued out from under the [door]." Under the door! The buried life, then, is only for the humblest. If we stoop low enough the waters will flow over us. Reaching the Bible's last book we have waters from under a throne (Rev. 22:1). Progress can only be ours as self is dethroned and we come to a God-enthroned life, which is like the river Ezekiel saw, causing everything to live wherever the river flows.

Marks of Lordship

Because the Bible is the most remarkable book in the world, there are various ways by which we can approach and study it. One profitable method is that of analyzing a theme as it is presented in the Bible as a whole, then in a book, and last of all, in a chapter. Take for example, the doctrine of the Holy Spirit. To trace out and classify what the Scriptures have to say about His person and mission is a blessed task indeed. Once we have the general sweep of such a sublime truth, we can particularize and condense the Spirit's activities in a group of books, like the Pentateuch or the Gospels, and then come to an outline of His work as given in certain chapters.

To illustrate the benefits of such a chapter study let us look at 2 Corinthians 3. In this portion, taken up as it is with the ministry, Paul gives us several cameos of the Spirit. Features of His varied operations are made to stand out in bold relief for our enlightenment and edification. Altogether, we have five distinct manifestations of His work in the life of the believer.

Letters from the Spirit

In the opening verses of 2 Corinthians 3 Paul uses, with telling effect, the arresting simile of a letter (vv. 1–5). At the outset of this paragraph the apostle confirms an apostolic custom of sending letters of commendation. It may be that he had in mind a passage like Acts 18:27, "When [Apollos] was disposed to pass into Achaia, the brethren wrote, exhorting the disciples to receive him. . . ." Adopting this custom, Paul looks upon his converts as his letters of recommendation. The figure of speech is a forceful one.

As "epistles" or "letters" we are written, not with ink, but by the Spirit of the living God (Luke 11:20; 2 Cor. 3:3). He is a wonderful letter-writer. His writing is always legible. It can be read of all men (which cannot be said of my actual writing—at least, so my friends tell me). Letters written by the Spirit are known and read—known, and then read. Very often we know whom a letter is from because a familiar handwriting is seen, but to read or decipher what is written may be another matter.

The Spirit writes His letters not on paper, but on the heart. And they are borne not by hands, but in lives. The question is, are we true letters of commendation? A letter speaks of the absence of the one who wrote. To express what he would have said, if present, he turns to pen, ink, and paper. Christ, our blessed Lord, is absent from the earth, and during His absence the Holy Spirit is active writing letters, that is, producing lives that express the truth of Christ.

There is no letter so attractive, no sermon so powerful as a truly consistent Christian life. Christlikeness is always legible and eagerly read. The eye of the world seems to take in more than the ear.

Ignatius wrote of the verse before us: "Give unbelievers the chance of believing through you. Consider yourselves employed by God; your lives the form of language in which He addresses them. Be mild when they are angry, humble when they are haughty; to their blasphemy oppose prayer without ceasing; to their inconsistency, a steadfast adherence to your faith."

May it be manifestly shown that we are an epistle of Christ, a letter coming from Christ and carried about and presented by us as its bearer to those for whom it is intended. The Spirit is the writer, then, and we form the letter of Christ's recommendation to a world of need.

Life by the Spirit

There are two phrases in this chapter declaring the Spirit to be "the Lord, the Life-Giver." Paul speaks of Him as "the Spirit of the living God," and as the One who "giveth life" (2 Cor. 3:3,6). In another place the apostle reminds us that He is "the Spirit of life in Christ Jesus" (Rom. 8:2). This is as it should be, seeing that everything associated with Christianity is living. Religions of the world are related to dead leaders and saints. Christianity, however, was founded by the living Lord, who is alive forevermore.

We recognize that the immediate application of this aspect of the Spirit's ministry is to the ancient Law. By it comes the knowledge of sin and then the pronouncement of death. "The letter killeth," in that it brings home the realization of guilt and its punishment by death (Rom. 7:6). The quickening or life-giving of the Spirit, on the other hand, imparts new spiritual life (Rom. 6:4,11).

That the Spirit is responsible for all life is evident from a study of His wonderful and manifold activities. He it is who produces *natural life:* "And the earth was without form, and void; and darkness was upon the face of the deep. And the Spirit of God moved upon the face of the waters" (Gen. 1:2). He produces *physical life:* "But if the Spirit of him that raised up Jesus from the dead dwell in you, he that raised up Christ from the dead shall also quicken your mortal bodies by his Spirit that dwelleth in you" (Rom. 8:11). He produces *spiritual life:* "The wind bloweth where it listeth, and thou hearest the sound thereof, but canst not tell whence it cometh, and whither it goeth: so is every one that is born of the Spirit" (John 3:8).

THE EVIDENCES OF A SPIRIT-FILLED LIFE

Life-giving Spirit, o'er us move,
    As on the formless deep,
Give life and order, light and love,
    Where now is death or sleep.

Lordship of the Spirit

Sharing the deity of the Godhead, the Holy Spirit has a Lordship few seem to recognize and revere. Paul, however, understood this obscured truth. "The Lord is that Spirit" (2 Cor. 3:17,18); the Spirit is Lord. Rotherham's *Emphasized Bible* makes the note, "Where the Spirit is LORD, there is [liberty]." And as we shall see when we come to the next point liberty cannot be experienced unless the Spirit's lordship is fully realized.

One cannot read Acts without being impressed with the presence and presidency of the Spirit throughout the book. I agree with A. T. Pierson that this fifth book of the New Testament ought to be renamed and called, the "Acts of the Holy Spirit through the Apostles."

Is the lordship of the Spirit a realized fact of our life? Are we absolutely obedient to His voice? Does He have the entire control of every part of our life? Is He *Lord*?

Liberty in the Spirit

David reminds us that the third person of the Trinity is God's "free Spirit" (Ps. 51:12). Truly, He is the emancipating Spirit causing bondage to give place to freedom. Three mediums of freedom there are: *The Word of God; the Truth of God,* "And ye shall know the truth, and the truth shall make you free . . . ye shall be free indeed" (John 8:32,36); and *the Spirit of God,* "Now the Lord is that Spirit, and where the Spirit of the Lord is, there is liberty" (2 Cor. 3:17).

With the full recognition of the Spirit's lordship comes:

Liberty in mind. Freedom from fear, ignorance, error, prejudice, jealousy, and legality forms one of His blessings. Free sonship takes the place of the spirit of bondage.

Liberty from sin. As the Holy Spirit, He deals with all that is alien to His will. He delivers from the trammeling influence of sin and the flesh.

Liberty in prayer. Prayers in the Spirit are never restrained, dry, or mechanical. When He is in control of our inner life, we are delivered from "saying" prayers. Prevailing intercession becomes ours.

Liberty of worship. As the inspirer of true worship, the Spirit frees us from all formality, superficiality, and restraint as we endeavor to approach God. A free, spontaneous expression of adoration becomes ours as we worship God in the Spirit.

Liberty in service. Instead of forcing ourselves to labor for Christ, we delight to do His will. Ours is no longer a treadmill existence. We do not serve God because we have to, seeing we are professed Christians. The Spirit puts joy into service.

Liberty in giving. When the Spirit is in full control, He also holds the purse and prompts our giving. When He is Lord, there is no withholding of our substance. Liberty means liberality. Having freely received, we freely give.

Is this daily transformation ours? Are we becoming more like Christ? Is the Lord, the Spirit, producing likeness to Christ in hatred of sin, prayerful dependence upon God, passion for the Scriptures, a loving, winsome disposition, and submission to the will of God?

> Work on, then, Lord, till on my soul,
>   Eternal light shall break,
> And in Thy likeness, perfected,
>   I satisfied shall wake.

Two things are to be noted about the transformation the Spirit affects.

First of all, He transforms us into the likeness He presents. The word *changed* in 2 Corinthians 3:18, meaning "transformed" or "transfigured," is the same used of our Lord at His transfiguration (Matt. 17:2). For a moment there was the outflashing of His inherent glory.

Further the word is in the present tense, "transformed

continually," indicating a present, daily process. The Spirit takes us "from one degree of radiant holiness to another" as Weymouth translates Paul's word. Is the gradual conformity to Christ's image, ours (Prov. 4:18)? Are we allowing the Spirit to take us through the stages of a progressive sanctification?

The next thought is, the Spirit enables us to reflect the likeness He presents and changes us into. "The glory which shines upon us is reflected by us." From glory, that is, the origin of transformation, "the glory shining upon us"—to glory, this is the effect of transformation, "the reflection of that glory by us."

If, then, we allow the Spirit to fill and flood the life, He will without effort or consciousness on our part produce the likeness of Christ in us. "The power to enjoy Christ, is the power to reflect Him. The reflection is no effort, but, the necessary effect of enjoyment" (cf. 2 Cor. 3:7). The more unconscious we are of likeness to Christ, the better. "Moses did not know that . . . his face shone" (Ex. 34:29 RSV).

Marks of Filling

Our basic text for the final theme is taken from Ephesians, in which the heavenly walk and work of the believer is described as being the outcome of the Spirit's infilling. Saturated as it is with the truth of the Spirit, this epistle builds to a climax when Paul commands the saints to be filled with the Spirit (5:18). Constant obedience to such a specific command means a liberation of divine power in and through our life.

The contrast

Extremes are combined by Paul in his exhortation. What a striking contrast there is between drunkards and Spirit-filled believers! "Be not drunk with wine, wherein is excess; but be filled with the Spirit." This combination can be traced in other Scriptures. Of John the Baptist it is said, "He shall be great in the sight of the Lord, and shall drink neither wine nor strong drink; he shall be filled with the Holy [Spirit], even from his mother's womb" (Luke 1:15). Christ, filled with the Spirit, was called a "winebibber" (Matt. 11:19). Of Peter and others it was said, "These men are full of new wine. . . . these are not drunken, as ye suppose" (Acts 2:13–15).

Is a deep truth not wrapped up in such a contrast and comparison? When filled with spirits, the drunkard is absolutely under their control and for the time being they completely master the man. The Holy Spirit has the same results upon the recipients of His fullness. When our personality is pervaded, dominated by the Spirit, He masters us, making us indifferent to what others may say, think, or do. Drunk men are dead to all around in a very negative way. But we, when God-intoxicated, become dead to the opinion of the world and abandon all concern about our reputation.

Drink begets a state of false happiness. Watch the drunkard as he sings and speaks to himself. When the effects are over, what sadness, remorse, and despair. When we "drink deeply of God's Spirit," as Weymouth translates our basic text, how different the results. Such drinking leaves no regrets or sorrow behind. There is an abiding joy, for the believer makes melody in his heart. Intelligible psalms, hymns, and spiritual songs are his (Eph. 5:19).

A man spirit-saturated, having the DT's, sees things others cannot see. The Spirit-filled sees divine things hidden from the unspiritual.

Alcohol, taken to excess, is ruinous and disastrous. It destroys heart, health, and home, and fills the world with sin, sorrow, and shame. But saints cannot have too much of the Holy Spirit. We are satisfied with so little; yet we cannot go to excess in spiritual things. A life more abundant is offered us—a life beyond the ordinary. Let us not be afraid of getting too holy. Let us have a fear of imperfection rather than of perfection. The more the Spirit has of us, and we of Him, the more do we reflect the likeness of Christ.

The command

A "but" links two commands in the verse before us. "Be not

drunk with wine, wherein is excess." Yes, we say, this is an imperative command, all ought to obey. Paul, however, continues. "But be filled with the Spirit." This second command is as binding as the first. "Be not . . . be."

It is not our privilege to be Spirit-filled, but our duty. It is a sin not to be Spirit-filled. Refusing the fullness of the Spirit we commit the sin of disobedience. As God's commands are His enablings, He is ever willing to fill our lives as we willingly submit to the sway of the Spirit. In the construction of the passage the passive verb is employed, suggesting that there must be the surrendered will, willing mind, and yielded body if we are to be filled.

We must bear in mind the fact that the Spirit fills by displacement. He empties as He fills. As water is poured into a glass, air is driven out. We do not have to try and empty ourselves in order to receive the Spirit's fullness. The more He has of us, the less there is of sin and self. Further, He increases our capacity as He fills. The more we receive, as we willingly obey the divine command to be filled, the more our capacity is enlarged. We are not as stone jars with a limited capacity. Rather, we become as india-rubber vessels, with an ever-expanding capacity.

The character

What actually is this "filling" Paul enjoins upon all believers? And let it be said, it is for all and not the privilege of a few elect souls (Acts 2:1–21). Such a "filling" is not temporary. It does not evaporate. We are not filled with an influence, or an energy, or even holy desire, but with a person; thus it is an infilling. The Holy Spirit is within, and when fully yielded to, He rises as the well and fills the life.

As there can be no gifts apart from the giver, so we cannot have power apart from this person. "Ye shall receive power, the Holy Spirit coming upon you" (cf. Acts 1:8). Power is simply the manifestation of the presence of the Spirit.

The need of such power is apparent to ourselves and others. We think of past failure or present powerlessness, and sigh for life which is life indeed. We have a lack of assurance, doubting our acceptance and salvation; we lack victory over sin and self and live an uneven, up and down life. We lack the fruits of holiness and are altogether destitute of the graces of the Spirit. We lack power in service and are weak, useless, and barren. We lack knowledge concerning the Scriptures. With shame, we confess we have lived as spiritual paupers, although so much wealth is at our disposal.

We must have the fullness of the Spirit to combat self. The great rival of the Spirit is self. If filled with the one, we cannot be filled with the other. And because there are two kinds of self, good and bad, we need the Spirit to deal with both.

The soul is the seat of the self-life. From our bad self spring self-energy, self-confidence, and self-pride, which give birth to sins and lusts of all kinds. "In me (that is, in my flesh,) dwelleth no good thing . . ." (Rom. 7:18).But, as the result of the Spirit's infilling, we are enabled to die daily so that we can say, "I live; yet not I . . ." (Gal. 2:20).

We must have fullness of the Spirit to deal with our good self. All of us have what we might call our righteous self, and this is ever the hardest part to yield. Jesus had no sinful self. Being holy, He had no sin, no pride, no selfish interests. But He did possess a good self. Yet He died to this phase of His self-life. He pleased not Himself. His confession was, "I do always those things that please [My Father]" (John 8:29).

Self is ready to surrender everything but itself. With Jesus, this was not so. "Himself He cannot save" (Mark 15:31). He could have provided comfortable lodgings for Himself, which would have been legitimate, but He had "no where to lay His head" (Matt. 8:20). Willingly, He died to self-comfort. Therefore Paul urges us "not to please ourselves . . . even Christ pleased not himself" (Rom. 15:1–3).

Our Lord has taught us to go the second mile: "Go with him twain" (Matt. 5:41). We do not sin if we please ourselves and do not go the second mile. There is no evil in refusing to do the little extra. But as we live under the Holy Spirit, we become more willing to surrender even our good comfortable self.

THE EVIDENCES OF A SPIRIT-FILLED LIFE

There comes the subjection of even the legitimate to the Lord for His Glory.

The conditions

Owing to the presence of so much error regarding the exact nature of the Spirit's work within the believer, it is necessary to examine one or two negatives. Earnest Christians make at least seven common mistakes as they strive after the Spirit's fullness. While it is true that God answers our heart's desires, although they may be wrongly expressed, yet it is always best to seek God's gifts in God's appointed way.

It is not scriptural to pray or sing, "Come, Holy Spirit, come." Dispensationally, He came as a Person at Pentecost (John 14:16,17; Acts 2:1,2). Experientially, He came to us in the hour and experience of regeneration. "If any man have not the Spirit of Christ, he is none of His" (Rom. 8:9).

It is not scriptural to affirm that we must tarry for the Spirit. The apostles were commissioned to wait for the Spirit because He was coming as the gift of the ascended Lord. The Spirit did not come in response to the prayerful waiting on the part of the apostles, but because He had been promised by Christ. Thus, as soon as Christ entered glory, the Spirit came (Luke 24:49–53; Acts 1;4; 2;1,2).

It is not scriptural to seek for power apart from the Spirit. The Lord never divorces power from the person. The Holy Spirit is the power. "Ye shall receive power, when the Holy Spirit is come upon you" (Acts 1:8 ASV; 8:17,19,21). Our goal must ever be God Himself: not so much the gift as the Giver.

It is not scriptural to pray, "Lord, help me!" Asking for help implies that we can go so far, but that we must have the Spirit's aid to complete what we commenced. The Spirit, however, undertakes to control us in every way. He does not operate on a 50-50 basis, partly the Spirit, partly the energy of the flesh. It must be all of the Spirit.

It is not scriptural to bargain with God for the Spirit. Simon the Sorcerer wanted to purchase with money the gift of the Spirit (Acts 8:18–25). But God does not run an exchange store.

He never condescends to mere bargaining. All the Spirit has is like salvation, without money and without price, except the price of a full surrender.

It is not scriptural to dictate terms to the Spirit. Sometimes we are guilty of telling the Spirit how we desire Him to use us in the Lord's service, but He never works that way. Being sovereign, He will use us just how and when He likes (Acts 2:4; 1 Cor. 12:4–11).

It is not scriptural to plead for the Spirit. To listen to some prayers, lacking nothing in earnestness, one would think that God was loathe to bestow upon all the blessings of the Spirit. He is more willing to give than we are to receive (Acts 2:1–13; 4:31; 10:44; 11:15).

Coming to the positive aspect of the Spirit's infilling, we have the divine and human sides of such a spiritual birthright.

The divine side

While the "filling" or "infilling," as we prefer to call it, is a transaction that can and will be repeated as one lives in the Spirit, it is ever the Lord who fills the earthen vessel. As Godet expresses it, "Man is a vessel destined to receive God, a vessel which must be enlarged in proportion as it is filled, and filled in proportion as it is enlarged."

One result of such an infilling is a kind of passive activity, as of one wrought upon and controlled by Another, rather than of one directed by his own efforts. One becomes a God-intoxicated person. Seeing the verb Paul uses is in the present tense, this "infilling," performed by the divine Filler, is an experience the believer may apprehend and enter into this very moment.

The human side

While it is true that God alone can fill us with His Spirit, He never fills us alone. There are conditions we must observe and fulfill if we would be filled fully with the Spirit. What, then, are some of these conditions making real to us all the promised gifts of the Spirit?

From the negative side, as we have seen already, if we would be filled with the Spirit we must not grieve, quench, or resist the Spirit.

From the positive side there are four simple keywords to follow.

We must acknowledge. There must come the frank and full confession of sin and the yielding up of all doubtful practices. Such a yielding implies the absolute surrender of ourselves to the control of Another. Further, this "yielding" is a definite, drastic act (Matt. 5:23–26; 1 John 1:9; James 5:16; Rom. 12:1,2).

We must ask (Luke 11:5–13). While it is true, as already indicated, the believer in this age does not have to plead with God for the Spirit, there is a sense in which we are to ask, seek, and receive. A personal Pentecost, however, is a different matter. The Spirit came upon those gathered in the upper room because certain conditions had been fulfilled. Too many of us live impoverished lives, seeing we fail to ask and receive. By faith we must claim all we have in the promise of the Spirit.

We must accept (Acts 2:38,39). Faith, apart from strange and strong emotions, high excitement and ecstatic joy, is the only channel of the Spirit's infilling. Believing that there is such a fullness for us, we must accept it by faith and go out and live as filled ones. We must reckon upon God's faithfulness to fulfill His Word and fill us as we trust and obey.

We must act (Acts 3:1–6). Action will inevitably follow the filling. Stepping out upon the promise and obeying instantly and implicitly all the known will of God, the act becomes an attitude. The crisis develops into a process. Instinctively and habitually we come to obey every revelation (Acts 5:32) as we observe the restful maintenance of all conditions negative and positive to the Spirit's infilling.

The consequences

One has only to study the context of Ephesians 5 to discover how wonderful and far-reaching, practical and spiritual the results of the Spirit-filled life are. In fact, chapters 5 and 6 must be studied together if we would know something of a radiant life in the Spirit.

There is joy (Eph. 5:19).

Such a Spirit-produced joy is of a threefold nature.

It is inward. "Speaking to [ourselves] . . . making melody in [our] heart." What do we know of the singing heart? Carlyle says, "Give me the man who sings at his work." If Spirit-filled, heart melody is ours at all times.

It is outward. ". . . to one another" (ASV). The manifestation of a "joy unspeakable and full of glory," so glorifying to the Lord, is another evidence of the Spirit's fullness. It is part of His fruit (Acts 2:4).

It is upward ". . . to the Lord." The Spirit prompts us to make Him the sole object of our praise and adoration.

There is gratitude (Eph. 5:20).

From the inner life of the Spirit-filled believer, thankfulness ascends to God always and for all things. "Always" and "all"! Whether the "things" be pleasant or otherwise, we bless God who knows what is best for His own. A willing, joyful submission is ours in all He may permit (Rom. 8:28; 1 Thess. 5:18).

There is sanctification (Eph. 5:21; 6:24).

When Spirit-filled, every relationship of life is transformed, enriched, and enveloped.

Generally, there is a give and take attitude. With the Spirit enthroned and self dethroned, we cease to clamor for attention, place, or position. We submit one to another in the fear of the Lord (Eph. 5:21).

Socially, too, life is lived on a higher plane, as Paul shows. Husbands and wives live as heirs together of the grace of life (Eph. 5:22–23). Home life is sanctified and delivered from all that is unkind, peevish, irritable, and inconsiderate. Spirit-filled, we make home a miniature heaven. Children and parents reveal a domestic life loving and fragrant (6:1–4). Employers and employees labor together as one in Christ (vv.

5–9). Spirit-filled executives do not overwork or underpay their employees, and Spirit-filled workers do not waste time or give mere eyeservice. They give a full day's work for a full day's pay. Surely, all our labor problems would cease if only the principles laid down in this chapter could be recognized by industry.

Spiritually, we become warriors when fully possessed by the Spirit (Eph. 6:10–24). Paul brings before us the warrior's armor, foes, and resources in this well-known portion. Spirit-filled, we become more than conquerors as we face the world, flesh, and the Devil.

Our final question is this, What do we know about this fullness? Have we allowed the Holy Spirit to infill our lives? Are we willing to confess, "Lord, I am not filled, I should be filled, I can be filled. I will be filled, here and now!"

As we plead for an immediate decision on the part of sinners, so Christians also must make a prompt, definite adjustment of our hearts, minds, and wills to the mind of the Spirit. Faith is taking God at His Word. Are we willing then to take God at His Word and allow Him to infill us with His Spirit? Is this to be our decision?

> I take the promised Holy Ghost
>   I take the Gift of Pentecost,
> To fill me to the uttermost,
>   I take—He undertakes.

It would seem as if the expressive lines of Ada R. Habershon fittingly conclude this meditation on "His Infilling."

> I need to be filled in the morning,
>   Each moment of every day,
> I need to be filled in the morning,
>   Ere starting upon my way.
>
> I need to be filled for the home-life,
>   I need it for work outside,
> I need it alone in God's presence,
>   That I may in Him abide.

I need to be filled with the Spirit,
 To hear or to read His Word,
I need to be filled when by speaking,
 I witness for Christ my Lord.

I need it, and oh, I may have it,
 For by His enabling power,
The Spirit whom He has once given,
 Can fill me this very hour.

Chorus:
I need to be filled, Lord Jesus,
 I need to be filled each day;
I need to be filled with the Spirit,
 Each moment along life's way.